Psychoanalytic
Criticism

Psychoanalytic Criticism

A Reader

EDITED BY SUE VICE

Polity Press

Copyright © this collection Polity Press 1996.
Introduction and introductory material copyright © Sue Vice 1996.
Reading 4 copyright © Peter Nicholls 1996.

First published in 1996 by Polity Press
in association with Blackwell Publishers Ltd.

2 4 6 8 10 9 7 5 3 1

Editorial office:
Polity Press
65 Bridge Street
Cambridge CB2 1UR, UK

Marketing and production:
Blackwell Publishers Ltd
108 Cowley Road
Oxford OX4 1JF, UK

Blackwell Publishers Inc.
238 Main Street
Cambridge, MA 02142, USA

ISBN 0–7456–1049–8
ISBN 0–7456–1050–1 (pbk)

A CIP catalogue record for this book is available from the British Library and
the Library of Congress.

Typeset in 10/12pt Times
by Wearset, Boldon, Tyne and Wear
Printed in Great Britain by T.J. Press (Padstow) Ltd, Padstow, Cornwall.

This book is printed on acid-free paper.

Contents

Part V   Julia Kristeva: the Abject and the Semiotic   151

Part VI   Luce Irigaray: Femininity, Film and the Masquerade   174

Sources and Acknowledgements

The editor and publishers wish to thank the following for permission to use copyright material:

Columbia University Press for material from Julia Kristeva, *Powers of Horror*, 1982. Copyright © 1982 by Columbia University Press; Mary Ann Doane for 'Women's Stake: Filming the Female Body', *October*, 17, Summer 1981, pp. 22–36; Farrar, Straus & Giroux, Inc. for material from Edmund Wilson, 'The Ambiguity of Henry James' from *The Triple Thinkers*. Copyright © 1938, 1948 by Edmund Wilson, renewed © 1975 by Elena Wilson; Harvester Wheatsheaf and Rutgers University Press for material from Makiko Minow-Pinkney, *Virginia Woolf and the Problem of the Subject*. Copyright © 1987 by Rutgers, The State University; Alfred A. Knopf, Inc. for material from Peter Brooks, *Reading for the Plot*. Copyright © 1984 by Peter Brooks; Macmillan Ltd and W. W. Norton & Company, Inc. for material from Jacqueline Rose, 'Introduction' and Jacques Lacan, 'The Meaning of the Phallus' from Jacques Lacan, *Feminine Sexuality*, eds J. Mitchell and J. Rose, trans. Jacqueline Rose, 1982. Copyright © 1966 Éditions du Seuil. English translation copyright © 1982 by Jacqueline Rose; Oxford University Press for material from Luce Irigaray, 'Women, the sacred, and money', from *Paragraph*, Vol. 8 (October 1986), pp. 6–18. Copyright © 1986 Luce Irigaray; Oxford University Press, Inc. for material from Harold Bloom, *The Anxiety of Influence: A Theory of Poetry*. Copyright © 1973 by Oxford University Press, Inc.; Random House UK Ltd for material from Maria Bonaparte, *The Life and Works of Edgar Allen Poe*, 1971, Chatto & Windus; and with Basic Books Inc., a division of

HarperCollins Publishers Inc., for Sigmund Freud, 'From the History of an Infantile Neurosis' from *The Collected Papers of Sigmund Freud, Vol. XVII*, authorized translation by Alix and James Strachey, published by Basic Books, Inc. 1959 by arrangement with the Hogarth Press Ltd and the Institute of Psycho-Analysis, London; Routledge for material from Elizabeth Grosz, *Jacques Lacan: A Feminist Introduction*, 1990, Routledge; and Toril Moi, *Sexual/Textual Politics*, 1985, Methuen & Co.; Yale French Studies for material from Shoshana Felman, 'Turning the Screw of Interpretation', *YFS*, #55/56, 1978; and Barbara E. Johnson, 'The Frame of Reference: Poe, Lacan, Derrida', *YFS*, #55/56, 1978;

Every effort has been made to trace all the copyright holders but if any have been inadvertently overlooked the publishers will be pleased to make the necessary arrangement at the first opportunity.

Thanks to the following for their expert editorial and production input: Helen Dore, Hilary Frost, Lin Lucas, Debbie Seymour, Pam Thomas and John Thompson.

Thanks also to the Department of English Literature, and the University of Sheffield for material assistance with completing the copyright permissions.

Editor's Note

References to the works of Sigmund Freud: all references to the *Standard Edition of the Complete Psychological Works of Sigmund Freud* (24 volumes, trans, and ed. James Strachey, with Anna Freud, assisted by Alix Strachey and Alan Tyson, Hogarth Press and the Institute of Psycho-Analysis, London, 1953–73), are abbreviated *SE*, followed by the relevant volume and page number, and date of publication in English.

Ellipses which are the result of editorial intervention are signalled by square brackets, thus [...]; all others are original. The endnotes in each part of the reader follow one sequence, which means that they are by the different authors of the various readings. Where any potential for confusion has arisen (use of first person, for example) I have supplied the original author's name.

Introduction

This collection of articles aims to do two things: to introduce the reader unfamiliar with psychoanalytic criticism to a range of material in the area; and to provide, for those with defined interests in psychoanalysis, an accessible anthology of some of the most interesting and exciting debates in the cultural uses of psychoanalysis since Freud's day. Psychoanalysis, as clinical practice or theoretical model, is an interpretative strategy, concentrating particularly on the language which tries to render the body's experiences, the role of sexuality in defining the self, and the construction of subjectivity and gender. It might seem strange to use a therapeutic, medical practice (Freud, after all, trained initially as a neurologist) as the basis for a literary theory. However, in both the kind of practice where the patient (analysand) lies on the couch talking about his or her psychic life with the analyst who sits behind, and the kind where a literary critic uses the terminology and approach of psychoanalysis to investigate a text, the workings of language are clearly very important, and it is this fundamental fact which links the two practices. This is true of Freudian psychoanalysis, often called the 'talking cure', and even more so of post-structuralist, Lacanian psychoanalysis, which takes as its object the speaking human subject, and assumes that this adult, speaking subject is constructed *in* language. Lacan's emphasis makes clearer the link between psychoanalysis as a therapy and as a critical practice: both are concerned with the workings of language and how the unconscious is expressed in it.

In her introduction to the collection *Psychoanalysis and Cinema*, E. Ann Kaplan usefully notes that three different senses of 'psychoanalysis' are always present in Freud's writing: psychoanalysis as a science, as a medical practice, and as a way of approaching literary and anthropological texts. The latter two senses of psychoanalysis are the ones which have been most heavily relied upon by textual criticism. That said, Kaplan observes that six further aspects of psychoanalysis, as it is used in critical practice, can be identified.[1] Several of these have a primarily, though not exclusively, historical function, and most are represented by at least one piece of writing in the present anthology.

These aspects are: first, psychoanalysis as a talking cure. This includes two different elements: the scene of analysis, in which the analyst interprets the analysand's utterances, characterized by transference, imaginary relations, and so on; and Freud's theory of human development, including the Oedipus complex, later reformulated by Lacan.

Second, psychoanalysis can be used to explain literary themes and characters; the critic acts as analyst to the authorial patient, as Marie Bonaparte does in her psychobiography of Edgar Allan Poe. Third, psychoanalysis can be seen structurally as itself an aesthetic discourse, the aesthetic being the realm neglected by the second usage. The use of fictionalizing as it occurs between analyst and analysand is likened to narrative fiction, as Peter Brooks, as we will see below, does with the psychoanalytic category of transference, and Peter Nicholls does to some extent in his use of the Freudian concept of *Nachträglichkeit* (deferred action), in his essay reproduced here.

Fourth, psychoanalysis may itself be the subject of representation, as it is in Philip Roth's novel *Portnoy's Complaint*, which turns out to be the record of one man's talking cure, and Marie Cardinal's account of her own illness and cure, *The Words to Say It*. Fifth, psychoanalysis may be treated as a historically defined discourse, and its appearance on the contemporary scene charted and evaluated, as for instance Kate Millett does in her *Sexual Politics*, where she discusses it as an oppressive force in women's lives. Finally, psychoanalysis as a collection of processes is used by critics as a discourse with which to approach literary or filmic texts, and the relationship between audience and text. This sense of psychoanalysis is the one which occurs most frequently here, in most of the literary critical and cinematic essays, particularly those which deal with post-Freudian approaches, whether these be Lacanian, Kristevan or Irigarayan.

If one concept were singled out as the most significant factor in making psychoanalysis central in both culture and criticism, it would probably be the unconscious. The unconscious is perhaps his most significant contribution not only to psychoanalysis and literary theory, but to twentieth-century thought in general, and the one which feminist (and other) critics of Freud's views on femininity and sexuality are least likely to jettison. It is perhaps easy at the end of the twentieth century to take for granted the idea that there is a layer of life in each person which is out of their conscious control, but at the beginning of the century it was a revolutionary and empowering one.

The subject's history, his or her prohibited desires, live on in a realm called the unconscious, where such impulses as the urge to incest, patricide, suicide, unconventional expressions of sexuality, are not subject to the negatives placed upon them by the conscious in the interests of 'civilized' behaviour. In his case history of Dora, Freud infamously observed that there is no word in the unconscious for 'no'. The unconscious works by its own logic and even language, and it is the task of analysis to tap into this logic (as it is one of the tasks of psychoanalytic criticism to tap into the text's unconscious logic). It expresses itself, as Freud suggested, most obviously in everyday life through dreams, bodily symptoms, jokes, slips of the tongue (the notorious 'Freudian slip'), small inexplicable interruptions in the smoothly regulated social flow. It would seem that we are not the autonomous, rational creatures that pre-Freudian (or some current strands of anti-Freudian) thought has suggested, for not everything we do is under our conscious control. The implications of this theory of a subject (and also text) which is split, divided between two realms, is one we will see followed through from Freud to Lacan and French feminist theory.[2]

This collection of essays offers a chronological selection of three kinds of psychoanalytic writing: conceptual writings by analysts such as Sigmund Freud, Jacques Lacan and Julia Kristeva; commentaries on these writings, by critics such as Elizabeth Grosz; and literary critical essays which take a psychoanalytic approach, by writers such as Edmund Wilson and Peter Nicholls. The boundaries between these kinds of writing are often indistinct, which shows clearly the close relation between psychoanalysis and literature. The analysts themselves often rely on literary instances to support or exemplify their theories, perhaps most famously in Freud's use of Sophocles' play *Oedipus Rex*, its earliest instance being in his 1908 essay 'Creative Writers and Daydreaming'. Similarly, critics concentrating on analytic writings do not only limit themselves to this area: Elizabeth Grosz, for instance, comments in passing on literary genre – the medieval courtly love tradition – and much of her argument has an indirect literary relevance. Equally the more literary writers have much to say which affects our view of the original psychoanalytic theory, as is the case for instance in Peter Nicholls's discussion of history's role in deferred memory.

The essays which appear here are not meant to be a definitive sample or history of psychoanalytic criticism, but all have an individual importance, and bring into relief particular concepts or approaches. Some essays, such as Barbara Johnson's 'The Frame of Reference: Poe, Lacan, Derrida', have been reprinted before, but it seemed worth adding them to this collection in view of their influence and importance. This is the main motive of this collection: to provide a representative gathering of psychoanalytic writings in one volume and thus to give both newcomers and those already familiar with the area one possible overview of developments in psychoanalytic thinking, without their having to consult ten different books and periodicals and make fifteen photocopies.

Not all essays have been reproduced in their entirety, for different reasons, some to do with copyright restrictions (clearly an area ripe for both psychoanalytic and legal analysis), some with keeping the anthology at a reasonable length. Only one essay was especially commissioned for this volume: Peter Nicholls's essay on Toni Morrison is an extended analysis using the Freudian notion of *Nachträglichkeit*, which it seemed well worth including in full as it is the only such piece of literary criticism expanding upon this literarily promising concept.

As this collection is not intended to be, nor could have been, all-inclusive, there are inevitably some omissions. Carl Jung's work is not represented, although it has had considerable influence on archetypal literary criticism and on the creative practice of a number of writers, including poets Ted Hughes and Peter Redgrove, and the novelist Doris Lessing. This is largely because Jung's theories fall outside the trajectory this collection sketches: Freud, re-read by Lacan, is taken up by feminist psychoanalysts in differing ways.

Melanie Klein herself has had to be excluded because of lack of space, although a 'turn to Klein' has been identified by feminist critics in particular. Ann Scott suggests that the shift from interest in Lacanian theory to Kleinian represents not just a change of perspective from Oedipal to pre-Oedipal, Lacanian lack to Kleinian plenitude, but from interest in the construction of the subject to construction of the subject's world. She suggests that this shift has come about for three main reasons: feminist difficulties with the valorization of the phallus in psychoanalytic theory; concern over the location of language and power in the masculine realm; and increasing interest in a specifically British, empirical tradition of psychoanalysis, as distinct from the European tradition of Lacan.[3] This turn to Klein has resulted in an even more unlikely pairing, which Jane Gallop calls a 'theoretical double date',[4] as post-structuralism joins up with feminist social science in questioning (in Kleinian manner) the objectivity of scientific theory.[5] Interesting recent work on Klein has included Meg Harris Williams and Margot Waddell's *The Chamber of Maiden Thought*, which concentrates on the works of George Eliot; and Michael O'Pray's work on the films of David Cronenberg.[6]

Another gap might be the fact that recent French feminist psycho-analysis is represented by Kristeva, Luce Irigaray and Michèle Montrelay; other, equally interesting theorists, such as Hélène Cixous, Sarah Kofman, Michèle Le Doeuff and others are not to be found here simply for reasons of space. In the introduction to *Revaluing French Feminism*, Nancy Fraser observes that despite the wide range of writers represented in Elaine Marks and Isabelle de Courtivron's 1980 anthol-ogy *New French Feminisms*, 'for many English-speaking readers today "French feminism" simply *is* Irigaray, Kristeva and Cixous'.[7] While not suggesting that this is a good thing, I am acknowledging that these are the theorists readers are most likely to have come across, or want to know more about. The same is true of the omission of much recent Anglo-American feminist writing by theorists such as Jane Flax and Diana Fuss; and slightly earlier writers in the British object-relations school, such as D. W. Winnicott, are also missing, although it is clearer in some of these cases either that their relevance for literary criticism is slighter than is so of the followers of Freud, or that they are less inter-esting. Part of the point of this collection of essays is to inspire the read-er to read further, in ways suggested by what does appear here, and this applies particularly to French feminist theory.

This volume differs from other introductions to psychoanalytic the-ory in that it is a reader, a chronological collection of representative writings, and not a critical history or an anthology of commissioned arti-cles. In this sense it is an introduction to the area, a basis for further reading. The issues raised here include the following: what are, or can be, the relations between psychoanalysis and both literature *and* film, an overlap seldom discussed in collections dealing with psychoanalysis and textual analysis? What is the object of a psychoanalytic approach to a text: what would such a reading look like? Are the two kinds of text separable? Why do they seem to fit so well together when psycho-analysis is in the first instance a clinical practice? How is it that femi-nism and feminist literary theory have taken up psychoanalysis, or vice versa, when there has been so much controversy about the patriarchal nature of psychoanalytic theory and practice? These are the kinds of question a reader would expect to see raised in any introduction to psy-choanalytic criticism, but the difference here from histories or commis-sioned collections is that, although each section has an editorial introduction, the extracts speak for themselves. Some of them respond overtly to earlier ones also reproduced here; others implicitly take up issues already covered in a different way. The editorial material is intended only to put each writer in context, rather than to guide the reader's opinion.

Psychoanalytic criticism

Post-structuralist, especially Lacanian, psychoanalytic theory has emphasized the priority of language over meaning; in other words, language *forms* meaning, it does not give expression to a meaning which is pre-existent. Thus there has been a shift away from earlier, more clearly Freudian kinds of psychoanalytic literary criticism, which often involved attempts to 'analyse' the text's author or its characters, or to liken literary devices to kinds of psychic activity described by Freud, such as dream logic or condensation.[8] A reaction against this partly accounts for more recent tendencies to neglect close readings of texts; in his introduction to *Psychoanalysis and the Question of the Text*, Geoffrey Hartman defends the absence of such readings in the collection by observing that the essays investigate 'what kind of event in the history of interpretation psychoanalysis is proving to be',[9] an activity which 'compensates us for a relative lack of new interpretations [. . .] theory must first conceive of itself as productive [. . .] rather than as a meta-language'.[10]

However, as some of the writing in this collection shows, it is possible to offer a detailed reading of a text at the same time as, or as part of the same project as, considering the wider implications of the psychoanalytic approach. This is true, for instance, of Minow-Pinkney's discussion of Virginia Woolf, and Felman's of Henry James. Psychoanalysts themselves are clearly aware that 'all discourse is inhabited by the unconscious',[11] as Lacan's essay 'The Meaning of the Phallus' shows: the unconscious informs the play of word and sense in Lacan's writing, and in all other texts.

Lacan's particular style helps to break down the distinction between literature and psychoanalysis, by encouraging the kinds of critical attention usually reserved for creative writing. It is now often agreed among writers on psychoanalytic literary practice that the relation between criticism and text should be not masterful but mutual. It is not a question of a superior critical knowledge being used to unlock the secrets of a literary text, with the latter as passive object and psychoanalytic criticism as metalanguage, but a polymorphous 'mutual entanglement'.[12] In the introduction to *Literature and Psychoanalysis*, Shoshana Felman claims that in the past the relation of the two discourses has been like Hegel's master–slave relation of struggle between two entities for recognition where psychoanalysis has been the subject, literature the object: a 'unilateral monologue of psychoanalysis *about* literature'.[13] Her anthology is entitled thus to show that the text's perspective will be literary, but, Felman says, the result will not be a reversal of the usual priority of psychoanalytic discourse over literary, but a deconstruction of the whole relation. Instead of applying to the text a scientific knowledge, the interpreter will allow the rather different activity of *implication* to take place, in which each of the two domains will find itself 'enlightened, informed, but also affected, displaced, by the other'.[14]

As Felman emphasizes, psychoanalysis should not be an 'answering service',[15] telling the reader what the text 'really' means and then putting down the receiver, or closing the book, but should recognize its own ability to be rhetorical and textual. Barbara Johnson's essay 'The Frame of Reference' demonstrates the truth of this insight; every 'framing' commentary on Poe's 'The Purloined Letter' leaves itself open to further analysis by yet another commentary, so that there is no single, definitive psychoanalytic critical statement to be made about the short story. As Robert Young says in his introduction to Johnson's essay in *Untying the Text*, she shows that in literary analysis 'there always remains an irreducible otherness which can never be placed',[16] some element which escapes the interpretation put upon it, and to some extent this is the 'meaning' of the story 'The Purloined Letter'. It is a trick; its mystery can never be solved. The same is true of some of Henry James's short stories, 'The Beast in the Jungle' and 'The Figure in the Carpet', and of course of the genre of the shaggy-dog story: the 'terminal discharge'[17] we have come to expect of fictions is so delayed that it does not take place within the text at all: this is what the text has to say, and is the joke's punchline. In the case of Poe, as Johnson's essay shows, neither a definite assertion of undecidability, which is Lacan's position, nor Derrida's equivocal assertion of decidability, sums up the effect of the story, and as Young says,[18] 'the letter, in fact, makes the reader perform, makes analysis a performative which repeats the reading of the letter, while the letter itself escapes into – insignificance'.

Johnson's own essay is of course in its turn equally open to such framing. The use of the same word, 'framing', for both crime story and critical activity allows us to 'remain within a crime story even when the genre seems to be critical interpretation'.[19] Again, the boundaries between different kinds of text turn out to be indistinct; both psychoanalytic and literary discourses are present in the story, but which is elucidating which? This is a particularly pertinent question in the case of

Poe's story, which itself turns out to have something to say about the workings of literature and language, usually the role of a critical rather than a creative text.

If psychoanalysis should not be seen as the privileged, explanatory discourse, then equally, the literary text should not be privileged as if only certain kinds of writing conform to Hartman's definition of literary language as 'the "lack" or "gap" in meaning that leads to figurative supplementation or overdetermined usage'.[20] The human psyche itself also works this way, not to mention the language of the psychoanalytic treatise (Freud's study of Dora, for instance, which has often been likened to a late-nineteenth-century novel) or the psychoanalytic literary–critical essay (Lacan's and Derrida's essays on Poe, quoted by Barbara Johnson). In all these cases the unconscious is present in the text's language. Freud, after all, produced his case history of Senatspräsident Schreber from the latter's own published memoirs, explaining that paranoid personalities in particular express clearly their unconscious meanings.[21] In all these cases psychoanalysis deals with language – the system of bodily utterances which constitute hysteria, the memoirs of a paranoid personality, literary criticism – whether spoken or written.

The changing perception of what constitutes psychoanalytic literary criticism can be summarized in a comparison of two articles: one the introduction to *Psychoanalysis and Literature*, a collection of essays edited by Hendrik M. Ruitenbeek and published in 1964; the other Peter Brooks's 'The idea of a psychoanalytic literary criticism', published in 1986.[22] Ruitenbeek justifies the straightforward title for his anthology (the two realms are together but separate) by pointing out first, that Freud wrote essays on literature; second, that psychoanalysis has drawn on literature; third, such effects as 'condensation, displacement, multiple determination, and secondary elaboration [...] are being consciously employed in poetic works';[23] fourth, American writers in particular have been enabled by psychoanalysis to deal with a greater variety of human behaviour in novels and plays; and, in short, psychoanalysis has increased our understanding of creative persons and literary works.

Brooks, on the other hand, casts doubt on all four of these points of comparison. His essay appears in an anthology, edited by Shlomith Rimmon-Kenan, self-consciously styled *Discourse in Psychoanalysis and Literature*, to emphasize the rhetorical and textual aspects of the encounter while not losing sight of a 'human dimension'[24] often absent in post-structuralist studies. Brooks points out that while Freud did indeed write about literature, his more interesting work, particularly for the purposes of psychoanalytic criticism, lies elsewhere, in his writings on jokes and dreams, and in the metapsychological essays such as 'Beyond the Pleasure Principle'. Brooks replaces the two-way model of influence Ruitenbeek summons up (either literature has influenced psychoanalysis, or the other way round), with a more circular model in which it is never clear which comes first: is 'narrativity' a literary term relevant to psychoanalysis, or vice versa, as Shlomith Rimmon-Kenan asks in her introduction?[25] Brooks sees the circle as encompassing the human psyche as well as psychoanalytic and literary practice: 'we sense that there [. . .] must be some correspondence between literary and psychic process, that aesthetic structure and form, including literary tropes, must somehow coincide with the psychic structures and operations they both evoke and appeal to'.[26] Writers use certain devices not because, as Ruitenbeek suggests, they had read about them in Freud, but because Freud's, their own and their readers' ability to recognize such devices is a constituent element of being human. While this argument depends on a more sophisticated model of the human psyche than Ruitenbeek's, its main point is that it cannot be disproved, as the phrase 'both evoke and appeal to' suggests. We cannot help but see things in the way our psyche allows us to, so it is not surprising, indeed is inevitable, that it looks as if the world (and the text) reflects this shape. Making this the basis of any theory therefore runs the risk of tautology. Of course in the case of the text it is not simply a case of looking for something and therefore finding it, as it has indeed been constructed according to the same linguistic principles which constitute human subjectivity, 'consciously' or not. Brooks's circulation of meaning between text, psychoanalytic discourse and human mind may actually be a short circuit.

Ruitenbeek's third point, as we saw, is that psychic mechanisms also appear in creative writing. Brooks suggests that this undeniable 'crossover between psychic operations and [literary] tropes' cannot simply be pointed out and left at that. In likening, say, a metaphor in a Victor Hugo novel to a symptom, the critic is not simply using metaphorical language, which would, Brooks says, be destructive of the mutual relationship of text and psychoanalysis, and a species of 'imperialism'.[27] He suggests the usefulness of the notion of 'transference'. This term comes from clinical practice, where it refers to the relation of analysand to analyst, and is also used, not as a metaphor but as a structural analogy, of the relation of reader to text, or viewer to film. In psychoanalytic practice, the analysand's early relations with formative people, principally parents or other carers, are acted out again in the person of the analyst. In terms of the textual encounter, the transferential model illuminates the interaction of speaker and listener, text and reader; the object of analysis is thus *reading*, not the author, reader or fictional character. Brooks suggests that, like the analysand on the couch, the reader experiences dramas of power and desire through interpreting and constructing the text, and that this indicates why psychoanalysis is not a random choice for a textual critical practice. Psychoanalysis allows us to engage with 'dramas of desire played out in tropes',[28] not simply better to understand a particular literary text, or even literary language itself, but to give us a better understanding of our own fictive and textual constructions as subjects. A similar point is made by Lennard J. Davis in *Resisting Novels*; he tries to explain the fascination fictional characters have for readers in terms of those readers' earliest relationships. Novels, he suggests, offer a painless interaction with textual entities; the reader has enjoyable, limited relationships which terminate smoothly and harmlessly at the end of the story.[29] The kind of pain and disappointment described by Freud need not always afflict the subject.[30] Again, this is analogous to clinical experience: in the transference, the analysand is supposed to go through all the stages of a past relationship which may have been painful and destructive, with the analyst as proxy, and as the analyst is not the real love-object, when the relationship is ended (that is, when analysis is terminated) the patient has learnt that not all relationships have to be angst-ridden and anxiety-provoking.

Ruitenbeek's fourth point is really just an amplification of his third, that writers since Freud have been given greater access to subjects such as homosexuality, Oedipal jealousy, the detailed ramifications of human sexuality, and so on, which they can now describe 'consciously'. Whether Ruitenbeek means that Freud has given licence to writers to refer to such subjects when they would have been shy of doing so before, or that they would not have even thought of them without Freud's prompting, is not entirely clear. Either way, Ruitenbeek's observation is a limited one. It partakes of the short circuit identified by Brooks; for instance, does a description of the Oedipal triangle, complete with details of phallically possessing the mother and stabbing the father in fantasy, occur in Virginia Woolf's *To the Lighthouse* because she was at that time engaged in publishing Freud's works in translation at the Hogarth Press,[31] or because, if the Oedipus complex does exist, then one would expect to find it routinely described in works of literature whether or not they precede Freud's description of it? As Freud himself pointed out, Oedipal jealousy finds expression in literature from centuries ago, by Sophocles and Shakespeare.

On the other hand, authors do clearly benefit from a climate in which psychoanalytic and other critical theories are circulating freely. The writing of contemporary British novelist Michèle Roberts, for example, is influenced by the theories of French feminist theorists Luce Irigaray and Hélène Cixous.[32] However, this is not primarily a matter of representation, of particular subjects covered, but of changing use and awareness of language.

Finally, Ruitenbeek claims that psychoanalysis has increased our (readers') understanding of texts and creative persons, following the 'myth of the sick artist'.[33] This is the opposite of the conclusion reached by Brooks, who says that it is the act of reading, and neither reader nor author, which is illuminated by psychoanalytic criticism; further, Brooks says that reading texts in the way he recommends speaks to our own subjective constitution. Ruitenbeek makes no claim for psychoanalysis that could not be made for other 'schools' of criticism, while Brooks makes the perhaps overly grandiose one that through psychoanalytic discourse, literary criticism could become 'the discourse of something anthropologically important'.[34]

As the shape of this anthology suggests, feminist psychoanalytic theory, or some configuration of what Jerry Aline Flieger has called the 'ménage à trois' of feminism, psychoanalysis and literature,[35] may be what follows on from Ruitenbeek's hope that psychoanalysis will illuminate literary art and artists, and Brooks's that it will turn out to be anthropologically significant. What is referred to as a monolithic practice – psychoanalytic feminist textual criticism – actually covers a variety of different positions. Elizabeth Wright summarizes these by dividing them generically: there are those feminist writers who 'search for psychoanalytic themes in literary texts' and those who perform a 'literary analysis of theoretical texts'[36] (in this volume, Minow-Pinkney's work on Woolf comes under the first category, Johnson's on Lacan's under the second).

Flieger distinguishes three kinds of psychoanalytic feminist writer, categorized according to their attitude towards the subject: first, the dutiful daughter, who emphasizes what is positive about Freudian theory for women, that it is descriptive and not prescriptive, and thus an essential tool for feminist understanding of patriarchy; second, a 'reaction against this phallic conceit and this paternal authority',[37] including turning to the maternal and pre-Oedipal realms instead of the paternal and Oedipal for a theoretical basis; and the third kind of feminist writer, called by Flieger the 'prodigal daughter', who alters the law before acceding to it.[38] In this volume, Marie Bonaparte is a kind of uncritically 'dutiful daughter' to Freud, although she does not consider how Freudian theory might aid a gender-aware reading of texts (Flieger cites Juliet Mitchell's *Psychoanalysis and Feminism* as the work of another typical dutiful daughter[39]); Luce Irigaray, a reactor against phallic conceit, has often been accused of simply reversing the Freudian and Lacanian valorization of masculine anatomy and authority in some of her works by putting in its place the female body and feminine myths;[40] while Dora, the subject of Freud's case history, is often thought of as a prodigal daughter because of her particular impact on psychoanalytic 'law', as are theorists Jacqueline Rose and Shoshana Felman (both represented here).

Ann Scott, writing from a Kleinian rather than a Freudian or Lacanian perspective, draws a chronological distinction between different feminist approaches to psychoanalysis: first came feminist interest in anthropological theories, both Lévi-Strauss's and Lacan's, in trying to understand the workings of patriarchy; followed by the 'mothering debate' in US theory, concentrating on understanding the lived experience of women (Nancy Chodorow and Dorothy Dinnerstein, for example, explicitly discuss Kleinian theory[41]); and then the recent 'explosion of cultural and feminist interest in the works of Klein herself';[42] all stages paralleled at the level of clinical practice by the growth of the Women's Therapy Centre in London.[43]

Flieger answers her own question about uniting feminism and psychoanalysis – 'How does unconsciousness raising tally with consciousness raising?'[44] – by claiming that, brought together and united with literature as well, the rewards of such a united practice include the politicization of aesthetics, and the contribution to theory as active subjects of a gender usually treated as the objects of study. Gender, its construction and social deployment, is one of the central areas of psychoanalytic investigation, and a feminist contribution to this endeavour can politicize psychoanalysis, raising to the surface – and into consciousness – its patriarchal assumptions. This is one reason why such interest has been shown in Freud's case history of Dora by feminist critics; put simply, while acting as if he could be her liberator, Freud was one of Dora's oppressors.[45] The unconscious dimension of the speech of a male analyst with a female patient has a particularly overt political identity.

Flieger suggests that transference can be a means of freeing up gender identity; as the original Oedipal drama is replayed, power positions shift between analyst and analysand, and both can occupy different gender roles successively or simultaneously.[46] She sees the recognition of the human subject as textual as a moment where psychoanalysis and feminism can join especially effectively. She emphasizes the potential for an understanding of the 'social aspects of intersubjective exchange', in which 'every human subject lays claim to his or her humanity by a *textual* process [...] a speaking or writing of desire *deflected* from the original short-circuit of the incestuous family foyer and diverted to the larger audience beyond'.[47] As the discussion of Johnson's essay on 'The Purloined Letter' above suggests, psychoanalytic discourse can be used to open up rather than close down debate; according to Flieger, Johnson's work 'opens a closed triangular circuit onto a never-ending social nexus',[48] that is, opens the Oedipal triad into the wider social world, by drawing attention to the surplus that can never be contained in the psychoanalytic, or any other, analysis. Jane Gallop's work on Freud's case history of Dora also widens the perspective outward, to include in her psychoanalytic reading of Freud's study a materialist account of the socio-economic position of the governess in fin-de-siècle Vienna, without which, she suggests, commentary on *Dora* remains incomplete.[49]

Kleinian theory has often been more explicitly aware than Freudian of the impact it may have on politics and social issues. In interviews, Hanna Segal (Klein's 'prodigal daughter') has discussed the implications for her practice of her founder-membership of International Psychoanalysts Against Nuclear Weapons.[50] She has pointed out that it would be peculiar if external influences on analysands did not turn out to include political and historical events, and in some of her quoted case studies this is clearly true.[51] Kleinian object-relations theory (and in this it is similar to Freudian theory) is concerned with analysis of such issues as the origins of political idealism in individuals, or even the motivations of wider political groupings.[52] As Scott puts it, if one believes with Klein that the infant world persists throughout adult life, then 'such a representation of the early months of life will have unavoidable repercussions for one's view of group processes, family life, political identifications, and social organization'.[53] Michael Rustin, in *The Good Society and the Inner World*, discusses various social issues, among them racism, from a Kleinian perspective.[54]

The broadening of the critical ménage à trois to include a materialist analysis of history along with feminism, psychoanalysis and literature seems to indicate the way psychoanalytic criticism will go in the future.[55]

The readings

The readings which make up this volume begin with Freud and end with Irigaray, by way of Lacan and Kristeva; this is one way of structuring the relationship between psychoanalysis and critical practice. I will give only a brief description of the readings themselves: however, an

overview of the collection as a whole should emphasis its particular trajectory, and give a rationale for its contents.

Part I introduces Freud's most widely known concept, that of Oedipal
conflict, and a late essay, 'Beyond the Pleasure Principle', in which
Freud tries to locate an instinct more basic than the imperative to seek
pleasure. The critics whose work is placed alongside these two areas are
Harold Bloom and Peter Brooks, both of whom use Freudian concepts
for constructing theories rather than simply as methods of criticism.
Detailed psychoanalytic readings are not the point here, and individual
texts appear only as exemplifications. Bloom makes use of the Oedipus
complex as a model for his theory of literary history: it is a battle fought
every generation as successive poets attempt to shake off the influence
of older writers, and to prove that they are superior and original. Like
the Oedipal child, the new poet tries to prove he (sic) is not indebted to
a parent for his appearance in the world, and to deny the 'anxiety of
influence' his precursors may at first cause him. Brooks uses Freud's
'Beyond the Pleasure Principle' to suggest why it is that we not only
enjoy but invest much emotional energy in narrative; like the organism,
the reader wants to reach the end of the book, and that is why he or she
starts reading, but, like an individual life, the book must run the most
effective course first in order to offer a pleasurable discharge at the end.

Part II includes short extracts from one of Freud's case histories,
known as 'The Wolf Man'. These are accompanied by Peter Nicholls's
'The Belated Postmodern', in which he takes up elements of Freud's
study of the Wolf Man, and arguments in contemporary postmodernist
theory, to analyse and historicize Toni Morrison's novels, particularly
Beloved.

Part III is designed to contrast the approaches generated by Freudian
and Lacanian psychoanalysis. An extract from Marie Bonaparte's classic Freudian reading of Poe is set beside Barbara Johnson's discussion
of Lacan and Derrida's debate on Poe's story 'The Purloined Letter', in
which she uses the debate as the occasion for a more general and far-
reaching meditation on interpretation itself. Edmund Wilson's Freudian
approach to Henry James's *The Turn of the Screw* is similarly contrast-
ed with Shoshana Felman's 'Turning the Screw of Interpretation',
which, like Johnson's essay on Poe, takes the opportunity to make not
only a Lacanian reading of James's novella, but an investigation into
the project of psychoanalytic criticism itself.

Part IV deals with Lacan, his idea that the unconscious is structured
like a language, and the role played in his theory by the phallus. Lacan's
rather difficult text is interpreted by the two extracts which go with it:
these are part of Jacqueline Rose's introduction to *Jacques Lacan and*

the Ecole Freudienne: Feminine Sexuality, in which her translation of 'The Meaning of the Phallus' appears, and a section from Elizabeth Grosz's *Jacques Lacan: A Feminist Introduction*, in which she distinguishes between the signifier phallus and the organ penis in Lacan's thought.

Part V, on Kristeva, begins with an extract on abjection from her book *Powers of Horror*; this is followed by Toril Moi's discussion of Kristeva's theory of how the abject may be part of a revolutionary, and therefore feminist, process. The extract from Makiko Minow-Pinkney is a Kristevan reading of Virginia Woolf's novel *Mrs Dalloway*, concentrating on such elements as the slipping subject position in the text.

Finally, French feminist psychoanalysis and film theory appear together in Part VI. The potentially liberatory aspects of the theory of masquerade are explored by Mary Ann Doane in relation to the representation of the female body on screen. Luce Irigaray's 'Women, the sacred and money' attempts to describe the nature of the feminine under patriarchy, and the implication of this position for representation by and of women.

Notes

1 E. Ann Kaplan, 'Introduction', in Kaplan (ed.), *Psychoanalysis and Cinema* (London: Routledge/AFI, 1990), pp. 12–13. Thanks to John Haffenden and Erica Sheen for critical comments on this introduction.

2 See Sigmund Freud, 'The Unconscious', *SE*, vol. 14, (1915); 'The Mystic Writing Pad', ibid., vol. 19, (1919); and Juliet Flower MacCannell's entry in Elizabeth Wright, (ed.) *Feminism and Psychoanalysis: A Critical Dictionary* (Oxford: Blackwell, 1992), p. 440ff.

3 Ann Scott, 'Melanie Klein and the Questions of Feminism', in *Women: A Cultural Review*, 1 (2) (Summer 1990), p. 129. For a critical view of Kleinian claims to empiricism, see Noreen O'Connor, 'Is Melanie Klein the One Who Knows Who You Really Are?', in *Women: A Cultural Review*, 1 (2) (Summer 1990); Scott herself points out that Klein allows us to break with the empirical (p. 132). Perry Anderson has given an account of the British psychoanalytic tradition and its marginalization in 'Components of the National Culture', *New Left Review*, 56 (1968).

4 Wright, (ed.), *Feminism and Psychoanalysis*, p. 225.

5 See, for instance, Mary Jacobus, Evelyn Fox Keller and Sally Shuttleworth (eds.), *Body/Politics: Women and the Discourses of Science* (London: Routledge, 1990).

6 Meg Harris Williams and Margot Waddell, *The Maiden Chamber of Thought* (London: Routledge, 1991); Michael O'Pray, 'Primitive Phantasy in David Cronenberg's Films', *BFI Film Dossier* (1981).

7 Nancy Fraser and Sandra Lee Bartky (eds.), *Revaluing French Feminism: Critical Essays on Difference, Agency, and Culture* (Bloomington: University of Indiana Press, 1992), p. 1.

8 Definitions of psychoanalytic terms, principally Freudian although also including a number of Lacanian and Kleinian entries, can be found in J. Laplanche and J. B. Pontalis, *The Language of Psychoanalysis*, trans. Donald Nicholson-Smith, With an introduction by Daniel Lagache (London: Karnac Books, 1988); see also R. D. Hinshelwood, *A Dictionary of Kleinian Thought* (London: Free Association Books, 1987); and Wright (ed.), *Feminism and Psychoanalysis*.

9 Geoffrey Hartman (ed.), *Psychoanalysis and the Question of the Text* (Baltimore and London: Johns Hopkins University Press, 1978), p. 9.

10 Ibid., p. xix.

11 Shlomith Rimmon-Kenan (ed.), *Discourse in Psychoanalysis and Literature* (London: Methuen, 1987), p. xii.

12 Ibid., p. XV.

13 Shoshana Felman, (ed.), *Psychoanalysis and Literature: The Question of Reading: Otherwise* (Baltimore and London: Johns Hopkins University Press, 1982), p. 6.

14 Ibid., pp. 8–9.

15 Ibid., p. 10.

16 Robert Young (ed.), *Untying the Text: A Post-Structuralist Reader* (London: Routledge & Kegan Paul, 1981), p. 226.

17 Peter Brooks, 'The Idea of a Psychoanalytic Literary Criticism', in Rimmon-Kenan (ed.), *Discourse in Psychoanalysis and Literature*, p. 7.

18 Young, *Untying the Text*, p. 227.

19 Hartman (ed.), *Psychoanalysis and the Question of the Text*, p. xii.

20 Ibid., p. x.

21 Sigmund Freud, 'Psycho-Analytic Notes on an Autobiographical Account of a Case of Paranoia', *SE*, vol. 12 (1911).

22 Hendrik M. Ruitenbeek (ed.), *Psychoanalysis and Literature* (New York: E. P. Dutton, 1964); Brooks, 'The Idea of a Psychoanalytic Literary Criticism'.

23 Ruitenbeek (ed.), *Psychoanalysis and Literature*, p. xi.

24 Rimmon-Kenan (ed.), *Discourse in Psychoanalysis and Literature*, p. xii.

25 Ibid., p. xi.

26 Brooks, 'The Idea of a Psychoanalytic Literary Criticism', p. 4.

27 Ibid., pp. 8,9.

28 Ibid., p. 17.

29 Lennard J. Davis, *Resisting Novels: Ideology and Fiction* (London: Methuen, 1987).

30 Sigmund Freud, 'The Development of the Libido', *SE*, vol. 7, (1905).

31 Rachel Bowlby, *Virginia Woolf: Feminist Destinations* (Oxford: Blackwell, 1988), p. 65.

32 See Helen Birch's review of Roberts's *In the Red Kitchen* (London: Methuen, 1990): 'The development from her first, self-referential

Bildungsroman, A Piece of the Night, to her last, fictional reworking of the theories of French feminists Julia Kristeva, Hélène Cixous and Luce Irigaray, *The Book of Mrs Noah*, shows her becoming more and more ambitious. She refuses stable subjectivities and signs, scrutinizes the rhythms of language, questions sexual difference and even writing itself' ('Whispers of Immortality', *New Statesman and Society*, 14 September 1990).

33 Hartman (ed.), *Psychoanalysis and the Question of the Text*, p. xvi.

34 Brooks, 'The Idea of a Psychoanalytic Literary Criticism', p. 4.

35 Jerry Aline Flieger, 'Entertaining the Ménage à Trois: Psychoanalysis, Feminism, and Literature', in Richard Feldstein and Judith Roof, (eds.), *Feminism and Psychoanalysis* (Ithaca and London: Cornell University Press, 1989).

36 Wright (ed.), *Feminism and Psychoanalysis*, p. 224.

37 Flieger, 'Entertaining the Ménage à Trois', p. 191; the phrase 'phallic conceit', as Flieger points out, is Jane Gallop's, from *Feminism and Psychoanalysis: The Daughter's Seduction* (London: Macmillan, 1982), ch. 2, 'Of Phallic Proportions: Lacanian Conceit'.

38 Flieger, 'Entertaining the Ménage à Trois', p. 192.

39 See Juliet Mitchell, *Psychoanalysis and Feminism* (Harmondsworth: Pelican, 1975).

40 Flieger places theorists in different categories: Irigaray and Mitchell, for instance, are both also labelled 'prodigal daughters'. This flexibility is an important aspect of Flieger's feminist enterprise.

41 See Nancy Chodorow, *The Reproduction of Mothering: Psychoanalysis and the Sociology of Gender* (Berkeley: University of California Press, 1978); and Dorothy Dinnerstein, *The Rocking of the Cradle and the Ruling of the World* (London: Souvenir Press, 1978).

42 Scott, 'Melanie Klein and the Questions of Feminism', p. 128. She gives some examples of the increased interest in Klein, including recent Virago reprints of Klein's works. (Thanks to Alex George, Daniel Isaacson and Michael O'Pray for bibliographical information on Klein.)

43 See Wright (ed.), *Feminism and Psychoanalysis*, p. 457ff.

44 Flieger, 'Entertaining the Ménage à Trois', p. 188.

45 Charles Bernheimer and Claire Kahane (eds.), *In Dora's Case: Freud, Hysteria, Feminism* (London: Virago, 1985), p. 103.

46 This relation has been luridly portrayed in film: *Dressed to Kill* (Brian De Palma, 1980), *Silence of the Lambs* (Jonathan Demme, 1991) and *Final Analysis* (Phil Joanou, 1992), among others, show gender and role flexibility resulting in sexual betrayal and violence.

47 Flieger, 'Entertaining the Ménage à Trois', p. 205.

48 Ibid., p. 207.

49 Jane Gallop, 'Keys to Dora', in Wright (ed.), *Feminism and Psychoanalysis*, ch. 8.

50 'Hanna Segal Interviewed by Jacqueline Rose', in *Women: a Cultural Review* and Jan Moir, 'A piece of her mind', *Guardian* (23 September 1992), p. 35.

51 The Holocaust appears in two case studies: Hanna Segal had a patient who dreamed of a mass grave as a part of depressive anxieties (*Introduction to the Work of Melanie Klein,* London: Karnac Books, 1988, pp. 93–4); and Margot Waddell cites a patient's dream about a chamber full of mutilated bodies, which she associates with the woman's guilt about damage done by her, a 'Holocaust chamber of her mind' ('Gender Identity: Fifty Years on from Freud', *Women: A Cultural Review* p. 155).

52 See Klein's interview with Rose in *Women: A Cultural Review,* p. 204, for a discussion of how to analyse Conservative and Labour policy.

53 *Women,* p. 131.

54 Michael Rustin, *The Good Society and the Inner World: Psychoanalysis, Politics and Culture* (London: Verso, 1991).

55 Terry Eagleton points out the absence of rigorous textual criticism based on an alliance of feminism and materialism in the second edition of his *Myths of Power: A Marxist Study of the Brontës* (London: Macmillan, 1988), although an example he gives, Judith Lowder Newton's *Women, Power and Subversion* (University of Georgia Press, 1981) is a notable exception.

Part I
The Oedipus Complex and the Pleasure Principle

The Oedipus complex

Freud is probably most commonly associated with the theory of the Oedipus complex. Aspects of it appear in all kinds of popular forms, from Woody Allen's short film *Oedipus Wrecks* about a King Kong-sized phantom mother,[1] to John Lennon's celebrated lyric, 'Mother, you had me but I never had you'.[2] It is unclear whether or not Freud would have taken such apparent acknowledgements of the Oedipus complex as testimony to genuine faith in its existence, as elsewhere he claims that passionate resistance to it in fact constitutes grounds for believing in it – 'its reconstruction in the work of analysis is met in adults with the most decided disbelief'[3] – which simply testifies to the effective repression of a psychic reality.

What is less well known is that nowhere does Freud present a systematic account of what he means by the Oedipus complex after his first mention of it in 1910.[4] References to and accounts of it appear in various places throughout Freud's works, each with different details or emphases, and even major theoretical shifts concerning particularly the role of the little girl in the complex, and the issue of infantile sexuality.

The Oedipus complex is Freud's 'founding' theory, as Laplanche and Pontalis put it;[5] he claims that it is formative in the construction of sexual difference, the superego, and later behaviour, the ' "nucleus of the neuroses" '[6]. It underpins not only the infancy of every person but the infancy of humanity itself, as Freud suggests in *Totem and Taboo*; Oedipal guilt is the reason for structures of religion and morality.[7]

Put briefly, the Oedipus complex is what Freud called the 'family romance': the little boy, aged between three and five, loves his mother and jealously hates his rival for her love, the father. The little girl analogously loves the father and hates the betraying mother, who has failed to provide her with a penis. The complex is resolved for the boy by the castration complex, that is, fear of castration by the father if the boy continues with his amorous attitude towards his mother; for the girl the complex is instead initiated by the castration complex as she is already 'castrated', that is, possesses no penis.

There are many issues of significance arising from this brief summary. In his essay 'An Example of Psycho-Analytic Work'[8] Freud discusses the complex in some detail, which is worth looking at here. He emphasizes the importance for the child of its early years, and describes influences from this time 'which do not apply to all children, though they are common enough – such as the sexual abuse of children by adults, their seduction by other children ... their being deeply stirred by seeing or hearing at first hand sexual behaviour between adults' which you would not expect them to understand (p. 187). This statement of Freud's is very interesting, as here he is clearly treating the scenes of 'seduction' (that is, child sexual abuse, or even rape) which many of his female patients recounted to him, as material facts. (He also noted several cases of male patients, including the Wolf Man, who claimed to have been 'seduced' or sexually initiated in some way by governesses and nurses.) In 1914 Freud abandoned this theory of real child abuse by male parents or relations, as he claimed that there could be no therapeutic access to the facts, and 'it was hardly credible that perverted acts against children were so general'.[9] It was in this way that Freud 'stumbled' across the theory of infantile sexuality: that children desire their parents, not necessarily the other way round, and fantasize these scenes of abuse or seduction. What had been a material reality in Freud's work became a psychic one.

As well as the use to which Harold Bloom puts the Oedipus complex in explaining literary history in the following reading, and its 'thematic' appearance in literary texts,[10] the process of remembering on which it depends is significant for literary criticism, as Peter Nicholls suggests (see Part II). In Sophocles' play *Oedipus Rex*, Oedipus's present is entirely formed by the past which he painfully reconstructs, and in which he finally sees his own role. Freud likens this process to the way psychoanalysis works: 'The work of the Athenian dramatist exhibits the way in which the long-past deed of Oedipus is gradually brought to light by an investigation ingeniously protracted and fanned into life by ever fresh relays of evidence. To this extent it has a certain resemblance to the progress of a psychoanalysis' ('Development of the Libido', p. 330).

As a transition to the following readings, it is worth pointing out that Freud's downgrading of the role of the mother in the Oedipus complex (all she can do is encourage either incest or regression) has been widely criticized.[11] Freud presents the mother as a figure whose role must be 'resolved' under a superior patriarchal law.[12] *Pace* Mitchell, as Martin Stanton points out, Freud's account of psycho-sexual development actively excludes anything specifically feminine: 'the phallus and castration, for example, determine not only the constitution of sexual difference, but "knowledge" of it, and its supposed heterosexual "resolution".'[13] Melanie Klein reacted against precisely this ignoring of the mother in suggesting that the triadic relationship of mother, father and child is importantly preceded by a dyadic one, between mother and child. Also in reaction to Freud, Luce Irigaray has constructed a psychoanalytic and literary theory which depends not on the male but the female body (see Part VI).

Harold Bloom and the anxiety of influence

Harold Bloom suggests that poets misread previous masters to produce a new work, and then deny their paternity, along the lines of Oedipal rivalry. He uses psychoanalytic theory not to analyse specific texts, although this follows from what he proposes: he aims for 'a poetics that will foster a more adequate practical criticism', as he states in the reading here. He uses psychoanalysis to construct a more general theory of both writing and reading, and ultimately of knowledge itself, suggesting that, as happens in the Oedipus complex, poets battle with their artistic fathers in order to gain authority for themselves, in the same way that Oedipus and all other male infants battle with their own fathers for supremacy as a necessary part of becoming adult men.

Just as sons may, and Oedipus did, imagine they are self-created, not even dependent on the father for their existence, so poets may also claim that they have no influences, as Wallace Stevens does here in the letter Bloom quotes. What they write is all their own work. Bloom is careful to avoid this trap himself, and states that 'Nietzsche and Freud are, so far as I can tell, the prime influences upon the theory of influence' he has constructed. As Bloom points out, 'influence' is not always a matter of either conscious design or of having read the influencing writer. Ideas and even phrases from certain works can be such common currency that everyone is familiar with the experience of discovering that they are inadvertently quoting Shakespeare ('Neither a borrower nor a lender be'), for instance, without necessarily having read, Shakespeare's works.

Bloom suggests that it is impossible to be one's own father, poetically just as biologically, and far from being an admission of failure, of an inability to create originally, the traces of a precursor poet's work in that of the following poet ('ephebe', as Bloom terms this figure) and the ways in which the earlier poet is misread ('misprised'), are actually what makes the poet's work interesting and valuable. According to Bloom, the extent to which the previous poet's voice has been subdued to the ephebe's own is the measure of how 'strong' a poet is. However, Bloom sees a kind of poetic entropy at work, as if all the re-reading of earlier poets actually wears out poetic value, so the ephebe can only produce a watered-down version of the earlier work: 'poetry in our tradition, when it dies, will be self-slain, murdered by its own past strength'.

Bloom states that he finds Freud's 'family romance' the most useful model for analysing relations between poets, and that the latter's account of 'the mechanisms of defense and their ambivalent functionings provide the clearest analogues I have found for the revisionary ratios that govern intra-poetic relations'. The anxiety provoked by the Oedipal condition reappears in matters of poetic influence, and the attitude of the ephebe to the precursor poet may well be ambivalent, if not hostile.

This takes the idea propounded by Peter Brooks a stage further: Brooks suggested that a psychoanalytic literary criticism would investigate the ways in which the workings of a text resemble those of the human psyche. Bloom is using a psychoanalytic developmental theory to suggest how literary history works, why there are particular schools or movements at particular times, and how to evaluate a writer according to their Oedipal success or failure. The 'revisionary ratios' Bloom mentions here are six psychic defences against the parent poet, the specific operations a poet makes on the precursor's work, and therefore recognizing these ratios at work becomes the critical tool for analysing the different elements texts are composed of: a kind of incestuous intertextuality. Bloom likens the methods adopted by poets to the structure of the psyche: in the rest of his book he 'work[s] through [...] the revisionary ratios as mechanisms of defense'. In *The Anxiety of Influence*, he produces a reading of Shelley's 'Ode to the West Wind' as it struggles with Wordsworth's 'Ode: Intimations of Immortality', which shows how each stanza of Shelley's poem uses different revisionary ratios in an effort to get away from the parent poem.[14] And as Bloom points out here, Wordsworth's poem is itself a misreading of Milton's *Lycidas*.

It might be true that, as Juliet Mitchell argues of Freud,[15] Bloom is being descriptive, not prescriptive; and simply observing the passionate struggle for supremacy which does occur between male, or masculine, poets. Examples of works which can be interestingly read in a Bloomian way include T. S. Eliot's *The Waste Land*, which is highly intertextual; or *Bonfire of the Vanities* by Tom Wolfe, that self-styled twentieth-century Dickensian. However, even if this is true, it does seem that Bloom's claim to have put forward a universal poetic theory cannot be correct, as it leaves a feminist collaboration model unaccounted for, and fails to discuss the way in which influence is a gendered concept.[16] Bloom makes no effort to explore how the Oedipus complex affects women. As Sandra Gilbert and Susan Gubar say, women poets have a different attitude to male and female precursors from that of most male poets, who, according to Bloom, may see the muse as female, the earlier poet as male.[17]

Sigmund Freud, 'Beyond the Pleasure Principle', and Peter Brooks, 'Freud's Masterplot'

Freud's essay 'Beyond the Pleasure Principle'[18] was written in 1920, in the shadow of the First World War, which clearly influenced his theorizing in this work. Its influence on critical practice has largely centred around the account in it of the game of disappearance and reappearance ('*fort-da*') played by a little boy, as it has implications for theories about the acquisition of language, symbolization and the child's relation to its mother.

Peter Brooks in *Reading for the Plot*,[19] in the chapter entitled 'Freud's Masterplot', reproduced here, takes Freud's discussion of what lies beyond the pleasure principle further, and uses elements from the whole essay, intertextually, as he says, to construct a model for explaining the pleasure to be gained from reading as it relates to novelistic plotting. He deliberately distances himself from structuralist accounts of narrative[20] which have concentrated on identifying 'minimal narrative units and paradigmatic structures' because he finds them unable to account for 'the play of desire in time that makes us turn pages and strive for narrative ends' (p. xiii). Brooks chooses psychoanalysis as his template instead because, as we have seen in relation to the role of memory in the Oedipus complex, it is a narrative art 'concerned with the recovery of the past through the dynamics of memory and desire' (p. xiv). Like Bloom, Brooks is not using psychoanalysis to study authors' neuroses or to attribute an unconscious to fictional characters, but to compare the function of psyche and text (p. 112). Again like Bloom, Brooks starts not with individual readings of texts, although this is what he aims for, but with a more general model for reading and interpreting texts.

1 HAROLD BLOOM

A Meditation upon Priority, and a Synopsis

This short book offers a theory of poetry by way of a description of poetic influence, or the story of intra-poetic relationships. One aim of this theory is corrective: to de-idealize our accepted accounts of how one poet helps to form another. Another aim, also corrective, is to try to provide a poetics that will foster a more adequate practical criticism.

Poetic history, in this book's argument, is held to be indistinguishable from poetic influence, since strong poets make that history by misreading one another, so as to clear imaginative space for themselves.

My concern is only with strong poets; major figures with the persistence to wrestle with their strong precursors, even to the death. Weaker talents idealize; figures of capable imagination appropriate for themselves. But nothing is got for nothing, and self-appropriation involves the immense anxieties of indebtedness, for what strong maker desires the realization that he has failed to create himself? Oscar Wilde, who knew he had failed as a poet because he lacked strength to overcome his anxiety of influence, knew also the darker truths concerning influence. *The Ballad of Reading Gaol* becomes an embarrassment to read, directly one recognizes that every lustre it exhibits is reflected from *The Rime of the Ancient Mariner*; and Wilde's lyrics anthologize the whole of English High Romanticism. Knowing this, and armed with his customary intelligence, Wilde bitterly remarks in *The Portrait of Mr W. H.* that: 'Influence is simply a transference of personality, a mode of giving away what is most precious to one's self, and its exercise produces a sense, and, it may be, a reality of loss. Every disciple takes away something from his master.' This is the anxiety of influencing, yet no reversal in this area is a true reversal. Two years later, Wilde refined this bitterness in one of Lord Henry Wotton's elegant observations in *The Picture of Dorian Gray*, where he tells Dorian that all influence is immoral:

> Because to influence a person is to give him one's own soul. He does not think his natural thoughts, or burn with his natural passions. His virtues are not real to him. His sins, if there are such things as sins, are borrowed. He becomes an echo of someone else's music, an actor of a part that has not been written for him.

To apply Lord Henry's insight to Wilde, we need only read Wilde's review of Pater's *Appreciations*, with its splendidly self-deceptive closing observation that Pater 'has escaped disciples'. Every major aesthetic consciousness seems peculiarly more gifted at denying obligation as the hungry generations go on treading one another down. Stevens, a stronger heir of Pater than even Wilde was, is revealingly vehement in his letters:

> While, of course, I come down from the past, the past is my own and not something marked Coleridge, Wordsworth, etc. I know of no one who has been particularly important to me. My reality-imagination complex is entirely my own even though I see it in others.

He might have said: 'particularly because I see it in others', but poetic influence was hardly a subject where Stevens' insights could center. Towards the end, his denials became rather violent, and oddly humored. Writing to the poet Richard Eberhart, he extends a sympathy all the stronger for being self-sympathy:

> I sympathize with your denial of any influence on my part. This sort of thing always jars me because, in my own case, I am not conscious of having been influenced by anybody and have purposely held off from reading highly mannered people like Eliot and Pound so that I should not absorb anything, even unconsciously. But there is a kind of critic who spends his time dissecting what he reads for echoes, imitations, influences, as if no one was ever simply himself but is always compounded of a lot of other people. As for W. Blake, I think that this means Wilhelm Blake.

This view, that poetic influence scarcely exists, except in furiously active pedants, is itself an illustration of one way in which poetic influence is a variety of melancholy or an anxiety-principle. Stevens was, as he insisted, a highly individual poet, as much an American original as Whitman or Dickinson, or his own contemporaries: Pound, Williams, Moore. But poetic influence need not make poets less original; as often it makes them more original, though not therefore necessarily better. The profundities of poetic influence cannot be reduced to source-study, to the history of ideas, to the patterning of images. Poetic influence, or as I shall more frequently term it, poetic misprision, is necessarily the study of the life-cycle of the poet-as-poet. When such study considers the context in which that life-cycle is enacted, it will be compelled to examine simultaneously the relations between poets as cases akin to what Freud called the family romance, and as chapters in the history of modern revisionism, 'modern' meaning here post-Enlightenment. The modern poet, as W. J. Bate shows in *The Burden of the Past and the English Poet*, is the inheritor of a melancholy engendered in the mind of the Enlightenment by its skepticism of its own double heritage of imaginative wealth, from the ancients and from the Renaissance masters. In this book I largely neglect the area Bate has explored with great skill, in order to center upon intra-poetic relationships as parallels of family romance. Though I employ these parallels, I do so as a deliberate revisionist of some of the Freudian emphases.

Nietzsche and Freud are, so far as I can tell, the prime influences upon the theory of influence presented in this book. Nietzsche is the prophet of the antithetical, and his *Genealogy of Morals* is the profoundest study available to me of the revisionary and ascetic strains in the aesthetic temperament. Freud's investigations of the mechanisms of defense and their ambivalent functionings provide the clearest analogues I have found for the revisionary ratios that govern intra-poetic relations. Yet, the theory of influence expounded here is un-Nietzschean in its deliberate literalism, and in its Viconian insistence that priority in divination is crucial for every strong poet, lest he dwindle merely into a latecomer. My theory rejects also the qualified Freudian optimism that happy substitution is possible, that a second chance can save us from the repetitive quest for our earliest attachments. Poets as poets cannot accept substitutions, and fight to the end to have their initial chance alone. Both Nietzsche and Freud underestimated poets and poetry, yet each yielded more power to phantasmagoria than it truly possesses. They too, despite their moral realism, over-idealized the imagination. Nietzsche's disciple, Yeats, and Freud's disciple, Otto Rank, show a greater awareness of the artist's fight against art, and of the relation of this struggle to the artist's antithetical battle against nature.

Freud recognized sublimation as the highest human achievement, a recognition that allies him to Plato and to the entire moral traditions of both Judaism and Christianity. Freudian sublimation involves the yielding-up of more primordial for more refined modes of pleasure, which is to exalt the second chance above the first. Freud's poem, in the view of this book, is not severe enough, unlike the severe poems written by the creative lives of the strong poets. To equate emotional maturation with

the discovery of acceptable substitutes may be pragmatic wisdom, particularly in the realm of Eros, but this is not the wisdom of the strong
poets. The surrendered dream is not merely a phantasmagoria of endless gratification, but is the greatest of all human illusions, the vision of
immortality. If Wordsworth's *Ode: Intimations of Immortality from
Recollections of Earliest Childhood* possessed only the wisdom found
also in Freud, then we could cease calling it 'the Great Ode'.
Wordsworth too saw repetition or second chance as essential for development, and his ode admits that we can redirect our needs by substitution or sublimation. But the ode plangently also awakens into failure,
and into the creative mind's protest against time's tyranny. A
Wordsworthian critic, even one as loyal to Wordsworth as Geoffrey
Hartman, can insist upon clearly distinguishing between *priority*, as a
concept from the natural order, and *authority*, from the spiritual order,
but Wordsworth's ode declines to make this distinction. 'By seeking to
overcome priority,' Hartman wisely says, 'art fights nature on nature's
own ground, and is bound to lose.' The argument is that strong poets
are condemned to just this unwisdom; Wordsworth's Great Ode fights
nature on nature's own ground, and suffers a great defeat, even as it
retains its greater dream. That dream, in Wordsworth's ode, is shad-
owed by the anxiety of influence, due to the greatness of the precursor-
poem, Milton's *Lycidas*, where the human refusal wholly to sublimate is
even more rugged, despite the ostensible yielding to Christian teachings
of sublimation.

For every poet begins (however 'unconsciously') by rebelling more
strongly against the consciousness of death's necessity than all other
men and women do. The young citizen of poetry, or ephebe as Athens
would have called him, is already the anti-natural or antithetical man,
and from his start as a poet he quests for an impossible object, as his
precursor quested before him. That this quest encompasses necessarily
the diminishment of poetry seems to me an inevitable realization, one
that accurate literary history must sustain. The great poets of the
English Renaissance are not matched by their Enlightened descendants,
and the whole tradition of the post-Enlightenment, which is
Romanticism, shows a further decline in its Modernist and post-
Modernist heirs. The death of poetry will not be hastened by any reader's broodings, yet it seems just to assume that poetry in our tradition,
when it dies, will be self-slain, murdered by its own past strength. An
implied anguish throughout this book is that Romanticism, for all its
glories, may have been a vast visionary tragedy, the self-baffled enterprise not of Prometheus but of blinded Oedipus, who did not know that
the Sphinx was his Muse.

Oedipus, blind, was on the path to oracular godhood, and the strong poets have followed him by transforming their blindness towards their precursors into the revisionary insights of their own work. The six revisionary movements that I will trace in the strong poet's life-cycle could as well be more, and could take quite different names than those I have employed. I have kept them to six, because these seem to be minimal and essential to my understanding of how one poet deviates from another. The names, though arbitrary, carry on from various traditions that have been central in Western imaginative life, and I hope can be useful.

The greatest poet in our language is excluded from the argument for several reasons. One is necessarily historical; Shakespeare belongs to the giant age before the flood, before the anxiety of influence became central to poetic consciousness. Another has to do with the contrast between dramatic and lyric form. As poetry has become more subjective, the shadow cast by the precursors has become more dominant. The main cause, though, is that Shakespeare's prime precursor was Marlowe, a poet very much smaller than his inheritor. Milton, with all his strength, yet had to struggle, subtly and crucially, with a major precursor in Spenser, and this struggle both formed and malformed Milton. Coleridge, ephebe of Milton and later of Wordsworth, would have been glad to find his Marlowe in Cowper (or in the much weaker Bowles), but influence cannot be willed. Shakespeare is the largest instance in the language of a phenomenon that stands outside the concern of this book: the absolute absorption of the precursor. Battle between strong equals, father and son as mighty opposites, Laius and Oedipus at the crossroads; only this is my subject here, though some of the fathers, as will be seen, are composite figures. That even the strongest poets are subject to influences not poetical is obvious even to me, but again my concern is only with *the poet in a poet*, or the aboriginal poetic self.

A change like the one I propose in our ideas of influence should help us read more accurately any group of past poets who were contemporary with one another. To give one example, as misinterpreters of Keats, *in their poems*, the Victorian disciples of Keats most notably include Tennyson, Arnold, Hopkins, and Rossetti. That Tennyson triumphed in his long, hidden contest with Keats, no one can assert absolutely, but his clear superiority over Arnold, Hopkins, and Rossetti is due to his relative victory or at least holding of his own in contrast to their partial defeats. Arnold's elegiac poetry uneasily blends Keatsian style with anti-Romantic sentiment, while Hopkins' strained intensities and convolutions of diction and Rossetti's densely inlaid art are also at variance with the burdens they seek to alleviate in their own poetic selves. Similarly, in our time we need to look again at Pound's unending match with Browning, as at Stevens' long and largely hidden civil war with the major poets of English and American Romanticism – Wordsworth, Keats, Shelley, Emerson, and Whitman. As with the Victorian Keatsians, these are instances among many, if a more accurate story is to be told about poetic history.

2 PETER BROOKS

Freud's Masterplot

Let us undertake, then, to read *Beyond the Pleasure Principle* (1920) in intertextual relation to narrative fictions and the processes of plotting as we have begun to understand them. We may find a general legitimation for this enterprise in the fact that *Beyond the Pleasure Principle* constitutes Freud's own masterplot, the essay where he lays out most fully a total scheme of how life proceeds from beginning to end, and how each individual life in its own manner repeats the masterplot and confronts the question of whether the closure of an individual life is contingent or necessary. It is indeed so difficult to say what Freud is talking about in this essay – and especially, what he is *not* talking about – that we are almost forced to acknowledge that ultimately he is talking about the very possibility of talking about life – about its very 'narratability'. His boldest intention may be to provide a theory of comprehension of the dynamic of the life span, and hence of its narrative understanding. It is also notable that *Beyond the Pleasure Principle* is plotted in ways which, Freud suggests, have little to do with its original intention: near the end of the essay he speaks of the need to 'throw oneself into a line of thought and to follow it wherever it leads'.[21] The plotting of the masterplot is determined by the structural demands of Freud's thought, and it is in this spirit that we must read it as speaking of narrative plots.

Narrative always makes the implicit claim to be in a state of repetition, as a going over again of a ground already covered: a *sjužet* repeating the *fabula*, as the detective retraces the tracks of the criminal.[22] This claim to an act of repetition – 'I sing of', 'I tell of' – appears to be initiatory of narrative. It is equally initiatory of *Beyond the Pleasure Principle*: it is the first problem and clue that Freud confronts. Evidence of a 'beyond' that does not fit neatly into the functioning of the pleasure principle comes first in the dreams of patients suffering from war neuroses or from the traumatic neuroses of peace: dreams that return to the moment of trauma, to relive its pain in apparent contradiction of the wish-fulfillment theory of dreams. This 'dark and dismal' example is superseded by an example from 'normal' life, and we have the celebrated moment of child's play: the toy thrown away, the reel on the string thrown out of the crib and pulled back, to the alternate exclamation of *fort* and *da*. When he has established the equivalence between making the toy disappear and the child's mother's disappearance, Freud is faced with a set of possible interpretations. Why does the child repeat an unpleasurable experience? It may be answered that by staging his mother's disappearance and return, the child is compensating for his instinctual renunciation. Yet the child has also staged disappearance alone, without reappearance, as a game. This may make one want to argue that the essential experience involved is the movement from a passive to an active role in regard to his mother's disappearance, claiming mastery in a situation to which he has been compelled to submit.

Repetition as the movement from passivity to mastery reminds us of another essay, 'The Theme of the Three Caskets' (1913), where Freud, considering Bassanio's choice of the lead casket in *The Merchant of Venice* – the correct choice in the suit of Portia – decides that the choice of the right maiden in man's literary play is also the choice of death; by this choice, he asserts an active mastery of what he must in fact endure. 'Choice stands in the place of necessity, of destiny. In this way man overcomes death, which he has recognized intellectually.'[23] If repetition is mastery, movement from the passive to the active, and if mastery is an assertion of control over what man must in fact submit to – choice, we might say, of an imposed end – we have already a suggestive comment on the grammar of plot, where repetition, taking us back again over the same ground, could have to do with the choice of ends.

But other possibilities suggest themselves to Freud at this point. The repetition of unpleasant experience – the mother's disappearance – might be explained by the motive of revenge, which would yield its own pleasure. The uncertainty that Freud faces here is whether repetition can be considered a primary event, independent of the pleasure principle, or whether there is always some direct yield of pleasure of another sort involved. The pursuit of this doubt takes Freud into the analytic experience, to his discovery of the analysand's need to repeat, rather than simply remember, the past: the analysand 'is obliged to *repeat* the repressed material as a contemporary experience instead of, as the physician would prefer to see, *remembering* it as something belonging to the past' (p. 18). In other words, as Freud argued in two papers that prepare the way for *Beyond the Pleasure Principle*, 'The Dynamics of the Transference' (1912) and 'Remembering, Repeating and Working Through' (1914), repetition – including the need to reproduce and to work through – is itself a form of remembering, brought into play when recollection properly speaking is blocked by resistance. Thus the analyst encounters a 'compulsion to repeat', which is the work of the unconscious repressed and becomes particularly discernible in the transference, where it can take 'ingenious' forms. (I note here, as a subject for later exploration, that the transference is itself a kind of metaphor, a substitutive medium for the analysand's infantile experiences, and thus approximates the status of a text.) The compulsion to repeat gives patients a sense of being fatefully subject to a 'perpetual recurrence of the same thing'; it can indeed suggest pursuit by a demonic power. We know from Freud's essay 'The Uncanny' (1919) that this feeling of the demonic, arising from involuntary repetition, is a particular attribute of the literature of the uncanny, of texts of compulsive recurrence.[24]

Thus in analytic work (as also in literary texts) there is slim but real evidence of a compulsion to repeat which can override the pleasure principle, and which seems 'more primitive, more elementary, more instinctual than the pleasure principle which it overrides' (p. 23). Now, repetition is so basic to our experience of literary texts that one is simultaneously tempted to say all and to say nothing on the subject. To state the matter baldly: rhyme, alliteration, assonance, meter, refrain, all the mnemonic elements of literature and indeed most of its tropes are in some manner repetitions that take us back in the text, that allow the ear, the eye, the mind to make connections, conscious or unconscious, between different textual moments, to see past and present as related and as establishing a future that will be noticeable as some variation in the pattern. Todorov's 'same-but-different' depends on repetition. If we think of the trebling characteristic of the folktale, and of all formulaic literature, we may consider that the repetition by three constitutes the minimal repetition to the perception of series, which would make it the minimal intentional structure of action, the minimum plot. Narrative, we have seen, must ever present itself as a repetition of events that have already happened, and within this postulate of a generalized repetition it must make use of specific, perceptible repetitions in order to create plot, that is, to show us a significant interconnection of events. An event gains meaning by its repetition, which is both the recall of an earlier moment and a variation of it: the concept of repetition hovers ambiguously between the idea of reproduction and that of change, forward and backward movement (as we shall consider further in the next chapter). Repetition creates a *return* in the text, a doubling back. We cannot say whether this return is a return *to* or a return *of*: for instance, a return to origins or a return of the repressed. Repetition through this ambiguity appears to suspend temporal process, or rather, to subject it to an indeterminate shuttling or oscillation that binds different moments together as a middle that might turn forward or back. This inescapable middle is suggestive of the demonic: repetition and return are perverse and difficult, interrupting simple movement forward. The relation of narrative plot to story may indeed appear to partake of the demonic, as a kind of tantalizing instinctual play, a re-enactment that encounters the magic and the curse of reproduction or 'representation'. But to say more about the operations of repetition, we need to read further in Freud's text.

'What follows is speculation' (p. 24). With this gesture, Freud, in the manner of Rousseau's dismissal of the facts in the *Discourse on the Origins of Inequality*, begins the fourth chapter and his sketch of the economic and energetic model of the mental apparatus: the system Pcpt-Cs (the perceptual-conscious system) and the unconscious, the role of the outer layer as shield against excitations, and the definition of trauma as the breaching of the shield, producing a flood of stimuli which knocks the pleasure principle out of operation. Given this situation, the repetition of traumatic experiences in the dreams of neurotics can be seen to have the function of seeking retrospectively to master the flood of stimuli, to perform a mastery or binding of mobile energy through developing that anxiety which earlier was lacking – a lack which permitted the breach and thus caused the traumatic neurosis. Thus the repetition compulsion is carrying out a task that must be accomplished *before* the dominance of the pleasure principle can begin. Repetition is hence a primary event, independent of the pleasure principle and more primitive. Freud now moves into an exploration of the theory of the instincts, or drives, the most basic forces of psychic life.[25] The instinctual is the realm of freely mobile, 'unbound' energy: the 'primary process', where energy seeks immediate discharge, where no postponement of gratification is tolerated. It appears that it must be 'the task of the higher strata of the mental apparatus to bind the instinctual excitation reaching the primary process' before the pleasure principle can assert its dominance over the psychic economy (pp. 34–5). We may say that at this point in the essay we have moved from a postulate of repetition as the assertion of mastery (as in the passage from passivity to activity in the child's game) to a conception whereby repetition works as a process of *binding* toward the creation of an energetic constant-state situation which will permit the emergence of mastery and the possibility of postponement.

That Freud at this point evokes once again the demonic and the uncanny nature of repetition, and refers us not only to children's play but to their demand for exact repetition in storytelling as well, points our way back to literature. Repetition in all its literary manifestations may in fact work as a 'binding', a binding of textual energies that allows them to be mastered by putting them into serviceable form, usable 'bundles', within the energetic economy of the narrative. Serviceable form must, I think, mean perceptible form: repetition, repeat, recall, symmetry, all these journeys back in the text, returns to and returns of, that allow us to bind one textual moment to another in terms of similarity or substitution rather than mere contiguity. Textual energy, all that is aroused into expectancy and possibility in a text, can become usable by plot only when it has been bound or formalized. It cannot otherwise be plotted in a course to significant discharge, which is what the pleasure principle is charged with doing. To speak of 'binding' in a literary text is thus to speak of any of the formalizations, blatant or subtle, that force us to recognize sameness within difference, or the very emergence of a *sjužet* from the material of *fabula*. As the word 'binding' itself suggests, these formalizations and the recognitions they provoke may in some sense be painful: they create a delay, a postponement in the discharge of energy, a turning back from immediate pleasure, to ensure that the ultimate pleasurable discharge will be more complete. The most effective or, at the least, the most challenging texts may be those that are most delayed, most highly bound, most painful.

Freud now moves toward a closer inquiry concerning the relation between the compulsion to repeat and the instinctual. The answer lies in 'a universal attribute of instincts and perhaps of organic life in general' that '*an instinct is an urge inherent in organic life to restore an earlier state of things*' (p. 36). Instincts, which we tend to think of as a drive toward change, may rather be an expression of 'the conservative nature of living things'. The organism has no wish to change; if its conditions remained the same, it would constantly repeat the very same course of life. Modifications are the effect of external stimuli, and these modifications are in turn stored up for further repetition, so that, while the instincts may give the appearance of tending toward change, they 'are merely seeking to reach an ancient goal by paths alike old and new' (p. 38). Hence Freud is able to proffer, with a certain bravado, the formulation: '*the aim of all life is death*'. We are given an evolutionary image of the organism in which the tension created by external influences has forced living substance to 'diverge ever more widely from its original course of life and to make ever more complicated *détours* before reaching its aim of death' (pp. 38–49). In this view, the self-preservative instincts function to assure that the organism shall follow its own path to death, to ward off any ways of returning to the inorganic which are not immanent to the organism itself. In other words, 'the organism wishes to die only in its own fashion'. It must struggle against events (dangers) that would help it to achieve its goal too rapidly – by a kind of short circuit.

We are here somewhere near the heart of Freud's masterplot for organic life, and it generates a certain analytic force in its super-imposition on fictional plots. What operates in the text through repetition is the death instinct, the drive toward the end. Beyond and under the domination of the pleasure principle is this baseline of plot, its basic 'pulsation', sensible or audible through the repetitions that take us back in the text. Yet repetition also retards the pleasure principle's search for the gratification of discharge, which is another forward-moving drive of the text. We have a curious situation in which two principles of forward movement operate upon one another so as to create retard, a dilatory space in which pleasure can come from postponement in the knowledge that this – in the manner of forepleasure? – is a necessary approach to the true end. Both principles can indeed become dilatory, a pleasuring in and from delay, though both also in their different ways recall to us the need for end. This apparent paradox may be consubstantial with the fact that repetition can take us both backward and forward because these terms have become reversible: the end is a time before the beginning.

Between these two moments of quiescence, plot itself stands as a kind of divergence or deviance, a postponement in the discharge which leads back to the inanimate. For plot starts (or must give the illusion of starting) from that moment at which story, or 'life', is stimulated from quiescence into a state of narratability, into a tension, a kind of irritation, which demands narration. I spoke earlier of narrative desire, the arousal that creates the narratable as a condition of tumescence, appetency, ambition, quest, and gives narrative a forward-looking intention.[26] This is to say as well that beginnings are the arousal of an intention in reading, stimulation into a tension, and we could explore the specifically erotic nature of the tension of writing and its rehearsal in reading in a number of exemplary texts, such as Rousseau's account, in the *Confessions*, of how his novel *La Nouvelle Héloïse* was born of a masturbatory reverie and its necessary fictions, or the similar opening of Jean Genet's *Notre-Dame des fleurs*. The ensuing narrative – the Aristotelian 'middle' – is maintained in a state of tension, as a prolonged deviance from the quiescence of the 'normal' – which is to say, the unnarratable – until it reaches the terminal quiescence of the end. The development of a narrative shows that the tension is maintained as an ever more complicated postponement or *détour* leading back to the goal of quiescence. As Sartre and Benjamin compellingly argued, the narrative must tend toward its end, seek illumination in its own death. Yet this must be the right death, the correct end. The complication of the detour is related to the danger of short circuit: the danger of reaching the end too quickly, of achieving the im-proper death. The improper end indeed lurks throughout narrative, frequently as the wrong choice: choice of the wrong casket, misapprehension of the magical agent, false erotic object choice. The development of the subplot in the classical novel usually suggests (as William Empson has intimated) a different solution to the problems worked through by the main plot, and often illustrates the danger of short circuit.[27] The subplot stands as one means of warding off the danger of short circuit, assuring that the main plot will continue through to the right end. The desire of the text (the desire of reading) is hence desire for the end, but desire for the end reached only through the at least minimally complicated detour, the intentional deviance, in tension, which is the plot of narrative.

Deviance, detour, an intention that is irritation: these are characteristics of the narratable, of 'life' as it is the material of narrative, of *fabula* become *sjužet*. Plot is a kind of arabesque or squiggle toward the end. It is like that arabesque from *Tristram Shandy*, retraced by Balzac, that suggests the arbitrary, transgressive, gratuitous line of narrative, its deviance from the straight line, the shortest distance between beginning and end – which would be the collapse of one into the other, of life into immediate death. The detour of life in fact creates a momentary detour in Freud's essay, in chapter 5, as he considers the sexual instincts, which are in a sense the true life instincts yet also conservative in that they bring back earlier states of living substance; yet again, they stand in dynamic opposition to the death instincts, and hence confer a 'vacillating rhythm' on the life of the organism: 'One group of instincts rushes forward so as to reach the final aim of life as swiftly as possible; but when a particular stage in the advance has been reached, the other group jerks back to a certain point to make a fresh start and so prolong the journey' (p. 41). Freud's description of the 'vacillating rhythm' may in particular remind us of how a highly plotted nineteenth-century novel will often leave one set of characters at a critical juncture to take up another where it left them, moving this set forward, then rushing back to the first, creating an uneven movement of advance, turning back the better to move forward. As with the play of repetition and the pleasure principle, forward and back, advance and return interact to create the vacillating and apparently deviant middle.

Freud's text will in a moment take us closer to understanding the formal organization of this deviance toward the end. But it also at this point offers further suggestions about the beginning. For when he has identified both the death instincts and the life (sexual) instincts as conservative, tending toward the restoration of an earlier state of things, Freud feels obliged to deconstruct the illusion of a human drive toward perfection, an impulsion forward and upward: a force that – this is where he quotes *Faust* as the classic text of man's striving – 'presses ever forward unsubdued'. As we have already noted, the illusion of a striving toward perfection is to be explained by instinctual repression and the persisting tension of the repressed instinct, and the resulting difference between the pleasure of satisfaction demanded and that achieved, the difference that 'provides the driving factor which will permit of no halting at any position attained' (p. 42). This process of subtraction, we saw, is fundamental to Lacan's theory of desire, born of the gap or split between need and demand. Lacan helps us to understand how the aims and imaginings of desire – its enactments in response to imaginary scenarios of fulfillment – move us from the realm of basic drives to highly elaborated fictions. Desire necessarily becomes textual by way of a specifically narrative impulse, since desire is metonymy, a forward drive in the signifying chain, an insistence of meaning toward the occulted objects of desire.

Notes

1 *Oedipus Wrecks* is one of three shorts shown together as *New York Stories* (Martin Scorsese/Francis Coppola/Woody Allen, 1989).
2 Thanks to Matthew Campbell for drawing this to my attention.
3 Sigmund Freud, 'An Example of Psycho-Analytic work', *SE*, vol. 23, p. 190.

4 Freud's first use of the term 'Oedipus complex' occurs in 'A Special Type of Object-Choice Made by Men', (*SE*, vol. 11, 1910, p. 171).

5 J. Laplanche and J. B. Pontalis, *The Language of Psychoanalysis*, trans. Donald Nicholson-Smith, with an introduction by Daniel Lagache (London: Karnac Books, 1988), p. 286.

6 Ibid., p. 285.

7 Sigmund Freud, *Totem and Taboo*, *SE*, vol. 13 (1912–13), pp. 1–161.

8 Freud, 'An Example'; further references to this work are given in the text.

9 J. N. Isbister, *Freud: An Introduction to his Life and Work* (Cambridge: Polity Press, 1985), p. 77. See Sue Robinson, *Child Sexual Abuse: Whose Problem? Reflections on the Cleveland Case* (London Venture Press, 1989).

10 See, for instance, D. H. Lawrence, *Sons and Lovers*, for a portrayal of a strong Oedipal attachment between mother and son; and even something as apparently insubstantial as the video for Madonna's song 'Papa Don't Preach' follows Oedipal lines as Freud sketches them for the little girl. The young woman in the video, who clearly cares for her father in the absence of a mother, proposes moving out and substituting for him another, non-incestuous 'bearer of the organ', her boyfriend. The ambiguity of whether the 'baby' ('I'm gonna keep my baby', she tells her father) is the boyfriend or a child also fits with Freudian theory, as they approximate the same thing: a way of gaining the phallus the girl has been denied. Andrew Ross interestingly discusses the ambiguity of who 'Papa' in the lyrics is; at one concert Madonna had a backdrop for the song featuring a photograph of the Pope (see his 'Poetry and Motion: Madonna and Public Enemy', in Antony Easthope and John O. Thompson (eds), *Contemporary Poetry Meets Modern Theory*, Hemel Hempstead: Harvester Wheatsheaf, 1991). Again, paternal authority is carried equally by father or Father.

11 See, for example, Jessica Benjamin, *The Bonds of Love: Psychoanalysis, Feminism, and the Problem of Domination* (London: Virago, 1990) Nancy Chodorow, *The Reproduction of Mothering: Psychoanalysis and the Sociology of Gender* (Berkeley: University of California Press, 1978); and of course the work of French feminist theorists, including Irigaray, Kristeva, Sarah Kofman and Hélène Cixous.

12 Elizabeth Wright (ed.), *Feminism and Psychoanalysis: A Critical Dictionary* (Oxford: Blackwell, 1992), p. 294.

13 Ibid., p. 291.

14 Harold Bloom, *The Anxiety of Influence: A Theory of Poetry* (New York: Oxford University Press, 1973), pp. 14–16.

15 Juliet Mitchell, *Psychoanalysis and Feminism* (Harmondsworth: Pelican, 1974).

16 See Cheryl B. Torsney, 'The Critical Quilt: Alternative Authority in Feminist Criticism', in G. Douglas Atkins and Laura Morrow (eds), *Contemporary Literary Theory* (London: Macmillan, 1989); Annette Kolodny, 'A Map for Rereading: or, Gender and the Interpretation of Literary Texts', first published in *New Literary History*, 11(3)(Spring 1980),

reprinted in Elaine Showalter (ed.), *The New Feminist Criticism* (London: Virago, 1986); Janice Doane and Devon Hodges, *Nostalgia and Sexual Difference: The Resistance to Contemporary Feminism* (New York and London: Methuen, 1987).

17 Sandra M. Gilbert and Susan Gubar, *The Madwoman in the Attic: The Woman Writer and the Nineteenth Century Literary Imagination* (New York and London: Yale University Press, 1979).

18 Freud, 'Beyond the Pleasure Principle', *SE*, vol. 18, pp. 1–64. All further references are given in the text.

19 Peter Brooks, *Reading for the Plot: Design and Intention in Narrative* (Oxford; Oxford University Press, 1984). All further references are given in the text. See also Brooks, *Body Works: Objects of Desire in Modern Narrative* (Cambridge, Mass. and London: Harvard University Press, 1993).

20 Such formalist critics include Vladimir Propp, Tzvetan Todorov and Roland Barthes.

Reading 2 (Brooks)

21 Freud, 'Beyond the Pleasure Principle', p. 59. All further references are in the text.

22 J. Hillis Miller has noted that the etymology of the term *diegesis*, used by Plato to designate the narrative of events – the summary of action, as opposed to its imitative reproduction or *mimesis* – suggests that narrative is the retracing of a line already drawn. See 'The Ethics of Reading: Vast Gaps and Parting Hours', in Ira Konigsberg (ed.), *American Criticism in the Poststructuralist Age* (Michigan Studies in the Humanities, 1981), p. 25.

23 Freud, 'The Theme of the Three Caskets', *SE*, vol. 12 (1911), p. 299.

24 See Freud, 'The Dynamics of the Transference', ibid., pp. 99–108; 'Remembering, Repeating and Working Through', ibid., pp. 147–56; 'The Uncanny', *SE*, vol. 17 (1918), pp. 219–52.

25 The dynamic model of psychic life, Freud wrote in 1926, 'derives all mental processes [. . .] from the interplay of forces, which assist or inhibit one another, combine with one another, enter into compromises with one another, etc. All of these forces are originally in the nature of instincts . . .' (*SE*, vol. 20, p. 265). I shall use the term 'instinct' since it is the translation of *Trieb* given throughout the *Standard Edition*. But we should realize that 'instinct' is inadequate and somewhat misleading since it loses the sense of 'drive' and 'force' associated (as the preceding quotation suggests) with Freud's conception of *Trieb*. The currently accepted French translation, *pulsion*, would be more to our purposes: the model that interests me here might indeed be called 'pulsional'.

26 On the question of the beginning as 'intention', see Edward Said, *Beginnings: Intention and Method* (New York; Basic Books, 1975). It occurs

to me that the exemplary narrative beginning might be that of Kafka's
Metamorphosis: waking up to find oneself transformed into a monstrous ver-
min.

27 See William Empson, 'Double Plots', in *Some Versions of Pastoral* (New
   York; New Directions, 1960), pp. 25–84.

Part II
Sigmund Freud: The 'Wolf Man'

Sigmund Freud, 'A Case of Infantile Neurosis', and Peter Nicholls, 'The Belated Postmodern'

Freud's case history of Sergei Pankiev, the 'Wolf Man',[1] concerns a young man who developed an animal phobia (an anxiety hysteria) which was later replaced by obsessional neuroses.[2] In terms of Freud's own theories, it provided four things: evidence in support of the contentious issue of infantile sexuality; a suggestion that there might be a relation between 'primal scenes' and 'primal phantasies', early imaginary scenes common to all; the early 'oral organization of the libido' (p. 5) which led to his later work on identification and introjection, concepts discussed by Peter Nicholls in relation to Toni Morrison's novel *Beloved*; and the universality of bisexuality.

The extracts from the case history show first, Freud's conviction that, while the primal scene might not have really taken place, the Wolf Man's seduction by his sister did; second, the meticulous manner in which Freud calculates the detail of the case history, and a footnote in which he sets out the meaning of 'deferred action'; third, Freud's distinction between recollection and reconstruction in analysis, and his attempt to explain why primal scenes seem so real to analysands.

The influence of the case history on literary criticism has also been significant. James Strachey, editor of the *Standard Edition*, comments on the 'extraordinary literary skill with which Freud has handled the case. He was faced with the pioneer's task of giving a scientific account of psychological events of undreamt-of novelty and complexity. The outcome is a work which not only avoids the dangers of confusion and obscurity but from first to last holds the reader's fascinated attention' (p. 6). Peter Brooks, in his essay 'Fictions of the Wolf Man: Freud and Narrative Understanding', suggests why this should be so: 'the narrativity of the structure of explanation deployed in this nonfictional genre, the case history, necessarily implicates the question of fictions through the very plotting of that narrativity', and for us as readers '[i]t is of overwhelming importance [...] that life still be narratable', despite the doubt cast on storytelling by modernism.[3] Peter Nicholls's essay here suggests a way in which psychoanalysis might have a historicized application, particularly in the case of a lost history which, like an infantile trauma, will not be forgotten but continues to haunt the present. Michael Holquist has pointed out that the very notions of *fabula* (the chronological story) and *sjužet* (the plot ordered from those events) are historical ones, and different ages will have different ways of perceiving both realms.[4] This is something which Brooks's reading of the Wolf Man's case history as a particularly acute fragmentation of different plots and stories, in the light of Nicholls's use of this fragmentation to comment on the 'rememory' of a lost history, certainly bears out.

The Wolf Man's history

As Freud says in his chronology, the Wolf Man was born in Russia on Christmas Day 1886 (6 January 1887, according to the non-Russian Gregorian calendar). He was the son of a 'wealthy landowner and liberal political leader'.[5] When he was eighteen months old he contracted malaria and spent a particular afternoon in his cot in his parents' bedroom, where he either witnessed intercourse between them or, as Freud puts it, observed 'the interview between them into which he later introduced his coitus phantasy' (p. 121). At the age of two and a half, he came upon a servant-woman, Grusha, kneeling on the floor to wash it with a broom of twigs and a pail beside her; the posture reminded him so strongly of his mother's (either real or fantasized) during intercourse with his father that in 'an attempt at seduction' (p. 93) of Grusha, he urinated on the floor. She threatened him with castration, 'just as though she had understood what he meant' (p. 93).

This response to posture remained with the Wolf Man throughout his life, and determined his object choice: he repeatedly fell in love with young women whom he saw in the posture which resembled either scrubbing the floor or sexual intercourse *a tergo*, from behind.

Before he was three and a quarter, the little boy overheard his mother's lament to the doctor, 'I cannot go on living like this', and later on applied them to himself, thus identifying with the mother. He was three and a quarter when his sister began her attempts to seduce him, following an invitation to '"show our bottoms" by playing with his penis' (p. 20). What is interesting about this incident is that although Freud is willing and even eager to reduce certain phenomena to the status of fantasies, he states unequivocally that the young boy's 'seduction by his sister was certainly not a phantasy' (p. 21). As we saw earlier, incidents of apparent child abuse can conveniently be ascribed to infantile sexual fantasies, as can primal scenes in which children think they remember seeing their parents engaging in intercourse; Brooks points out that this retreat to phantasy also applies in Freud's discussion of the killing of the primal father in *Totem and Taboo*.[6] In this case, however, it seems clear to Freud that the Wolf Man's sister really did what he says, as she was 'a forward and sensual little thing' (p. 21). It seems possible that Freud does not mind allowing cases of women abusing male children, as admitting (or inventing) this hardly disturbs the façade of patriarchy in the way that admitting to wholesale sexual abuse by male adults would; and it draws attention away from the real cause for concern. In any case, as Freud allows a little later, for a little girl to behave in such a way with her brother and an older cousin might well betoken some kind of trauma in her own experience; if her brother witnessed parental intercourse, may not she also have? 'This hypothesis would also give us a hint of the reason for her own sexual precocity' (p. 57).[7]

Soon after the sisterly seduction, the little boy's Nanya, his beloved nurse, was caused to threaten him with castration when, in 'an attempt at seduction' of his own, he tried to masturbate before her (p. 24). Her threat that 'children who did that [...] got a "wound" in the place' (p. 24) initiated in him both an interest in castration and a sexual regression to 'pregenital organization' (p. 25) because of the prohibition against masturbation. When he was three and a half, an English governess was engaged by his family, and the change in his character began for which the governess was largely blamed. The little boy became very naughty and often flew into rages, even after the governess was dismissed. Freud suggests that in fact the child was trying to force punishment from his father (p. 28), in keeping with the anal-sadistic area into which his sexuality had been diverted.

At four the boy had the wolf dream after which he is named, which was the '[o]rigin of the phobia' (p. 121), the child's fear of wolves. Freud's discussion and elucidation of the dream, in which the small boy saw his bedroom window swing open on to a walnut tree full of six or seven motionless, staring white wolves with bushy tails, is both fascinating and ingenious. In an extended footnote, he explains every detail of the dream (pp. 42–4, n. 2), showing that it was a complex reordering of the child's ideas about wolf fairy-tales, castration, his own birthday (the walnut tree could also be a Christmas tree), his powerful wolfish father, and a memory of witnessing parental coitus: if the details are reversed, it is the child who is staring, not the wolves, at a scene of activity and motion.

From four and a half years onwards, the little boy's obsessional symptoms took hold; these included a compulsion to breathe out, a profound but sceptical interest in the story of the Crucifixion accompanied by a compulsion to think blasphemous thoughts involving excrement, both related to the original complex of ideas which inspired the wolf-dream. At eight and ten, the boy suffered the '[f]inal outbreaks of obsessional neurosis' (p. 121), and at seventeen a breakdown, 'precipitated by gonorrhoea' (ibid.)

When he began treatment with Freud at the age of twenty-three, the Wolf Man was completely dependent on his valet and personal physician for all the routines of life, including daily enemas.[8] He was unable to control his own finances, and experienced life at a remove, as if it were 'hidden in a veil' (p. 75). Again, Freud's explication of all these apparently disparate, meaningless disorders appears to be satisfyingly coherent and cogent;[9] he observes that 'during the analytic treatment, it became possible to liberate his shackled homosexuality [. . .] and it was a most remarkable experience to see how [. . .] each piece of homosexual libido which was set free sought out some application in life and some attachment to the great common concern of mankind' (p. 71).

Story and plot

A quick comparison of page numbers shows that this last statement, positive and moving as it is, is made in the middle of the account of the case history about the end stages of the analysis. The Russian formalist distinction between plot and story is again helpful in disentangling what is going on in Freud's narration of an analysis. 'Plot' is the artificial, literary ordering of the straightforward historical events of the 'story'; for example, Malcolm Lowry's *Under the Volcano* is the plotted version of the story which critics Chris Ackerley and Lawrence J. Clipper have disentangled into chronological form.[10] In the case of 'From the History of an Infantile Neurosis', however, the relations between story and plot are even more complex, and not only because it is not always clear whether some elements of the story really happened, or only exist in terms of the plot.

Freud says, 'I am unable to give either a purely historical or a purely thematic account of my patient's story; I can write a history neither of the treatment nor of the illness, but I shall find myself obliged to combine the two methods of presentation' (p. 13). His distinction between 'historical' and 'thematic' corresponds to that of 'story' and 'plot', but, as Brooks points out, matters are even more complicated than this suggests.

There are in fact four temporal and expository layers at work in the case history: (1) the history of the neurosis; (2) the reasons for the neurosis; (3) the history of the treatment and how these events came out during analysis; (4) the order of the case history in presenting these other three categories. That is, Freud must 'manage to tell, both "at once" and "in order", the story of a person, the story of an illness, the story of an investigation, the story of an explanation: and "meaning" must lie in the effective interrelationship of all of these'.[11] As in relation to the '*fort-da*' episode of 'Beyond the Pleasure Principle', what looked like a straightforward instance of Freud the analyst reporting a fragment of a case history in fact involved three roles: as (unnamed) grandfather, as observer of the child, and as narrator of the observation. In the case of the Wolf Man, the reporting analyst's role is itself so fragmented that it becomes almost dialogic, in Mikhail Bakhtin's term: as Brooks says, '[t]ruth, then, arises from a dialogue among a number of *fabula* [stories] and number of *sjužet* [plots], stories and their possible organizations, as also between two narrators, analysand and analyst'.[12]

It is also germane here to consider Stanley Fish's suggestion that Brooks's analysis of the case history shows that he has fallen under the spell of rhetorical control so carefully wrought by Freud, and that the real drama here is that of 'Freud's rhetorical mastery'.[13] The elements of the case history are simply representations of that mastery; the anal erotic, for instance, which Freud spends some time discussing with reference to the Wolf Man's condition, is merely a 'metaphor for persuasion'.[14] The case history is the case history of its own production.

3 SIGMUND FREUD

The Seduction and its Immediate Consequences

It is easy to understand that the first suspicion fell upon the English governess, for the change in the boy made its appearance while she was there. Two screen memories had persisted, which were incomprehensible in themselves, and which related to her. On one occasion, as she was walking along in front of them, she said, 'Do look at my little tail!' Another time, when they were on a trip, her hat flew away, to the two children's great satisfaction. This pointed to the castration complex, and might permit of a construction being made to the effect that a threat uttered by her against the boy had been largely responsible for originating his abnormal conduct. There is no danger at all in communicating constructions of this kind to the person under analysis; they never do any damage to the analysis if they are mistaken; but at the same time they are not put forward unless there is some prospect of reaching a nearer approximation to the truth by means of them. The first effect of this supposition was the appearance of some dreams, which it was not possible to interpret completely, but all of which seemed to centre around the same material. As far as they could be understood, they were concerned with aggressive actions on the boy's part against his sister or against the governess and with energetic reproofs and punishments on account of them. It was as though ... after her bath ... he had tried ... to undress his sister ... to tear off her coverings ... or veils – and so on. But it was not possible to get at any firm content from the interpretation; and since these dreams gave an impression of always working over the same material in various different ways, the correct reading of these ostensible reminiscences became assured: it could only be a question of phantasies, which the dreamer had made on the subject of his childhood at some time or other, probably at the age of puberty, and which had now come to the surface again in this unrecognizable form.

This explanation came at a single blow, when the patient suddenly called to mind the fact that, when he was still very small, 'on the first estate', his sister had seduced him into sexual practices. First came a recollection that in the lavatory, which the children used frequently to visit together, she had made this proposal: 'Let's show our bottoms', and proceeded from words to deeds. Subsequently the more essential part of the seduction came to light, with full particulars as to time and place. It was in spring, at a time when his father was away; the children were in one room playing on the floor, while their mother was working in the next. His sister had taken hold of his penis and played with it, at the same time telling him incomprehensible stories about his Nanya, as though by way of explanation. His Nanya, she said, used to do the same thing with all kinds of people – for instance, with the gardener: she used to stand him on his head, and then take hold of his genitals.

Here, then, was the explanation of his phantasies whose existence we had already divined. They were meant to efface the memory of an event which later on seemed offensive to the patient's masculine self-esteem, and they reached this end by putting an imaginary and desirable converse in the place of the historical truth. According to these phantasies it was not he who had played the passive part towards his sister, but, on the contrary, he had been aggressive, had tried to see his sister undressed, had been rejected and punished, and had for that reason got into the rage which the family tradition talked of so much. It was also appropriate to weave the governess into this imaginative composition, since the chief responsibility for his fits of rage had been ascribed to her by his mother and grandmother. These phantasies, therefore, corresponded exactly to the legends by means of which a nation that has become great and proud tries to conceal the insignificance and failure of its beginnings.

The governess can actually have had only a very remote share in the seduction and its consequences. The scenes with his sister took place in the early part of the same year in which, at the height of the summer, the Englishwoman arrived to take the place of his absent parents. The boy's hostility to the governess came about, rather, in another way. By abusing the nurse and slandering her as a witch, she was in his eyes following in the footsteps of his sister, who had first told him such monstrous stories about the nurse; and in this way she enabled him to express openly against herself the aversion which, as we shall hear, he had developed against his sister as a result of his seduction.

But his seduction by his sister was certainly not a phantasy. Its credibility was increased by some information which had never been forgotten and which dated from a later part of his life, when he was grown up. A cousin who was more than ten years his elder told him a conversation about his sister that he very well remembered what a forward and sensual little thing she had been: once, when she was a child of four or five, she had sat on his lap and opened his trousers to take hold of his penis.

[...]

From his tenth year onwards he was from time to time subject to moods of depression, which used to come on in the afternoon and reached their height at about five o'clock. This symptom still existed at the time of the analytic treatment. The recurring fits of depression took the place of the earlier attacks of fever or languor; five o'clock was either the time of the highest fever or of the observation of the intercourse, unless the two times coincided. Probably for the very reason of this illness, he was in his parents' bedroom. The illness, the occurrence of which is also corroborated by direct tradition, makes it reasonable to refer the event to the summer, and since the child was born on Christmas Day, to assume that his age was $n + 1\frac{1}{2}$ years.[15] He had been sleeping in his cot, then, in his parents' bedroom, and woke up, perhaps because of his rising fever, in the afternoon, possibly at five o'clock, the hour which was later marked out by depression. It harmonizes with our assumption that it was a hot summer's day, if we suppose that his parents had retired, half undressed,[16] for an afternoon *siesta*. When he woke up, he witnessed a coitus *a tergo* [from behind], three times repeated;[17] he was able to see his mother's genitals as well as his father's organ; and he understood the process as well as its significance.[18] Lastly he interrupted his parents' intercourse in a manner which will be discussed later.

[...]

The view, then, that we are putting up for discussion is as follows. It maintains that scenes from early infancy, such as are brought up by an exhaustive analysis of neuroses (as, for instance, in the present case), are not reproductions of real occurrences, to which it is possible to ascribe an influence over the course of the patient's later life and over the formation of his symptoms. It considers them rather as products of the imagination, which find their instigation in mature life, which are intended to serve as some kind of symbolic representation of real wishes and interests, and which owe their origin to a regressive tendency, to a turning-away from the tasks of the present. If that is so, we can of course spare ourselves the necessity of attributing such a surprising amount to the mental life and intellectual capacity of children of the tenderest age.

Besides the desire which we all share for the rationalization and simplification of our difficult problem, there are all sorts of facts that speak in favour of this view. It is also possible to eliminate beforehand one objection to it which may arise, particularly in the mind of a practising analyst. It must be admitted that, if this view of these scenes from infancy were the right one, the carrying-out of analysis would not in the first instance be characteristic of diverting their interest from the present and of attaching it to these regressive substitutes, the products of their imagination. Then there is absolutely nothing for it but to follow upon their tracks and bring these unconscious productions into consciousness; for, leaving on one side their lack of value from the point of view of reality, they are of the utmost value from our point of view, since they are for the moment the bearers and possessors of the interest which we want to set free so as to be able to direct it onto the tasks of the present. The analysis would have to run precisely the same course as one which had a *naïf* faith in the truth of the phantasies. The difference would only come at the end of the analysis, after the phantasies had been laid bare. We should then say to the patient: 'Very well, then; your neurosis proceeded *as though* you had received these impressions and spun them out in your childhood. You will see, of course, that that is out of the question. They were products of your imagination which were intended to divert you from the real tasks that lay before you. Let us now enquire what these tasks were, and what lines of communication ran between them and your phantasies.' After the infantile phantasies had been disposed of in this way, it would be possible to begin a second portion of the treatment, which would be concerned with the patient's real life.

4 PETER NICHOLLS

The Belated Postmodern: History, Phantoms, and Toni Morrison

'The narrative into which life seems to cast itself surfaces most forceful-ly in certain kinds of psychoanalysis': so writes Toni Morrison in the introduction to her new volume of essays, *Playing in the Dark*.[19] Morrison's preoccupation with themes of time, memory and mourning – especially in *Beloved* (1987) – makes it tempting to frame a reading of her work with concepts drawn from psychoanalysis (Freud's notion of 'working through', for example).[20] Morrison herself has so far said little about the relevance of psychoanalysis to her fiction, but the remark quoted above occurs in an account of Marie Cardinal's *The Words to Say It*: 'More than the enthusiasm of the person who suggested the book,' Morrison writes, 'I was persuaded by the title: five words taken from Boileau that spoke the full agenda and unequivocal goal of a novelist' (*PD*, p. v). A celebration of the talking cure, Cardinal's 'autobiographical novel' offers a striking model of therapeutic narration which may well have affected Morrison's attempts to present Sethe's process of 'remembering something she had forgotten she knew'.[21]

In the context of the lectures which make up *Playing in the Dark*, Cardinal's story of her illness has, too, a particular relevance to Morrison's archeology of the black presence in white American culture. Cardinal's account of her first anxiety attack records her feeling of panic at a concert given by Louis Armstrong. For Morrison, this first moment of *possession* by the illness which Cardinal would later come to call 'the Thing' provides a powerful figure for the intermittent invasion of white culture by 'the associative language of dread and love that accompanies blackness' (*PD*, p. x). Morrison reports her growing fasci-nation with 'the way black people ignite critical moments of discovery or change of emphasis in literature not written by them' (*PD*, p. viii), and much of *Playing in the Dark* is an attempt to outline the multiple ways in which a mythological Africanism was constructed as an ideolog-ical and psychic defense against such disruptive incursions into white American culture:

What became transparent were the self-evident ways that Americans choose to talk about themselves through and within a sometimes allegorical, sometimes metaphorical, but always choked representation of an Africanist presence. (*PD*, p. 17)

This metaphysical Africanism is 'choked', as Morrison puts it, by 'unspeakable thoughts, unspoken',[22] and the implication is that the counter-narrative of black fiction may have the capacity to recall what the historical record has 'forgotten', much as in psychoanalysis (in Ned Lukacher's words) 'The patient's speech "remembers", while the patient himself remains oblivious and utterly resists all the analyst's efforts to bring the "memory" to consciousness.'[23] To imagine Morrison's project in this way is to emphasize her sense of American history as irredeemably compromised by its metaphysical imperative to construct a white self (Africanism, she argues, has become 'a metaphysical necessity' [*PD*, p. 64]). 'History' has functioned like Lacan's Imaginary to provide 'an ego-reinforcing presence' (*PD*, p. 45), its fictions of wholeness and self-presence dependent on the 'duties of exorcism and reification and mirroring' that have fallen to the 'Africanist persona' (*PD*, p. 39) whose tabooed blackness has allowed 'the projection of the not-me', a veritable 'playground for the imagination' (*PD*, p. 38) in white American culture. Morrison's recent work might thus be read as a reversal of this 'exorcism', a shattering of the mirror through which the spectre of difference may suddenly emerge into the light.

When Marie Cardinal's narrator flees from the jazz concert it is with the feeling of being 'svelte in appearance but torn apart inside',[24] and while Morrison reads this internal violence as a figure for the relation of 'the cultural associations of jazz ... to Cardinal's "possession"' (*PD*, p. viii) it is tempting to connect it also to a particular sense of the postmodern. The term is not one that Morrison tends to use in her critical writings, although her comments in one interview suggest that she understands it primarily in relation to a dissolution of stable patterns of social and psychic identity.[25] There may seem little to be gained in designating Morrison's fiction as 'postmodern', especially as in its weaker forms the term frequently connotes exercises in aimless self-reflexivity which are worlds apart from the passionate historical imagination at work in a novel like *Beloved*. Perhaps for that reason, however, our sense of the postmodern might be productively sharpened by thinking it along the lines of Morrison's argument in *Playing in the Dark*. We might, in fact, discover an alternative postmodernism, one which is fully historical and obsessively cognizant of that fact, by reading Morrison's fiction as its outer limit, as the point at which the postmodern signals the invasion of a cultural centre from its margins.[26] As in the case of

Marie Cardinal's 'possession', a forgotten history has the power to shake the social and metaphysical forms against which it breaks,[27] and this idea of history as a violent intrusion from somewhere else is clearly very different from the familiar forms of stylistic appropriation and unmotivated pastiche which have given us the more comfortable worlds of 'faction' and nostalgia movies. More specifically, the nature of that intrusion is one which refigures 'History' along the lines of a psychic temporality for which memory is less a matter of cultural allusion than of shock and trauma.[28]

From this point of view, the most productive formulation of the post-modern is surely that which regards it not as some new epoch succeeding the modern, but rather (following Lyotard) as a disruptive mode *within* the modern.[29] The postmodern and the modern thus coexist, inhabiting the same conceptual and historical space, and producing a tension which rends History from within. As Gianni Vattimo puts it, 'the post-modern displays, as its most common and most imposing trait, an effort to free itself from the logic of overcoming, development and innovation'.[30] Aesthetic forms have the capacity to release us from that particular logic of History, because they allow, in Heidegger's sense, 'the ungrounding of historicity, which is announced as a suspension of the hermeneutic continuity of the subject with itself and with history' (p. 125). And if, in Foucault's words, 'Continuous history is the indispensable correlative of the founding function of the subject',[31] any 'strong' concept of the postmodern will have less to do with forms of indeterminacy than with those of unresolvable *contradiction*. The dismantling of a racial metaphysics by causing it to be invaded by its other will thus amount to a violent 'possession' of its thematics of time and memory, leaving them also, we might say, 'torn apart inside'.

II

'The narrative into which life seems to cast itself surfaces most forcefully in certain kinds of psychoanalysis.' How, though, might the intimacies of the analyst's couch provide us with a way of talking about a history no longer grounded in metaphysics? One tempting answer to that question is to invoke Freud's concept of the 'return of the repressed', as Mae G. Henderson has done in one of the best discussions of *Beloved*.[32] The danger here, though, is that we begin to think of the 'repressed' as simply a lost fact or datum, a link which once restored will return us to a form of historical continuity. Yet psychoanalysis is concerned not so much with the discovery of a hidden content as with, in the words of

Laplanche and Leclaire, 'an interpretive elaboration or working-through whose role is to weave around a rememorated element an entire network of meaningful relations that integrate it into the subject's explicit apprehension of himself'. From this point of view, then, 'the Freudian experience of "memory" has less to do with the recollection of an "event" than with the repetition of a structure'.[33] And for psychoanalysis, of course, memory leads a double life since it is (in David Krell's words) both 'the source of the *malady* with which it is concerned and the *therapy* it proffers'.[34] To remember is thus not simply to restore a forgotten link or moment of experience, nor is it unproblematically to 'repossess' or re-enact what has been lost.[35] That idea of recovering an occluded or 'buried' past derives from a traditional association of knowledge with recollection and depends on a thoroughly metaphysical 'presencing' of what is absent. The development of Freud's theory of memory is actually away from this phantasmatic form of recollection, and while his use of 'acting out' (*Agieren*) in therapy might seem tied to a form of 'presence', this is complicated, as Dominick LaCapra has argued, by a concept of memory which 'allowed for the distinction between mnemic trace and phantasm'.[36]

The distinction is a momentous one, connecting a major strand of Freud's thought to subsequent poststructuralism and to a certain theory of the postmodern for which concepts of time and memory are of central importance.[37] In the wake of Lacan, attention has recently been focussed on a related concept of deferral in Freud's theory which is codified in the word *Nachträglichkeit*, 'belatedness', or, in its usual technical translations, 'deferred action' and 'retroaction'. The concept is best known from the case history of the Wolf Man, though it is foreshadowed in the *Studies on Hysteria* and in some of Freud's early letters to Wilhelm Fliess. The Wolf Man, we recall, witnesses at the age of one and a half an act of sexual intercourse between his parents but the shock of this impression is deferred until some sexual understanding of its import is possible. As Freud puts it:

> At the age of one and a half the child receives an impression to which he is unable to react adequately; he is only able to understand it and to be moved by it when the impression is revived in him at the age of four; and only twenty years later, during the analysis, is he able to grasp with his conscious mental processes what was then going on in him.[38]

As Lacan observes, 'the event remains latent in the subject',[39] thereby giving rise to a complex temporality in which the subject is always in more than one place at any time. Deferred action is, then, a product of the excessive character of the first event which requires a second event to release its traumatic force ('only the occurrence of the second scene can endow the first one with pathogenic force').[40] John Forrester neatly defines this movement as 'the articulation of two *moments* with a time of delay'.[41] It is not simply a matter of recovering a lost memory, but rather of the restructuring which forms the past in retrospect as 'the original site [. . .] comes to be reworked'.[42]

What is involved, then, is not just a time-lapse between stimuli and response, but, as Laplanche and Pontalis are careful to point out, a particular kind of 'working over', a 'work of recollection'.[43] So too *Nachträglichkeit* must be distinguished from Jung's theory of 'retrospection' (*Zurückfantasieren*), for, as Laplanche explains, while the latter

> simply means the fact of creating a past to meet current needs, perhaps in an attempt to avoid present difficulties and to conceal them from oneself [. . .] Freud insists upon the tension between the old scene and the recent scenario.[44]

It is this 'tension' which implies a radical unsettling of that 'philosophy of representation – of the original, the first time, resemblance, imitation, faithfulness'[45] which postmodernism will also seek to disrupt. *Nachträglichkeit* calls into question traditional notions of causality – the second event is presented now as the 'cause' of the first[46] – and its retroactive logic refuses to accord ontological primacy to any originary moment. Since the shock of the first scene is not felt directly by the subject but only through its later representation in memory we are dealing with, in Derrida's words, 'a past that has never been present'.[47] Belatedness, in this sense, creates a complex temporality which inhibits any nostalgia for origin and continuity – the 'origin' is now secondary, a construction always contained in its own repetition (as Andrew Benjamin puts it, 'The original event is thus no longer the same as itself. The effect of the present on the past is to cause a repetition of the "event" within which something new is taking place').[48]

III

The abstractness of these ideas may seem a far cry from the dramatic tension of Morrison's writing, but her search for an alternative, 'ungrounded' historicity has some affinity with the critique of metaphysics outlined here. Let us return for a moment to Derrida's notion of 'a past which has never been present': in a later passage of *Memoires for Paul de Man*, he calls this particular past 'historicity itself – an historicity which cannot be historical, an "ancientness" without history, without anteriority, but which produces history'.[49] In contrast to the 'unfolding of presence'[50] which is 'history', 'historicity' is the movement of temporal difference, or, as Derrida puts it in *Dissemination*, 'a series of temporal differences without any central present, without a present of which the past and the future would be but modifications'.[51] This historicity shares with the temporality of the subject the qualities of self-division and disunity, but it must not be construed in terms of the empirical time of consciousness. For historicity, like the time of the unconscious, is a construction (Freud observes in his study of the Wolf Man that 'these scenes from infancy are not reproduced during the treatment as recollection, they are the products of construction'[52]). This is not necessarily to suggest that the traumatic event never took place, but rather that it has never been *present* and hence that it exists only as a repetition.[53] It is in this sense that what is 'remembered' can come to seem something *foreign* to the subject's lived experience, a fragment from another time when the subject was different, but a fragment which has the power drastically to restructure the self in its present moment (Lyotard speaks figuratively of 'this stranger in the house ... his clandestine entry and unnoticed stay' (*H*, p. 17)).

Historicity, then, in the sense used here, does not constitute itself as a unified object (or 'moment') which can be repossessed by a contemplative subject. In fact, it is precisely that particular present of contemplation which is torn by the intrusion of a different time. It is not fortuitous that Althusser, in defining his own conception of a 'differential temporality' which breaks decisively with the 'ontological category of the present'[54] should find a helpful model in Freud's theory:

> We have known, since Freud, that the time of the unconscious cannot be confused with the time of biography. On the contrary, *the concept of the time of the unconscious must be constructed* in order to obtain an understanding of certain biographical traits. In exactly the same way, it is essential to construct the concepts of the different historical times which are never given in the ideological obviousness of the continuity of time (which need only be suitably divided into a good periodization to obtain the time of history), but must be constructed out of the differential nature and differential articulation of their objects in the structure of the whole.[55]

Of particular interest here is Althusser's conception of historicity as a disruption of the subject's continuous, lived temporality (mired in 'ideological obviousness'). The contrast between empirical and historical time might in fact allow us to draw a broad distinction between modernist and postmodernist conceptions of temporality. As Lyotard has observed, a characteristically 'modern' approach to the past is to scrutinize it for its 'errors' and 'crimes', and thus to master it through interpretation.[56] To this we can add a related tendency to conceive the past as a phantasmatic space to be reinhabited and repossessed (historical events become the object of a desire which promises to draw them into some sort of symbiotic union with the present).[57] Both modes frequently depend upon a reformulation of the nineteenth-century poetic of epiphanies and arrested moments, and both stalk the past in search of 'ego-reinforcing' models of authority and insight. By way of contrast, a postmodern historicity – Morrison's *Beloved* is an almost overwhelming example – conceives the subject as shaken out of its secure metaphysical time and exposed to the shock of a temporality which is always self-divided. For the postmodern text, this is the subject's 'real' time, though it would be more accurate to say that the subject is possessed by it than that she or he possesses it.

Now we can begin to see why Freud's concept of *Nachträglichkeit* and traumatic memory might provide a way of thinking about this postmodern historicity. For, as Laplanche puts it, 'the recall of the first scene [...] sets off the upsurge of sexual excitation, *catching the ego in reverse*, and leaving it disarmed, incapable of using the normally outward-directed defenses, and thus falling back on a pathological defense, and "posthumous primary process".'[58] The ego is caught 'in reverse' partly because, in Lacan's words, 'the past [...] reveals itself reversed in repetition',[59] but also because the degree of excitation felt is disproportionate to the (second) event which appears to have occasioned it. It is precisely this effect of deferred action which Lyotard has developed to define a postmodern historicity. In *Heidegger and 'the jews'*, for example, he proposes memory as anamnesis in contrast to a memorializing history which 'forgets' through discursive ordering ('one forgets as soon as one believes, draws conclusions, and holds for certain' (*H*, p. 10). 'Memorial history' functions as 'a protective shield' (*H*, p. 8), providing a series of psychic defenses which guarantee 'the diachrony of the self-assured spirit' (*H*, p. 26)

Belatedness as the constitutive element of the unconscious will therefore present a contrasting temporality in which anachronism is the principal feature. 'History' here is no longer a sort of container in which events are serially disposed, but a collision of two temporalities – following Freud's model of traumatic memory, Lyotard speaks of a first moment of shock without affect and a second moment of affect without shock (*H*, p. 12) This first moment, which Lyotard compares to the sublime, marks the irruption of the 'figural' which is always 'beyond' representation.[60] But can we remember without memorializing? As Lyotard observes, 'One *must*, certainly, inscribe in words, in images. One cannot escape the necessity of representing' (*H*, p. 26). None the less, the avant-garde will always pursue the 'sublime feeling' (*H*, p. 32) which lies beyond representation, and Lyotard characterizes such artistic projects as

> an aesthetics of shock, an anaesthetics. It is a shock that, in the Kantian *Gemüth* and in the Freudian apparatus, defies the power that is nevertheless constitutive of the mind according to Kant (i.e., that which synthesizes the manifold, its elementary memory). Not only does the imagination, required to present sensibly something that would re-present the Absolute, fail in its task but it falls into an 'abyss'. . . . (*H*, p. 31)

This is 'shock' conceived not in its weaker sense (the modernist 'shock of the new') but as equivalent to 'trauma', and Lyotard alludes to Freud's early account of Emma to indicate the kind of excess of affect involved:

> Something, however, *will make* itself understood, 'later' [. . .] It will be represented as something that has never been presented. Renewed absurdity. For instance, as a symptom, a phobia (Emma in the store). This will be understood as feeling, fear, anxiety, feeling of a threatening excess whose motive is obviously not in the present context. A feeling, it seems, born of nothing that can be verified in the 'present' situation in a perceptible, verifiable, or falsifiable way, and which therefore necessarily points to an elsewhere that will have to be located outside this situation, outside the present contextual situation, imputed to a different site than this one. (*H*, p. 13)[61]

Emma's phobic reaction ('a trauma *after the event*', in Freud's words)[62] provides a sort of figure for a postmodern 'history': excessive affect cannot be properly integrated into a present context of meanings, and the past which seems now not to have been directly experienced (it is not remembered as 'present')[63] suddenly surges back into the self, causing pain and anxiety. Much of what Lyotard has written about Auschwitz has sought to present this sense of history as trauma, as the opening of a wound within the subject. The problem is always to acknowledge the 'protective shield' which our culture invokes against this resurgent past while at the same time recognizing (without 'memorializing') the alien and unassimilable nature of what is remembered. In contrast to the modernist desire to inhabit the past, in Lyotard's account of the postmodern it is the past which inhabits us, invading 'an apparatus constitutively unprepared to receive it' (*H*, p. 17). Perhaps it is not simply, then, that the ego is caught 'in reverse', but that it is opened to a vertigo in which defenses fall and something foreign lodges in what was formerly the 'centre' of the self.

IV

This trope of a return cannot but remind us of Morrison's *Beloved*, the text in which Morrison has explored most vividly what we might call the insistence of historicity in the self. There is a ghost here and a persistent haunting, as Morrison uncovers the intricate relations between love and possession, using the resources of fiction to free us from a metaphysical History.

The theme of possession, of a force invading the self, has itself haunted postmodern American writing, being first definitively broached in William Burroughs' *The Naked Lunch* (1959) and operating as a persistent metaphor of social control in experimental fiction of the last three decades.[64] Yet while *Beloved* also explores ways in which the body can be possessed by something external to it, Morrison tends to see the workings of power as inseparable from the disjunctive operations of a 'belated' temporality. This is the full force of 'unspeakable thoughts, unspoken', for feeling, understanding and speaking never seem to occur in the same moment. The fluid shifts between different times in this novel and in *Jazz* thus do not work to enforce some deterministic reading of the past's effects upon the present, but rather to evoke the traumatic force of a historicity which splits the subject, compelling it to live in different times rather than in a secure, metaphysical present.

Who is Beloved? A revenant, someone who comes back, she seems to offer precisely what we have always yearned for, the past made good, an origin restored, 'my girl come home' (*B*, p. 201), with 'new skin' (*B*, p. 50) to match her 'new shoes' (*B*, p. 66). But she is not that; or at least she is always more than that, at once Sethe's daughter and an African lost in the Middle Passage – and even as Sethe's daughter, she is not what she was, but grown to the age she would have been, her neck bearing 'the little curved shadow' left by the handsaw (*B*, p. 239). This play of contradiction seems now the very mark of the postmodern, issuing in an insistence that something (someone) can be two things at once, that two things can occupy the same space, that the origin is irreducibly doubled.

And there is more: for this haunting is but one of many (as Baby Suggs points out, ' "Not a house in the country ain't packed to its rafters with some dead Negro's grief. We lucky this ghost is a baby" ' [*B*, p. 5]), and the voices heard in 124 are quickly understood by Stamp Paid: 'although he couldn't cipher but one word, he believed he knew who spoke them. The people of the broken necks, of fire-cooked blood and black girls who had lost their ribbons. What a roaring' (*B*, p. 181). So Beloved is also a figure of thwarted love, of the body literally possessed by others, of the entire tragedy of slavery which cannot adequately be spoken. Her belated appearance is traumatic in Freud's sense precisely because it embodies an overwhelming desire, a now unrepresentable excess of the emotional need suppressed under slavery ('to love anything that much was dangerous' [*B*, p. 45], and 'not to need permission for desire – well now, *that* was freedom' [*B*, p. 162]).[65]

Beloved returns, then, *nachträglich*, but she will be forever 'unaccounted for' (*B*, p. 275), impossible to memorialize in some metaphysical History. In her figure, historicity comes back with all the force of bewildering, unfulfilled desire, playing havoc with temporal and symbolic schemes. That force permeates the texture of Morrison's writing which, as in the later *Jazz*, makes powerful use of retroactive effects, embedding signs and images which will only become clear at a later stage. In some cases these are darkly proleptic of a story to be filled in later; in others Morrison constructs a complex sequence of displaced affect – early on we hear, for example, that Sethe's hurt 'was always there – like a tender place in the corner of her mouth that the bit left' (*B*, p. 9), but it is not until we have penetrated further into the narrative that we associate this portentous but unlocated image with the suffering of both Sethe's mother and Paul D. The distinctive rhythms of Morrison's prose create an intricate cross-weaving of times in which each moment comes to signify only in relation to at least one other. To re-read *Beloved* forewarned of this is to become increasingly attuned to the flickering trail of such emotional intensities, one illuminating another in a time which can never constitute a full present. This brief exchange between Denver and Beloved, for example:

'What is it?' asks Denver.
'Look,' she points to the sunlit cracks.
'What? I don't see nothing.' Denver follows the pointing finger. (*B*, p. 125)

But Beloved does, as we later know: 'at night I cannot see the dead man on my face daylight comes through the cracks and I can see his locked eyes' (*B*, p. 210). This is not some facile trick of composition, one time 'rhyming' with or passively echoing another;[66] rather, Morrison evokes the texture of a temporality which makes anachronism the condition of the psychic life, embedding its effects in the very detail of narration ('Sethe feels her eyes burn and it may have been to keep them clear that she looks up' (*B*, p. 261).

If belatedness is a condition recognized in the local detail of the writing, it also frames the larger movement of the narrative. Beloved first exists in 124 as a troublesome ghost, 'not evil, just sad' (*B*, p. 8).

Whereas the community tends to assume that 'the haunting was done by an evil thing looking for more', 'None of them knew the downright pleasure of enchantment, of not suspecting but *knowing* the things behind things' (*B*, p. 37). It is Paul D who 'beat[s] the spirit away', but 'in its place he brought another kind of haunting' which seems to conjure up the full horror of slavery (*B*, p. 96). 'Paul D ran her off so she had no choice but to come back to me in the flesh' (*B*, p. 200), and it is in this new embodiment that Beloved begins to play her ambiguous role in the narrative. At first she is a 'sweet, if peculiar guest' (*B*, p. 57) but as the very incarnation of a boundless desire (*B*, p. 58) she soon imposes intolerable demands upon Sethe.

The partial demonizing of Beloved runs parallel to a shifting conception of memory in the novel. In the opening stages, Sethe is troubled by frozen images of the past – 'I was talking about time. It's so hard for me to believe in it. Some things go. Pass on. Some things just stay' (*B*, pp. 35–6) – and the 'glittering' headstone which is her memorial to Beloved seems a way of 'keeping the past at bay' (*B*, p. 42). With the 'miraculous resurrection' (*B*, p. 105) of her lost daughter, however, Sethe begins to remember 'something she had forgotten she knew' (*B*, p. 61). Yet the process of remembering is at once a release and a bondage, snaring the mind in a deadly repetition even as it brings a part of the psyche back to life ('Anything dead coming back to life hurts' (*B*, p. 35)). The danger becomes clearer as the novel proceeds and the narcissistic identification with Beloved becomes stronger: 'But her brain was not interested in the future, loaded with the past and hungry for more, it left her no room to imagine, let alone plan for the next day' (*B*, p. 70). With her recognition of Beloved, Sethe is finally freed from the need to remember and left 'smiling at the things she would not have to remember now' (*B*, p. 182). But this release from 'rememory' is another kind of prison, bringing a claustrophobic introversion ('The world is in this room' (*B*, p. 183)) and leaving Sethe 'wrapped in a timeless present' (*B*, p. 184).[67]

Now we begin to see the darker effects of the 'miraculous resurrection' (*B*, p. 105), for having dropped her defences on the departure of the 'chastising ghost' (*B*, p. 86),[68] Sethe is, as it were, invaded by the spirit of her murdered daughter. It is the violence of this intrusion of one world into another which will later appal the pragmatic Ella:

> As long as the ghost showed out from its ghostly place – shaking stuff, crying, smashing and such – Ella respected it. But if it took flesh and came in her world, well, the shoe was on the other foot. She didn't mind a little communication between the two worlds, but this was an invasion. (*B*, p. 257)

The force of Beloved's desire, strongly marked by a language of orality and ingestion (chewing and swallowing), threatens to consume Sethe from within. 'Beloved ate up her life, took it, swelled up with it, grew taller on it' (*B*, p. 250), and the momentum of this desire, excessive and unspeakable because so long pent up by slavery, begins to carry us back into the past. If the novel opens with a grim rewriting of the primal scene (here a *dead* child witnesses the sexual act), now an equally macabre reversal takes place as 'Beloved bending over Sethe looked the mother, Sethe the teething child' (*B*, p. 250). To complete this traumatic looping back of the narrative we have the final sight of Beloved facing the singing women:

> The devil-child was clever, they thought. And beautiful. It had taken the shape of a pregnant woman, naked and smiling in the heat of the afternoon sun. Thunderblack and glistening, she stood on long straight legs, her belly big and tight. (*B*, p. 261)

Pregnant with ... Paul D's child? Or – the suggestion is ludicrous – with Sethe herself?

Perhaps one way of understanding this peculiar moment in the novel is to consider more closely the work of mourning which frames the story. Sethe's initial attempt to 'keep the past at bay' (*B*, p. 42) is in one sense a refusal to mourn which we might understand with the help of a distinction drawn by Nicolas Abraham and Maria Torok between 'incorporation' and 'introjection'.[69] Whereas introjection assimilates to the self what is lost, incorporation perpetuates the existence of the lost object as something alive and foreign within the self. As Derrida explains in his introduction to Abraham and Torok's study of the Wolf Man:

> Sealing the loss of the object, but also marking the refusal to mourn, such a maneuver [incorporation] is foreign to and actually opposed to the process of introjection. I pretend to keep the dead alive, intact, *safe (save) inside me*, but it is only in order to refuse, in a necessarily equivocal way, to love the dead as a living part of me, dead *save in me*, through the process of introjection, as happens in so-called normal mourning.[70]

The dead person is thus not an object of identification but a phantasmatic presence within the self which gives rise to a topography which Abraham and Torok call the 'crypt':

> Grief that cannot be expressed builds a *secret vault* within the subject. In this crypt reposes – alive, reconstituted from the memories of words, images, and feelings – the objective counterpart of the loss, as a complete person with his own topography, as well as the traumatic incidents – real or imagined – that had made introjection impossible.[71]

This 'crypt' is equivalent to 'a split in the Ego',[72] a rift from which emerges 'a false unconscious filled with phantoms – to wit, fossilized words, live corpses, and foreign bodies'.[73] The lost object is thus incorporated as something live and present, 'fantasmatic, unmediated, instantaneous, magical, sometimes hallucinatory'.[74] The terms Derrida uses here are certainly suggestive in the context of *Beloved*, and indeed Morrison herself has spoken of her novel in a way which further confirms the relevance of this idea of incorporation as some sort of fragmentation of the self. In an interview with Gloria Naylor given when she was at work on *Beloved*, Morrison spoke of her interest in a theme connecting two stories (one was that of Margaret Garner, model for Sethe, the other would form the basis of Dorcas's story in *Jazz*):

> Now what made those stories connect, I can't explain, but I do know that, in both instances, something seemed clear to me. A woman loved something other than herself so much. *She had placed all of the value of her life in something outside herself.* That the woman who killed her children loved her children so much; they were the best part of her and she would not see them sullied.[75]

Is this, then, the major theme of *Beloved* and the one which ties it to *Jazz* (apparently the second novel of a projected trilogy)? If the crypt is a split in the ego, then Morrison's account suggests that in the case of *Beloved* the central problem for Sethe is to come to terms with 'what it is that really compels a good woman to displace the self, her self' (p. 584). Morrison explains to Naylor:

> So what I started doing and thinking about for a year was to project the self not into the way we say 'yourself', but to put a space between those words, as though the self were really a *twin* or a thirst or a friend or something that sits right next to you and watches you, which is what I was talking about when I said 'the dead girl'. (p. 585)

So for Morrison, it seems, the genesis of *Beloved* lay partly in that sense that 'the best thing that is in us is also the thing that makes us sabotage ourselves, sabotage in the sense that our life is not as worthy of our perception of the best part of ourselves' (p. 585). Beloved has striven to destroy the boundaries of her mother's self ('I want the join' (*B*, p. 213), seeking now to possess – to incorporate – Sethe.[76] If Sethe's only hope lies in 'claiming ownership of [her] freed self' (*B*, p. 95) it is ultimately by managing, as Derrida puts it, to 'love the dead as a living part of me, dead *save in me*' that she will do so (Morrison has described the main problem in *Beloved* as 'how to own your own body and love somebody else').[77] The crucial recognition then will be Paul D's, that 'you your best thing, Sethe. You are' (*B*, p. 273).

But as Morrison emphasized in a recent talk,[78] something remains after the end of this particular story ('There is a loneliness that can be rocked ...' (p. 274)). In the gap between Sethe's final words ('Me? Me?') and the name which closes the narrative ('Beloved') the contradictions reappear. Beloved is exorcized, but in the last two pages of the novel she returns (again). This particular haunting is not over:

> Down by the stream in back of 124 her footprints come and go. They are so familiar. Should a child, an adult place his feet in them, they will fit. Take them out and they disappear again as though nobody ever walked there. (*B*, p. 275)

'Familiar', familial: this ghost seems the product of what Abraham and Torok term 'transgenerational haunting' in which something repressed is transmitted across several generations.[79] This phantom, writes Abraham, 'is not related to the loss of a loved one, it cannot be considered the effect of unsuccessful mourning, as is the case of melancholics or all those who carry a tomb within themselves' (p. 76). In line with his theory of 'transgenerational haunting', Abraham concludes instead that

> It is the children's or descendants' lot to objectify these buried tombs through diverse species of ghosts. What comes back to haunt are the tombs of others. The phantoms of folklore merely objectify a metaphor active within the unconscious: the burial of an unspeakable fact *within the loved one*. (p. 76)

The desire to forget is strong, but while 'This is not a story to pass on' (*B*, p. 275) the memory of 'Sixty Million and more' is somehow encrypted within us, in our time and in our bodies:

> So they forgot her. Like an unpleasant dream during a troubling sleep. Occasionally, however, the rustle of a skirt hushes when they wake, and the knuckles brushing a cheek in sleep seem to belong to the sleeper. Sometimes the photograph of a close friend or relative – looked at too long – shifts, and something more familiar than the dear face itself moves there. They can touch it if they like, but don't, because they know things will never be the same if they do. (*B*, p. 275)[80]

V

This figure of belatedness seems to return in *Jazz* (1992), the second volume of the projected trilogy that begins with *Beloved*. In the 1985 interview with Naylor, Morrison hints at a continuity between the two books:

> I just imagined her [Beloved] remembering what happened to her, being someplace else and returning, knowing what happened to her. And I call her Beloved so that I can filter all these confrontations and questions that she has in that situation, which is 1851, and then to extend her life, you know, her search, her quest, all the way through as long as I care to go, into the twenties where it switches to this other girl. Therefore I have a New York uptown-Harlem milieu in which to put this love story, but Beloved will be there also. (p. 585)

The elusive presence will linger on, then, to be discovered yet again fifty years later in the accelerated rhythms of the Jazz Age. But on this question even the narrative voice of *Jazz* is misled, for the hectic pace of the twenties seems to imply that 'the bad stuff' of the past has gone: 'Forget that. History is over, you all, and everything's ahead at last.'[81] Perhaps the City has invented new plots, plots which may repeat each other but which have no connection to a darker, more distant past. This is the 'error' of the narrative voice who, having told us the story of Joe, Violet and Dorcas, is confident that 'the three of them, Felice, Joe and Violet' will prove to be some sort of 'mirror image of Dorcas, Joe and Violet' (*J*, p. 221): 'I was so sure that it would happen. That the past was an abused record with no choice but to repeat itself at the crack and no power of earth could lift the arm that held the needle' (*J*, p. 220). But the narrator gets it wrong: this particular narrative does not repeat itself because all along it has concealed another, older story. The jazz rhythms of the twenties are counterpointed by a darker rhythm, an elusive presence which leads a phantom existence within the new:

> Both the warning and the shudder come from the snapping fingers, the clicking. And the shade. Pushed away into certain streets – just there – at the edge of the dream, or slips into the crevices of a chuckle. It is out there in the privet hedge that lines the avenue. Gliding through rooms as though it is tidying this, straightening that. It bunches on the curb-stone, wrists crossed, and hides its smile under a wide-brim hat. Shade. Protective, available. Sometimes not; sometimes it seems to lurk rather than hover kindly, and its stretch is not a yawn but an increase to be beaten back with a stick. Before it clicks, or taps or snaps its fingers. (*J*, p. 227)

Is this the presence of Beloved once again? At first sight (and following Morrison's remarks in the interview with Naylor) we might conclude that she is reborn in Dorcas, another 'beloved' who is killed by the one who loves her. But Dorcas is in fact only a pretext here, and Joe Trace, 'bound to the track' (*J*, p. 120) which will end in the girl's murder, is unaware that this is the same 'trail' (*J*, p. 130) which he had once followed in pursuit of the woman Wild who is his mother: as the narrative voice confesses, 'To this moment I'm not sure what his tears were really for, but I do know they were for more than Dorcas. All the while he was running through the streets in bad weather I thought he was looking for her, not Wild's chamber of gold' (*J*, p. 221). It is at the end of this trail that we seem to encounter Beloved again, for is not the first appearance of Wild strongly reminiscent of the pregnant 'devil-child' at the end of the previous novel? Beloved there is naked and 'thunderblack', while Wild is 'a naked berry-black woman' (*J*, p. 144) whose stomach is, in the very words of *Beloved* (*B*, p. 261) 'big and tight'. So too Wild has a 'babygirl laugh' (*J*, p. 167) and Golden Gray fears that she will 'explode in his arms' (*J*, p. 153), much, perhaps, as Beloved 'Disappeared some say, exploded right before their eyes' (*B*, p. 263).[82] And what of the child? If, to follow the more 'logical' of the two readings I suggested above, Beloved was indeed bearing Paul D's child, it is perhaps not surprising to find that Wild's offspring, Joe Trace, seems to 'inherit' certain qualities from Paul D.[83]

With these possible connections in mind we can begin to map the coincidence of larger themes across the two novels. In each book Morrison is concerned with the power of the dead to fixate the living – as Violet is told early on in *Jazz*, 'Can't rival the dead for love. Lose every time' (*J*, p. 15). So too in each novel someone murders her or his 'best thing' or 'necessary thing' (*J*, p. 28), and it is this act of violence which occasions the traumatic opening of historicity. When we read the two novels in sequence we can see even more clearly that Morrison's sense of the self's invasion by the past is closely bound up with a complex negotiation of the question of mothering. In *Beloved*, Sethe must overcome the incorporation of her dead daughter as a living presence, and the exploration of belatedness here finally allows a sort of dissolution of Beloved's bodily existence. As John Forrester puts it in his discussion of Freud's concept of *Nachträglichkeit*, 'the past dissolves in the present, so that the future becomes (once again) an *open question*, instead of being specified by the fixity of the past'.[84] In *Jazz*, Beloved's quest for Sethe is reworked, and the lives of Joe, Dorcas and Violet are all profoundly marked by the early loss of a mother. To complicate matters, the dead Dorcas also makes Violet recall the daughter she miscarried many years before ('Was she the woman who took away the man, or the daughter who fled her womb?' (*J*, p. 109)). In the lyrical conclusion which so 'surprises' the narrator, Morrison draws together the different strands of the novel, linking the murder of Dorcas not only with the elusive presence of Wild (marked by the red birds which attend her much as the hummingbirds circle Sethe's head), but also with the suicide of Violet's mother and the return of her 'phantom father' (*J*, p. 100):

Lying next to her, his head turned toward the window, he sees through the glass darkness taking the shape of a shoulder with a thin line of blood. Slowly, slowly it forms itself into a bird with a blade of red on the wing. Meanwhile Violet rests her hand on his chest as though it were the sunlit rim of a well and down there somebody is gathering gifts (lead pencils, Bull Durham, Jap Rose Soap) to distribute to them all. (*J*, p. 225)[85]

To reach this state in which Violet and Joe 'are [each] inward toward the other' (*J*, p. 228) it has once again been necessary to undo the work of incorporation. For Violet has carried another within herself (christened Violent after her attack on Dorcas's body): 'Afterward she sat in the drugstore sucking malt through a straw and wondering who on earth that other Violet was that walked about the City in her skin; peeped out through her eyes and saw other things' (*J*, p. 89). This is not just 'another self', for Violet has been possessed by someone else, by the imaginary presence of Golden Gray. As she explains to Felice:

My grandmother fed me stories about a little blond child. He was a boy, but I thought of him as a girl sometimes, as a brother, sometimes as a boyfriend. He lived inside my mind. Quiet as a mole. But I didn't know it till I got here. the two of us. Had to get rid of it. (*J*, p. 208)

Felice understands these stories 'About having another you inside that isn't anything like you' and asks:

'How did you get rid of her?'
'Killed her. Then I killed the me that killed her.'
'Who's left?'
'Me.' (*J*, p. 209)

So Dorcas, with her 'high-yellow skin' (*J*, p. 97), is somehow paired with the 'golden boy' of True Belle's stories, 'the tricky blond kid living inside Mrs Trace's head' who reminds Felice of 'A present taken from whitefolks' (*J*, p. 211).

What seems to be important here is the idea adumbrated much earlier in the novel that both Joe and Violet have compensated for the loss of a mother by incorporating the image of another:

Standing in the cane, he was trying to catch a girl he was yet to see, but his heart knew all about, and me, holding on to him but wishing he was the golden boy I never saw either. Which means from the beginning I was a substitute and so was he. (*J*, p. 97)

To move beyond these destructive 'substitutions' it is necessary once again to let the past make its disruptive way into the present, to allow the country rhythms of a shadowy past to surge back into the modernist riffs of the City. For the final peace between Joe and Violet – 'They are under the covers because they don't have to look at themselves any-more; there is no stud's eye, no chippie glance to undo them' (*J*, p. 228) – cancels the phantom presences which have stood between them, allowing them to take charge of their lives and their bodies. And so the narrative voice admits its error:

> I believed I saw everything important they did, and based on what I saw I could imagine what I didn't; how exotic they were, how driven. Like dangerous children. That's what I wanted to believe. It never occurred to me that they were thinking other thoughts, feeling other feelings, putting their lives together in ways I never dreamed of. (*J*, p. 221)

Jazz, then, does not teach some grim Faulknerian lesson about the past's power to determine the present; rather, it asserts the surviving *trace* of the past in a present which purports to be sufficient to itself. While *Jazz* celebrates the sensual freedoms of the twenties and 'the flesh that is now yours',[86] it is with the recognition that the 'shade' of Beloved will linger on. But the form of the narrative parallels Joe's 'trail' in this respect, reminding us that the past is not monolithic but somehow yielding, capable of bringing release through the very experience of *Nachträglichkeit*:

> He felt peace at the beginning, and a kind of watchfulness, as though something waited. A before-supper feeling when someone waits to eat. Although it was a private place, with an opening closed to the public, once inside you could do what you pleased: disrupt things, rummage, touch and move. Change it all to a way it was never meant to be. (*J*, p. 184)

If the figure of belatedness links the two novels, it is because Morrison grasps the persistence of an enslaved past as both a violent intrusion into the self *and* as the very possibility of the black self's release into some form of agency. This last theme is one which Morrison has recently emphasized in relation to both novels, observing, for example, of *Jazz*'s Joe Trace that he is 'moving on a course because of his past, and he does not understand who he is hunting. But he does understand what is in his hand and takes the consequences of his own action with or without the police [...] he assumes responsibility for that.'[87] In the rhythms of Morrison's narrative, then, the past, now loosed from fixity, is no longer phantasmal or encrypted, but can contain the promise of a future which will be, precisely, an open question.

Notes

1 Sigmund Freud, 'From the History of an Infantile Neurosis', *SE*, vol. 17, (1918); all page references given in the text. I would like to thank John Forrester for invaluable bibliographical help in approaching the Wolf Man.
2 Juliet Mitchell, *Psychoanalysis and Feminism* (Harmondsworth: Penguin, 1974), p. 65.
3 Peter Brooks, *Reading for the Plot: Design and Intention in Narrative* (Oxford: Oxford University Press, 1984), pp. 279, 285.
4 Michael Holquist, *Dialogism: Bakhtin and His World* (London: Methuen, 1990), p. 148.
5 Brooks, *Reading for the Plot*, p. 265.
6 Ibid., p. 354 n. 9.
7 *Feminist Review Special Issue: Family Secrets, Child Sexual Abuse*, 28 (Spring 1988). I am grateful to Agnes McAuley for this reference.
8 Brooks, *Reading for the Plot*, p. 267.
9 This may also be the impression given by Freud's virtuoso reading of the case history of Schreber, where apparently unanalysable chaos is given form and meaning (again, the meaning is that of homosexuality), although subsequently critics have questioned Freud's analysis by pointing to a material substratum of abuse by Schreber's father: see Morton Schatzman, *Soul Murder* (Harmondsworth: Penguin, 1978) and William G. Niederland, *The Schreber Case: Psychoanalytic Profile of a Paranoid Personality* (New York: Quadrangle, 1974).
10 Chris Ackerley and Lawrence J. Clipper, *A Companion to 'Under the Volcano'* (Vancouver: University of British Columbia Press, 1984).
11 Brooks, *Reading for the Plot*, p. 273.
12 Ibid., p. 284.
13 Stanley Fish, 'Withholding the Missing Portion: Psychoanalysis and Rhetoric', in F. Meltzer, (ed.), *The Trials of Psychoanalysis* (Chicago: University of Chicago Press, 1988), pp. 192, 198.
14 Ibid., p. 200.

Reading 3 (Freud)

15 [It might perhaps be clearer to say '$n + \frac{1}{2}$'. The point is that owing to the interval of 6 months between the patient's birthday and the summer, his áge at the time of the trauma must have been 0 years + 6 months, or 2 years – 6 months, etc.] [*James Strachey's note*]
16 In white underclothes: the *white* wolves.
17 Why three times? He suddenly one day produced the statement that I [Freud] had discovered this detail by interpretation. This was not the case. It was a spontaneous association, exempt from further criticism; in his usual way he passed it off on to me, and by this projection tried to make it seem more trustworthy.

18 I [Freud] mean that he understood it at the time of the dream when he was four years old, not at the time of the observation. He received the impressions when he was one and a half; his understanding of them was deferred, but became possible at the time of the dream owing to his development, his sexual excitations, and his sexual researches.

Reading 4 (Nicholls)

19 *Playing in the Dark: Whiteness and the Literary Imagination* (Cambridge, Mass. and London: Harvard University Press, 1992), p. v. (hereafter cited in the text as *PD*).

20 See Mae G. Henderson, 'Toni Morrison's *Beloved*: Re-Membering the Body as Historical Text', in Hortense J. Spillers (ed.), *Comparative American Identities* (London: Routledge, 1991), p. 74.

21 *Beloved* (London: Pan Books, 1988), p. 61 (hereafter cited in the text as *B*). Bruno Bettelheim calls the work an 'autobiographical novel' in his Introduction. Morrison apparently discovered Cardinal's account in 1983. Without enforcing the connection too rigorously, there are several other aspects of *The Words to Say It* which may have resonated with Morrison's work on *Beloved*, not least, perhaps, the account of Marie's mother's illness which is closely tied to the early death of a daughter: 'She no longer needed to come as often because, little by little, her dead baby had again begun to grow inside her and would live there for ever.' See below, pp. 61–2.

22 *Beloved*, p. 199. See also 'Unspeakable Things Unspoken: The Afro-American Presence in American Literature', *Michigan Quarterly Review*, 28 (1) Winter 1989, pp. 1–34.

23 Ned Lukacher, *Primal Scenes: Literature, Philosophy, Psychoanalysis* (Ithaca and London: Cornell University Press, 1986), p. 12.

24 Marie Cardinal, *The Words to Say it*, trans. Pat Goodheart (London: Pan Books, 1983), p. 36: 'The beauty of those thick, glossy flowers! I was running, they were already far behind, and yet the heart of one of these that I had glimpsed for a fraction of a second stayed with me, keeping me company in my race, as calm as I was agitated, svelte in appearance but torn apart inside.' Morrison (p. ix) quotes the last phrase in her account.

25 'Living Memory' (Interview with Toni Morrison by Paul Gilroy), *City Limits* (31 March/7 April, 1988), p. 11: 'From a woman's point of view, in terms of confronting the problems of where the world is now, black women had to deal with "post-modern" problems in the nineteenth century and earlier. These things had to be addressed by black people a long time ago. Certain kinds of dissolution, the loss of and the need to reconstruct certain kinds of stability.'

26 Cf. Robert Young, *White Mythologies: Writing History and the West* (London: Routledge, 1990), pp. 19–20 for the view that postmodernism designates 'not just the cultural effects of a new stage of "late" capitalism', but 'European culture's awareness that it is no longer the unquestioned and

dominant centre of the world'. See also Thomas Docherty, *After Theory: Postmodernism/postmarxism* (London: Routledge, 1990).

27 Cf. *The Words to Say It*, p. 15: 'The Thing, which on the inside was made of a monstrous crawling of images, sounds, and odours, projected in every way by a devastating pulse making all reasoning incoherent, all explanation absurd, all efforts to order tentative and useless ...'

28 See also the discussion of 'time-lag' and its relation to *Beloved* in Homi K. Bhabha, '"Race", Time and the Revision of Modernity', *Oxford Literary Review*, 13 (1–2), 1991, pp. 193–219, especially pp. 215–16.

29 Jean-François Lyotard, 'Answering the Question: What Is Postmodernism?', in *The Postmodern Condition: A Report on Knowledge*, trans. Geoff Bennington and Brian Massumi (Manchester: Manchester University Press, 1984), pp. 71–82.

30 Gianni Vattimo, *The End of Modernity: Nihilism and Hermeneutics in Postmodern Culture*, trans. Jon R. Snyder (Cambridge: Polity Press, 1988), p. 105.

31 Michel Foucault, *The Archeology of Knowledge*, trans. A. M. Sheridan Smith (London: Tavistock Publications Ltd, 1982), p. 12.

32 Mae G. Henderson, 'Toni Morrison's *Beloved*', p. 63.

33 Jean Laplanche and Serge Leclaire, 'The Unconscious: A Psychoanalytic Study', *Yale French Studies*, 48 (1972), p. 128. Cf. John Forrester, *The Seductions of Psychoanalysis: Freud, Lacan, and Derrida* (Cambridge: Cambridge University Press, 1990), p. 199 on 'Freud's theory that it was a *way* of remembering that was traumatic, rather than *what* was remembered'.

34 David F. Krell, *Of Memory, Reminiscence, and Writing: On the Verge* (Bloomington and Indianapolis: Indiana University Press, 1990), p. 106.

35 Cf. Mae G. Henderson, 'Toni Morrison's *Beloved*', p. 64: 'Morrison seeks to repossess the African and slave ancestors after their historic violation.' And ibid., pp. 80–1 on Sethe's ability to '"relive" or re-enact the past'.

36 Dominick LaCapra, 'History and Psychoanalysis', in Françoise Meltzer (ed.), *The Trial(s) of Psychoanalysis* (Chicago and London: University of Chicago Press, 1988), p. 18.

37 This particular view of the postmodern is to be distinguished from that of Fredric Jameson who has argued consistently that postmodernity is characterized by a 'waning' of a thematics of time and memory ('memory has been weakened in our time', as he puts it in *Postmodernism, or the Cultural Logic of Late Capitalism* Verso, 1991 [London and New York: p. 364]). For a critique, see my 'Divergences: Modernism, Postmodernism, Jameson and Lyotard', *Critical Quarterly*, 33(3) (Autumn 1991), pp. 1–18.

38 *Pelican Freud Library*, 9 (Harmondsworth: Penguin Books, 1981), p. 278 n. 2. Cf. the letter to Fliess of 15 October 1895, in *The Origins of Psycho-Analysis: Letters to Wilhelm Fliess, Drafts and Notes: 1887–1902* (London: Imago, 1954), p. 127: 'Have I revealed the great clinical secret to you ... ? Hysteria is the consequence of presexual *sexual shock*. Obsessional neurosis is the consequence of presexual *sexual pleasure* later transformed into guilt.' Freud goes on to observe that 'the relevant events become effective only as *memories*'.

39 *Ecrits: A Selection*, trans. Alan Sheridan (London: Tavistock, 1977), p. 48.

40 Jean Laplanche and J. B. Pontalis, *The Language of Psychoanalysis*, trans. Donald Nicholson-Smith, with an introduction by Daniel Lagache (London: Karnac Books, 1988), p. 113. Cf. Laplanche, *New Foundations for Psychoanalysis*, trans. David Macey (Oxford: Blackwell, 1989), p. 112: 'This theory postulates that nothing can be inscribed in the human unconscious except in relation to at least two events which are separated from one another in time by a moment of maturation that allows the subject to react in two ways to an initial experience or to the memory of that experience.'

41 Forrester, *The Seductions of Psychoanalysis*, p. 206.

42 Andrew Benjamin, *Art, Mimesis and the Avant-Garde* (London: Routledge, 1991), p. 197. Cf. Lacan, *Ecrits*, p. 48: '... the effect of full speech is to reorder past contingencies by conferring on them the sense of necessities to come, such as they are constituted by the little freedom through which the subject makes them present.'

43 Laplanche and Pontalis, *The Language of Psychoanalysis*, p. 114.

44 Laplanche, *New Foundations for Psychoanalysis*, p. 118.

45 Michel Foucault, *Language, Counter-Memory, Practice: Selected Essays and Interviews*, ed. Donald F. Bouchard (Ithaca: Cornell University Press, 1977), p. 172.

46 See Lukacher, *Primal Scenes*, p. 35: 'Deferred action demands that one recognize that while the earlier event is still to some extent the cause of the later event, the earlier event is nevertheless also the effect of the later event. One is forced to admit a double or "metaleptic" logic in which causes are both causes of effects and the effect of effects.'

47 *Memories for Paul de Man*, rev. ed., trans. Cecile Lindsay et al. (New York: Columbia University Press, 1989), p. 58: 'Memory stays with traces, in order to "preserve" them, but traces of a past that has never been present, traces which themselves never occupy the form of presence and always remain, as it were, to come.' Cf. *Margins of Philosophy*, trans. Alan Bass (Brighton: Harvester Press, 1986), p. 21. The same point is stressed by Lyotard in *Heidegger and 'the jews'*, trans. Andreas Michel and Mark Roberts (Minneapolis: University of Minnesota Press, 1990), p. 13 (hereafter cited in the text as *H*): 'It will be represented as something that has never been presented.' David Krell, *Of Memory, Reminiscence, and Writing*, p. 6 observes of Merleau-Ponty's elaboration of a similar idea in *The Phenomenology of Perception* that it 'heralds the passing of an epoch of mnemic metaphysics. It marks the inception of a memory beneath the traditional ontotheological uses of recollection, a memory no longer in thrall to presence.'

48 Andrew Benjamin, 'Translating Origins: Psychoanalysis and Philosophy', in L. Venuti (ed.), *Rethinking Translation: Discourse, Subjectivity Ideology* (London: Routledge, 1992), p. 30. This logic is perhaps inscribed in the etymology of the verb 'to remember', from the Latin *rememorari*, 'call to mind again, remember *again*'; Morrison's 'rememory' is not, as is sometimes thought, a coinage, but an archaism which the *OED* defines as 'remembrance'.

49 *Mémoires*, p. 95.

50 Jacques Derrida, *Of Grammatology*, trans. Gayatri Chakravorty Spivak (Baltimore and London: Johns Hopkins University Press, 1976), p. 85. 'the word history has no doubt always been associated with a linear scheme of the unfolding of presence, where the line relates the final presence to the originary presence according to the straight line or the circle.'

51 Jacques Derrida, *Dissemination*, trans. Barbara Johnson (Chicago: University of Chicago Press, 1981), p. 210. See also *Writing and Difference*, trans. Alan Bass (London: Routledge, 1978), p. 212 for the connection of this central theme with Freud's *Nachträglichkeit*: 'That the present in general is not primal but, rather, reconstituted, that it is not the absolute, wholly living form which constitutes experience, that there is no purity of the living present – such is the theme, formidable for metaphysics, which Freud, in a conceptual scheme unequal to the thing itself, would have us pursue.'

52 *Pelican Freud Library*, 9, p. 284.

53 See Philippe Lacoue-Labarthe and Jean-Luc Nancy, 'Le peuple juif ne reve pas', in *La Psychanalyse est-elle une histoire juive?* (Paris: Seuil, 1981), pp. 86–7.

54 Louis Althusser and Etienne Balibar, *Reading Capital*, trans. Ben Brewster (London: Verso, 1979), pp. 100, 95. Althussser's argument is underpinned by his critique of Hegel's 'historical present': 'the structure of historical existence is such that all the elements of the whole always co-exist in one and the same time, one and the same present, and are therefore contemporaneous with one another in one and the same present' (p. 94).

55 Ibid., p. 103 (Althusser's emphases).

56 See *L'inhumain: Causeries sur le temps* (Paris: Editions Galilée, 1988), pp. 35–8. The main question here is 'the insinuation of will into reason' – see Lyotard, *Tombeau de l'intellectuel et autres papiers* (Paris: Editions Galilée, 1984), p. 81.

57 For a discussion of these aspects of Modernism, see my 'Apes and Familiars: Modernism, Mimesis, and the Work of Wyndham Lewis', *Textual Practice* (forthcoming).

58 Jean Laplanche and J. B. Pontalis, 'Fantasy and the Origins of Sexuality', *International Journal of Psycho-Analysis*, 49, (1)1968, p. 4 (my italics).

59 *Ecrits*, p. 103.

60 Cf. *Heidegger and 'the jews'*, p. 15: 'the force of the excitation cannot be "bound", composed, neutralized, fixed in accordance with other forces "within" the apparatus, and to that extent it does not give rise to a *mise-en-scène*'.

61 For the case of Emma, see *Project for a Scientific Psychology*, in *The Origins of Psychoanalysis*, pp. 410–14.

62 Ibid., p. 413 (Freud's italics).

63 Compare Lyotard's account (*Heidegger and 'the jews'*, p. 11) of a past 'which is not an object of memory like something that might have been forgotten and must be remembered with a view to a "good end", to correct knowledge'.

64 See *The Naked Lunch* (London: Corgi, 1974), p. 247: ' "Possession" they call it [...] Sometimes an entity jumps in the body [...] As if I was usually there but subject to goof now and again [...] *Wrong! I am never here* [...] Never that is *fully* in possession ...' Thomas Pynchon's *Gravity's Rainbow* (1973; Harmondsworth: Penguin, 1987) provides one definitive exploration of the 'interiorization' of control: 'All these things arise from one difficulty: control. For the first time it was *inside*, do you see. The control is put inside. No more need to suffer passively under "outside forces"' (p. 30).

65 For Beloved as the force of desire, see p. 58: 'A touch no heavier than a feather but loaded with desire. Sethe stirred and looked around. First at Beloved's soft new hand on her shoulder, then into her eyes. The longing she saw there was bottomless. Some plea barely in control.' The implications of the last phrase become clear as Beloved becomes increasingly demanding (p. 240): 'when Sethe ran out of things to give her, Beloved invented desire'.

66 For the temporal relation trivialized as 'echo', see, for example, Peter Ackroyd, *Hawksmoor* (1985) and *Chatterton* (1987).

67 Cf. *Beloved*, p. 244: 'like Sweet Home where time didn't pass'.

68 *Beloved*, p. 86: 'Her heavy knives of defense against misery, regret, gall and hurt, she placed one by one on a bank where clear water rushed on below.' But we have already had a forewarning (p. 57) of the conflict to come between Sethe and Beloved: 'In lamplight, and over the flames of the cooking stove, their two shadows clashed and crossed on the ceiling like black swords.'

69 As Laplanche and Pontalis explain (*The Language of Psychoanalysis*, p. 211), Freud uses 'incorporation' to define the 'Process whereby the subject, more or less on the level of phantasy, has an object penetrate his body and keeps it "inside" his body. Incorporation constitutes an instinctual aim and a mode of object-relationship which are characteristic of the oral stage ...' 'Introjection' (a term which Freud borrowed from Ferenczi) is 'closely akin to identification' and while 'close in meaning to incorporation [...] does not necessarily imply any reference to the body's real boundaries (introjection into the ego, into the ego-ideal, etc.)' (ibid., p. 229).

70 '*Fors*: The Anglish Words of Nicolas Abraham and Maria Torok', trans. Barbara Johnson, in Abraham and Torok, *The Wolf Man's Magic Word: A Cryptonymy*, trans. Nicholas Rand (Minneapolis: University of Minnesota Press, 1986), pp. xvi–xvii. Cf. ibid, pp. xxi–ii: 'By resisting introjection, it prevents the loving, appropriating assimilation of the other, and thus seems to preserve the other *as* other (foreign), but it also does the opposite. It is not the *other* that the process of incorporation preserves, but a certain topography it keeps safe, intact, untouched by the very relationship with the other to which, paradoxically, introjection is more open.'

71 Nicolas Abraham and Maria Torok, 'Introjection – Incorporation: *Mourning* or *Melancholia*', in S. Lebovici and D. Widlocher (eds), *Psychoanalysis in France* (New York: International University Press, 1980), p. 8. See also Maria Torok, 'Maladie du deuil et fantasme du cadavre exquis', in Abraham and Torok, *L'Ecorce et le noyau* (Paris: Flammarion, 1987), pp. 229–51.

72 *The Wolf Man's Cryptonomy*, p. 81: 'For the crypt *is already* constructed, and the Ego cannot quit the place where it had once been; it can only withdraw into seclusion and construct a barrier separating it from the other half of the Ego.'

73 Elisabeth Roudinesco, *Jacques Lacan & Co.: A History of Psychoanalysis in France, 1925–1985* (London: Free Association Books, 1990), p. 599.

74 Derrida, '*Fors*', p. xvii.

75 Gloria Naylor and Toni Morrison, 'A Conversation', *Southern Review*, 21 Summer 1985, p. 584 (my emphases). Further references will be given in the text.

76 Note how the struggle between them is permeated with images of orality and ingestion. The image of Beloved as pregnant reverses the phantasmal moment earlier in the novel when Sethe's water seems to break for the *second* time when she first sees Beloved (p. 51).

77 Interview with Salman Rushdie, *The Late Show* (BBC2), June 1992.

78 Bloomsbury Theatre, London, 6 June 1992.

79 Nicolas Abraham, 'Notes on the Phantom: A Complement to Freud's Metapsychology', trans. Nicholas Rand, in Meltzer (ed.), *The Trial(s) of Psychoanalysis*, pp. 75–80; further references will be given in the text. See also the use made of this idea in Jacqueline Rose, *The Haunting of Sylvia Plath* (London: Virago, 1991).

80 Cf. Abraham, 'Notes on the Phantom', pp. 77–8: 'The phantom's periodic and compulsive return lies beyond the scope of symptom-formation in the sense of a return of the repressed; it works like a ventriloquist, like a stranger within the subject's own mental topography. The phantom's periodic and compulsive return lies beyond the scope of symptom-formation in the sense of a return of the repressed; it works like a ventriloquist, like a stranger within the subject's own mental topography.'

81 *Jazz* (London: Chatto and Windus, 1992), p. 7 (hereafter cited in the text as *J*).

82 Cf. *Beloved*, p. 133: 'she had two dreams: exploding, and being swallowed'.

83 Joe is 'A nice, neighborly, everybody-knows-him man [...] the sort women ran to when they thought they were being followed [...] Women teased him because they trusted him' (*Jazz*, p. 73). Cf. Felice's view of Joe, ibid., p. 206.

84 Forrester, *The Seductions of Psychoanalysis*, p. 206 (his italics).

85 Cf. *Jazz*, p. 228, where Joe and Violet are 'bound and joined by carnival dolls', the same 'clothespin dolls' which are lost in the fire which kills Dorcas's mother.

86 Interview with Salman Rushdie, *The Late Show* (BBC2), June 1992.

87 Ibid. Morrison also observed that a central concern of *Beloved* is 'how to exert individual agency under this huge umbrella of determined life'.

Part III
Sigmund Freud versus Jacques Lacan: Edgar Allan Poe and Henry James

---

Marie Bonaparte and Barbara Johnson on Edgar Allan Poe's 'The Purloined Letter'

Edgar Allan Poe's macabre stories, which feature mysterious murder, blackmail, return from the dead, hints at incest, dramas of trapped consciousnesses and addiction, are clearly tempting to analyse psychoanalytically. The extract here from Marie Bonaparte's *Life and Works of Edgar Allan Poe* links Poe's life overtly and rather unquestioningly to his writing, in a species of psychoanalytic criticism which could be called 'psychobiography'[1] or 'applied psychoanalysis'.[2] Barbara Johnson's essay ingeniously incorporates essays on Poe's story 'The Purloined Letter' by Lacan and Derrida, while also providing a commentary on both; this view of Poe suggests that his story is about its own workings, and that, like the psyche, it can only keep retelling the story of its own origins in signification.

The story

'The Purloined Letter'[3] (1845) is the third in a series with 'The Murders in the Rue Morgue' (1841) and 'The Mystery of Marie Rogêt' (1842) of short detective stories featuring C. Auguste Dupin; it is narrated by his unnamed commonsensical friend, who explains how the Prefect of Parisian police burst in on them one evening, asking for help with a '"*very* simple"' (p. 7) business. The Perfect describes how Minister D— has purloined a '"document of the last importance"' from the royal apartments, and must still possess it as certain effects have not yet taken place: '"the disclosure of the document to a third person, who shall be nameless, would bring in question the honour of a personage of most exalted station"' (p. 8). The thief took the document openly, in the presence of the recipient and '"the other exalted personage from whom especially it was her wish to conceal it"' (ibid.): she could not stop him.

The narrator comments on the '"ascendancy"' offered in this scenario by '"the robber's knowledge of the loser's knowledge of the robber"' (ibid.), and the narrator observes that power resides in keeping hold of the letter: once it is more than a threat, and is used, its power is lost.

On a second visit, the Prefect describes the extraordinary searches for the letter conducted on the Minister's home: every inch has been searched, the cushions probed with needles, furniture joints examined with a microscope, the moss between the bricks outside inspected. The '"prodigious"' reward is one reason for such zeal, and the Prefect offers a large part of it to anyone who can obtain the letter – the appearance of which he describes minutely. Dupin says that the Prefect may as well sign the cheque to him right away, and then hands the Prefect the letter.

Dupin explains to his sidekick that the police had gone about the search in the wrong way: '"Had the letter been deposited within the range of their search, these fellows would, beyond a question, have found it"' (p. 14). Dupin has worked out the whereabouts of the letter by the mechanism of '"an identification of the reasoner's intellect with that of his opponent"', as the narrator interprets it. The Prefect's problem was largely in supposing the Minister to be a fool because he is also a poet; but, Dupin points out, he is also a mathematician, and has therefore been '"driven, as a matter of course, to *simplicity*"' (p. 19). He offers his theory that some things, '"like the over-largely lettered signs and placards of the street, escape observation by dint of being excessively obvious"' (p. 20).

Dupin describes how, with these ideas in mind, he visited the Minister's hotel wearing a pair of green spectacles to hide his eyes, and found the Minister, pretending lassitude, lounging at home. Looking secretly round, Dupin sees '"a trumpery filagree card-rack of pasteboard [...] dangling [...] from a little brass knob just beneath the middle of the mantel-piece"' (p. 21), in which was a dirty, crumpled letter. Although different from the Prefect's description, Dupin knew it was the letter he sought, and realized it had been turned inside out. Returning the next day on the pretext of having left behind a snuffbox, a prearranged scream in the street gave Dupin the chance to take the letter and substitute for it a facsimile. Dupin thinks with pleasure of the shock the

Minister, who once did him an evil turn, will get when he sees the quotation therein, in Dupin's handwriting, from Crébillon's play *Atrée*.

Marie Bonaparte

Bonaparte (1882–1962) was an analysand of Freud's, a personal friend, and responsible for helping him and others escape the Nazis in 1939.[4] Her book, *The Life and Works of Edgar Allan Poe: A Psycho-Analytic Interpretation* gives much attention to the details of Poe's life. Edgar was born in Boston in 1809; his father, David Poe, deserted the family two years later, and his actress mother Elizabeth, née Arnold, died of tuberculosis a year after that. He was brought up by foster-parents, who took him with them to Britain between the ages of six and eleven. The young Poe fell out with his adoptive father John Allan (whose surname he took as his own middle name) when the latter had to pay gambling debts accrued by Poe at university, and to support himself joined the army. He engineered his own dismissal, and went to live in Baltimore with his aunt and other family members. He married his cousin Virginia when he was twenty-six: she was half his age. She died of tuberculosis ten years later, and Poe himself died aged forty, an alcoholic and impoverished. Following the logic of dreams, Bonaparte claims that Poe's pathology is clear in his stories, which tend to follow narratives of either hatred for the father or hopeless love for the mother. Her discussion of 'The Purloined Letter' here is extremely interesting, and elements of it, such as likening the fireplace to the female body, are picked up by Lacan in his very different reading. Similarly, Bonaparte's point about Poe's shifting the Oedipal battle over the mother to the realm of the intellect is something Norman N. Holland emphasizes: he says the characters are like small boys, and convert a story about sex, murder, cannibalism and adultery into 'an intellectual game'.[5] He also repeats Bonaparte's insight about the battle in the story between the Minister and Dupin, however intellectualized, being over a woman.[6]

Barbara Johnson

Johnson, by contrast, discusses Poe's story in terms of its processes of meaning, and as a possible model for how psychoanalysis can approach any text. The story is, in Johnson's phrase, an 'allegory of the signifier', or letter, and is 'about' the language out of which it is constructed. Felman calls it an 'allegory of analysis'[7] in that repetition affords a position for understanding an earlier state: Dupin, who restores the letter/symptom[8] to the Queen, is in the position of the analyst. She also suggests that the story is 'an allegory of poetic writing', in that the poet is by definition one who hides things well, making possible the uncovering of questions rather than answers by readers and critics.[9] It is clearly true that all three Dupin tales are 'less interesting for their detective plots than for their theories about how detection works'; they are already about the processes of their own working.[10]

A 'letter' can mean a typographical character; an epistle; or the institution of literariness ('What makes a man of letters'), as Lacan points out,[11] and in Poe's tale all these meanings overlap. In the sense of 'letter' as a 'phoneme which differentiates sound' and makes meaning possible,[12] the story is about the relationship between the self and signification.[13] As a signifier, the letter is the conscious manifestation of the signifieds of the unconscious; as Catherine Belsey points out, the letter (epistle) in the story is a sign of contradiction and scandal, the source of the 'divided, contradictory subject'.[14] Johnson relies on the debate between Lacan and Derrida about the story, and also offers her own observations on both it and the other theorists' positions.

Edmund Wilson, 'The Ambiguity of Henry James'; Shoshana Felman, 'Turning the Screw of Interpretation'

Henry James's novella *The Turn of the Screw* (1898), although exhibiting features of his later style, such as complex sentence structure and limited point of view, was received with widespread enthusiasm when it was published ('Human imagination can go no further into infamy, literary art could not be used with more refined subtlety of spiritual defilement'; 'what story in the whole region of fiction can match its deliberate, intentional, insidious horror, the sense and presence of gloating, atrocious, destructive evil which it conveys', as contemporary reviewers put it[15]), and continues to be popular. There are film versions of it – *The Innocents* (Jack Clayton, 1961) – and an opera, Benjamin Britten's *The Turn of the Screw*, both of which raise interesting issues about the portrayal of ambiguity in a visual rather than a textual medium.

Henry James

James famously disavowed[16] the power of his own story; he wrote of it to H. G. Wells, 'the thing is essentially a pot-boiler and a *jeu d'esprit*';[17]

to F. W. H. Myers that it 'is a very mechanical matter [...] an inferior, a merely *pictorial* subject';[18] and, in the New York Preface, 'it is a piece of ingenuity pure and simple, of cold artistic calculation, an *amusette* to catch those not easily caught (the "fun" of the capture of the witless being ever but small), the jaded, the disillusioned, the fastidious'.[19] Many critics have questioned and mulled over these possibly disingenuous comments, including Shoshana Felman, as we shall see; and Edmund Wilson noted, '[James] has carried his ambiguous procedure to a point where we almost feel that the author does not want the reader to get through to the hidden meaning'.[20]

'The Turn of the Screw'

The story has elements that are clearly promising for a psychoanalytic interpretation: a female narrator is convinced she sees sexually evil ghosts, which, she becomes convinced, are communicating in some way with the children whose governess she is.

It is revealing that any summary of the story presupposes a particular interpretation, as Wilson's summary at the beginning of his essay shows, especially as the story is structured around ambiguities which can only be approached on the basis of the text's language, not its plot; but here are the bare bones of it.

An unnamed young man reads out from a manuscript a description of events written by the woman who was subsequently his sister's governess. In this narrative, the governess explains how she took up a previous post at Bly, taking care of two children, Miles and Flora: their uncle (also their guardian) wanted to be relieved entirely of responsibility for them. The governess accepts the post partly because of her attraction to the uncle – the Master – and when walking in the grounds of the house thinking about him, looks up and sees a male figure standing on a tower. The figure seems malevolent; she describes him to the housekeeper, Mrs Grose, who, rather unnerved, identifies him as Peter Quint, who used to be the Master's valet. When pressed for further details, Mrs Grose reveals that Quint is now dead.

While he was alive, Quint had a relationship with the then governess, Miss Jessel, and as the children went everywhere with the pair, there is a suggestion that Miles and Flora have become corrupted by adult knowledge. The governess is convinced that Quint and Miss Jessel, whose ghost she also (thinks she) sees, have come back for the children, who seem angelic, although Miles has been sent home from school for an unspecified reason. She spends much time trying to persuade

Mrs Grose of the truth of the ghosts' presence, while also trying to
work out what the children know and what their attitude is to the
revenants.

Ultimately the governess becomes convinced that the children wel-
come the servants' ghosts; a scene by the lake seems evidence that Flora
is in communication with Miss Jessel, but the governess's reaction
frightens Flora so much that she begs not to have to see her any more.
The governess has a similar confrontation with Miles, whom she imagines she can 'save' from the ghost of Quint, but she stifles him to death
instead.

Edmund Wilson

The 'meaning' of the story has long been hotly debated, and relatively
early a self-defining strand of 'Freudian criticism' developed around the
debate: is *The Turn of the Screw* a ghost story or something else, perhaps worse; a story about madness or deliberate evil? This debate
focused particularly around the question of whether the ghosts are real
or not. If they are hallucinations of the governess, the tale is a psychological study, not simply a thriller. Christine Brooke-Rose describes the
'overdetermination of the enigma (ghosts versus hallucinations)' in the
tale, which is 'constant yet unresolved and can be read both ways each
time'.[21] As Wilson points out, the view that there was a 'clever, psychological'[22] James at work rather than simply a spinner of a ghost-yarn was
signalled early on (1924) by Edna Kenton.[23] Wilson introduced explicit
Freudian terminology to the view that the subject of the story is the
governess's mind, not objective ghosts, and after his article was published in the 1934 issue of *Hound and Horn* devoted to James, there followed a 'literary controversy which, over the years, has become itself
almost as compelling as the tale'.[24]

In the essay reproduced here, Wilson not only says definitively that
the governess suffers from delusions, and that therefore the story is not
about ghosts but a psychological study, he also identifies clearly the
source of these delusions: 'the governess who is made to tell the story is
a neurotic case of sex repression, and [. . .] the ghosts are not real ghosts
but hallucinations of the governess'. He proceeds to analyse elements
of the story in a 'Freudian' manner: the scene where Flora makes a
boat by fixing a mast into a flat piece of wood may be further evidence
of the fact that the children have been 'corrupted', as he puts it in the
reading here, but more that the governess sees signs of her passion
everywhere.

Shoshana Felman

Felman uses her critique of Wilson's essay on *The Turn of the Screw* to discuss what she thinks the tale is about, and simultaneously to mount an investigation into the workings and limitations of the kind of psychoanalytic criticism used by Wilson. As she points out, the irony of a psychoanalytic criticism which refuses to become 'a *dupe* of literature' is that the urge to such mastery ends up undoing itself, stifling ambiguity, the unconscious, which should be its very province, just as the governess stifles Miles in trying to prise his knowledge from him. The child represents unconscious knowledge because he knows things he should not ("'They know – it's too monstrous: they know, they know!'" ', as the governess cries to Mrs Grose; clearly the use of the verb 'to know' depends on its own ambiguity, as it means both specifically sexual knowledge and knowledge of facts; the same double meaning occurs in the title and text of James's *What Maisie Knew* (1897).). However, to try to grasp this knowledge is to grasp death.[25] 'Grasp' is used both literally and metaphorically by the governess,[26] and this is a locution repeated by Wilson: 'When one has once got hold of the clue to this meaning of *The Turn of the Screw*, one wonders how one could ever have missed it'. (Even more recent suggestions, that the 'secret' the text has to impart is the hidden horror of child abuse, practised by Quint and Jessel and continued by the governess, or that the ghosts represent the propensity of evil to continue after death, are deadening interpretative gestures, which pin down the text and show that the reader has, again, fallen into the trap.[27]) The troubling nature of the-child-who-knows is clear for example in horror films, where a sexually aware or murdering child is a figure of particular dread; this is the case in *Hallowe'en* (John Carpenter, 1978), in which the murderer is the victim's small brother, and *The Shining* (Stanley Kubrick, 1980), where what seem to be the ghosts of twin sisters try to entice the small psychic boy to come and 'play' with them.

Elizabeth Wright also points out some unanswered, and unraised, questions in Felman's essay. Wright asks why Felman never questions · James's wish to catch out his readers – what of his repression and transference? And why should readers enjoy, or at least accept, this state of affairs?[28] It is as if, Wright suggests, Felman is so keen to disrupt the hierarchy of text over psychoanalysis that she has not noticed herself replacing it with a different priority, that of text over psyche: 'The text lies in wait, ready to occupy the subject'.[29]

5 MARIE BONAPARTE

Tales of the Mother

Others tales by Poe also express, though in different and less aggressive fashion, regret for the missing maternal penis, with reproach for its loss. First among these, strange though it seems, is 'The Purloined Letter'.

The reader will remember that, in this story, the Queen of France, like Elizabeth Arnold, is in possession of dangerous and secret letters, whose writer is unknown. A wicked minister, seeking a political advantage and to strengthen his power, steals one of these letters under the Queen's eyes, which she is unable to prevent owing to the King's presence. This letter must at all costs be recovered. Every attempt by the police fails. Fortunately Dupin is at hand. Wearing dark spectacles with which he can look about him while his own eyes are concealed, he makes an excuse to call on the Minister and discovers the letter openly displayed in a card rack, hung 'from a little brass knob just beneath the middle of the mantelpiece'.

By a further subterfuge, he possesses himself of the compromising letter and leaves a similar one in its place. The Queen, who will have the original restored to her, is saved.

Let us first note that this letter, very symbol of the maternal penis, also 'hangs' over the fireplace, in the same manner as the female penis, if it existed, would be hung over the cloaca which is here represented – as in the foregoing tales – by the general symbol of fireplace or chimney. We have here, in fact, what is almost an anatomical chart, from which not even the clitoris (or brass knob) is omitted. Something very different, however, should be hanging from that body!

The struggle between Dupin and the Minister who once did Dupin an 'ill turn' – a struggle in which the latter is victorious – represents, in effect, the Oedipal struggle between father and son, though on an archaic, pregenital, and phallic level, to seize possession, not of the mother herself, but of a part: namely, her penis.

We have here an illustration of that 'partial love' and desire, not for the whole of the loved being but for an organ, which characterizes one stage of infantile libidinal development.

Yet though the Minister, impressive father figure and 'man of genius' as he is, is outwitted by the ratiocinatory and so more brilliant son, he presents one outstanding characteristic which recalls that very 'son', for he, too, is a poet! He is a composite figure, combining characteristics of the two 'wicked' fathers; first of Elizabeth Arnold's unknown lover, her castrator in the child's eyes, and then of John Allan.

For did not John Allan, too, appear to the child as the ravisher castrator of a woman, Frances. Edgar's beloved and ailing 'Ma'? More still, had he not impugned his true mother's virtue and injured her reputation, as the blackmailing Minister planned to do with the Queen's?

The Minister also reminds us of John Allan by his unscrupulous ambition. And it was John Allan again, who, to Poe as a child, represented that *'monstrum: horrendum* – an unprincipled man of genius', not far removed from the 'criminal' of 'vast intelligence' figured in the Man of the Crowd. So does the father often appear to the small boy, at once admired and hated.

Most striking of all, the Minister exhibits Poe's outstanding feature, his poetic gift. And here Poe, in fact, identifies himself with the hated though admired father by that same gift of identification whose praises he sings in 'The Purloined Letter' as being the one supremely effective way of penetrating another's thoughts and feelings.

Poe, impotent and a poet, could never so wholly identify himself with the orangutang in 'The Murders in the Rue Morgue', for there the father conquers the mother only by reason of his overwhelming strength. But, in his unconscious, Poe could achieve this with the Minister, for though the latter, once more, triumphs by superior strength, this time it is of the intellect.

As to the King whom the Queen deceives, he must again be David Poe, Elizabeth's husband. Small wonder that Dupin, embodying the son, should declare his 'political sympathies' with the lady! Finally, in return for a check of 50,000 francs, leaving to the Prefect of Police the fabulous reward, Dupin restores to the woman her symbolic letter or missing penis. Thus, once more, we meet the equation gold = penis. The mother gives her son gold in exchange for the penis he restores.

6 Barbara Johnson

The Frame of Reference:
Poe, Lacan, Derrida[30]

A literary text that both analyses and shows that it actually has neither a self nor any neutral metalanguage with which to do the analysing calls out irresistibly for analysis. And when that call is answered by two eminent thinkers whose readings emit an equally paradoxical call to analysis of their own, the resulting triptych, in the context of the question of the act of reading (literature), places its would-be reader in a vertiginously insecure position.

The three texts in question are Edgar Allan Poe's short story 'The Purloined Letter'[31], Jacques Lacan's 'Seminar on "The Purloined Letter"',[32] and Jacques Derrida's reading of Lacan's reading of Poe, 'The Purveyor of Truth' (Le Facteur de la Vérité).[33] In all three texts, it is the act of analysis that seems to occupy the centre of the discursive stage and the act of analysis of the act of analysis that in some way disrupts that centrality, subverting the very possibility of a position of analytical mastery. In the resulting asymmetrical, abysmal structure, no analysis – including this one – can intervene without transforming and repeating other elements in the sequence, which is thus not a stable sequence, but which nevertheless produces certain regular effects. It is the functioning of this regularity, and the structure of these effects, that will provide the basis for the present study.

Any attempt to do 'justice' to three such complex texts is obviously out of the question. But it is precisely the nature of such 'justice' that is the question in each of these readings of the act of analysis. The fact that the debate proliferates around a crime story – a robbery and its undoing – can hardly be an accident. Somewhere in each of these texts, the economy of justice cannot be avoided. For in spite of the absence of mastery, there is no lack of effects of power.

I shall begin by quoting at some length from Lacan's discussion of 'The Purloined Letter' in order to present both the plot of Poe's story and the thrust of Lacan's analysis. Lacan summarizes the story as follows:

> There are two scenes, the first of which we shall straightway designate the primal scene, and by no means inadvertently, since the second may

be considered its repetition in the very sense we are considering today.

The primal scene is thus performed, we are told, in the royal boudoir, so that we suspect that the person of the highest rank, called the 'exalted personage', who is alone there when she receives a letter, is the Queen. This feeling is confirmed by the embarrassment into which she is plunged by the entry of the other exalted personage, of whom we have already been told prior to this account that the knowledge he might have of the letter in question would jeopardize for the lady nothing less than her honour and safety. Any doubt that he is in fact the King is promptly dissipated in the course of the scene which begins with the entry of the Minister D –. At that moment, in fact, the Queen can do no better than to play on the King's inattentiveness by leaving the letter on the table 'face down, address uppermost'. It does not, however, escape the Minister's lynx eye, nor does he fail to notice the Queen's distress and thus to fathom her secret. From then on everything transpires like clockwork. After dealing in his customary manner with the business of the day, the Minister draws from his pocket a letter similar in appearance to the one in his view, and, having pretended to read it, he places it next to the other. A bit more conversation to amuse the royal company, whereupon, without flinching once, he seizes the embarrassing letter, making off with it, as the Queen, on whom none of his manoeuvre has been lost, remains unable to intervene for fear of attracting the attention of her royal spouse, close at her side at that very moment.

Everything might then have transpired unseen by a hypothetical spectator of an operation in which nobody falters, and whose quotient is that the Minister has filched from the Queen her letter and that – an even more important result than the first – the Queen knows that he now has it, and by no means innocently.

A remainder that no analyst will neglect, trained as he is to retain whatever is significant, without always knowing what to do with it: the letter, abandoned by the Minister, and which the Queen's hand is now free to roll into a ball.

Second scene: in the Minister's office. It is in his hotel, and we know – from the account the Prefect of Police has given Dupin, whose specific genius for solving enigmas Poe introduces here for the second time – that the police, returning there as soon as the Minister's habitual, nightly absences allow them to, have searched the hotel and surroundings from top to bottom for the last eighteen months. In vain – although everyone can deduce from the situation that the Minister keeps the letter within reach.

Dupin calls on the Minister. The latter receives him with studied nonchalance, affecting in his conversation romantic ennui. Meanwhile Dupin, whom this pretence does not deceive, his eyes protected by green glasses, proceeds to inspect the premises. When his glance catches a rather crumpled piece of paper – apparently thrust carelessly in a division of an ugly pasteboard card-rack, hanging gaudily from the middle of the mantelpiece – he already knows that he's found what he's looking for. His conviction is reinforced by the very details which seem to contradict the description he has of the stolen letter, with the exception of the format which remains the same.

Whereupon he has but to withdraw, after 'forgetting' his snuffbox on the table, in order to return the following day to reclaim it – armed with a facsimile of the letter in its present state. As an incident in the street, prepared for the proper moment, draws the Minister to the window, Dupin in turn seizes the opportunity to snatch the letter while substituting the imitation, and has only to maintain the appearances of a normal exit.

Here as well all has transpired, if not without noise, at least without all commotion. The quotient of the operation is that the Minister no longer has the letter, but, far from suspecting that Dupin is the culprit who has ravished it from him, knows nothing of it. Moreover, what he is left with is far from insignificant for what follows. We shall return to what brought Dupin to inscribe a message on his counterfeit letter. Whatever the case, the Minister, when he tries to make use of it, will be able to read these words, written so that he may recognize Dupin's hand: '... Un dessein si funeste/S'il n'est digne d'Atrée est digne de Thyeste',[34] whose source, Dupin tells us, is Crébillon's *Atrée*.

Need we emphasize the similarity of these two sequences? Yes, for the resemblance we have in mind is not a simple collection of traits chosen only in order to delete their difference. And it would not be enough to retain those common traits at the expense of the others for the slightest truth to result. It is rather the intersubjectivity in which the two actions are motivated that we wish to bring into relief, as well as the three terms through which it structures them.

The special status of these terms results from their corresponding simultaneously to the three logical moments through which the decision is precipitated and the three places it assigns to the subjects among whom it constitutes a choice.

That decision is reached in a glance's time. For the manoeuvres which follow, however stealthily they prolong it, add nothing to that glance, nor does the deferring of the deed in the second scene break the unity of that moment.

This glance presupposes two others, which it embraces in its vision of the breach left in their fallacious complementarity, anticipating in it the occasion for larceny afforded by that exposure. Thus three moments, structuring three glances, borne by three subjects, incarnated each time by different characters.

The first is a glance that sees nothing: the King and the police.

The second, a glance which sees that the first sees nothing and deludes itself as to the secrecy of what it hides: the Queen, then the Minister.

The third sees that the first two glances leave what should be hidden exposed to whoever would seize it: the Minister and finally Dupin.

In order to grasp in its unity the intersubjective complex thus described, we would willingly seek a model in the technique legendarily attributed to the ostrich attempting to shield itself from danger; for that technique might ultimately be qualified as political, divided as it here is among three partners: the second believing itself invisible because the first has its head stuck in the ground, and all the while letting the third calmly pluck its rear; we need only enrich its proverbial denomination by a letter, producing 'la politique de l'autruiche',[35] for the ostrich itself to take on forever a new meaning.

Given the intersubjective modulus of the repetitive action, it remains to recognize in it a repetition automatism in the sense that interests us in Freud's text. (SPL, pp. 41–4)

Thus, it is neither the character of the individual subjects, nor the contents of the letter, but the position of the letter within the group that decides what each person will do next. It is the fact that the letter does not function as a unit of meaning (a signified) but as that which produces certain effects (a signifier) that leads Lacan to read the story as an illustration of 'the truth which may be drawn from that moment in Freud's thought under study – namely, that it is the symbolic order which is constitutive for the subject – by demonstrating ... the decisive orientation which the subject receives from the itinerary of a signifier' (SPL, p. 40). The letter acts like a signifier precisely to the extent that its function in the story does not require that its meaning be revealed: 'the letter was able to produce its effects *within* the story: on the actors in the tale, including the narrator, as well as outside the story: on us, the readers, and also on its author, without anyone's ever bothering to worry about what it *meant'*.[36] 'The Purloined Letter' thus becomes for Lacan a kind of allegory of the signifier.

Derrida's critique of Lacan's reading does not dispute the validity of the allegorical interpretation on its own terms, but questions rather its implicit presuppositions and its modus operandi. Derrida aims his objections at two kinds of targets: (1) what Lacan puts into the letter, and (2) what Lacan leaves out of the text.

(1) What Lacan puts into the letter: While asserting that the letter's meaning is lacking, Lacan, according to Derrida, makes this lack into *the* meaning of the letter. But Derrida does not stop there: he goes on to assert that what Lacan means by that lack is the truth of lack-as-castration-as-truth: 'The truth of the purloined letter is the truth itself. ... What is veiled/unveiled in this case is a hole, a nonbeing (non-étant); the truth of being (l'être), as nonbeing. Truth is "woman" as veiled/unveiled castration' (PT, pp. 60–1). Lacan himself, however, never uses the word 'castration' in the text of the original seminar. That it is suggested is indisputable, but Derrida, by filling in what Lacan left blank, is repeating precisely the gesture of blank-filling for which he is criticizing Lacan.

(2) What Lacan leaves out of the text: This objection is itself double: on the one hand, Derrida criticizes Lacan for neglecting to consider 'The Purloined Letter' in connection with the other two stories in what Derrida calls Poe's 'Dupin Trilogy'. And on the other hand, according to Derrida, at the very moment Lacan is reading the story as an allegory of the signifier, he is being blind to the disseminating power of the signifier in the text of the allegory, in what Derrida calls the 'scene of writing'. To cut out part of a text's frame of reference as though it did not exist and to reduce a complex textual functioning to a single meaning are serious blots indeed in the annals of literary criticism. Therefore it is all the more noticeable that Derrida's own reading of Lacan's text repeats precisely the crimes of which he accuses it: on the one hand, Derrida makes no mention of Lacan's long development on the relation between symbolic determination and random series. And on the other hand, Derrida dismisses Lacan's 'style' as a mere orna- ment, veiling, for a time, an unequivocal message: 'Lacan's "style", moreover, was such that for a long time it would hinder and delay all access to a unique content or a single unequivocal meaning determinable beyond the writing itself' (PT, p. 40). The fact that Derrida repeats the very gestures he is criticizing does not in itself invalidate his criticism of their effects, but it does render problematic his statement condemning their existence. And it also illustrates the transfer of the repetition compulsion from the original text to the scene of its reading.

In an attempt to read this paradoxical encounter more closely, let us examine the way in which Derrida deduces from Lacan's text the fact that, for Lacan, the 'letter' is a symbol of the (mother's) phallus. Since Lacan never uses the word 'phallus' in the seminar, this is already an interpretation on Derrida's part, and quite an astute one at that. Lacan, as a later reader of his own seminar, implicitly agrees with it by placing the word 'castrated' – which had not been used in the original text – in his 'Points' presentation. The disagreement between Derrida and Lacan thus arises not over the validity of the equation 'letter = phallus', but over its meaning.

How, then, does Derrida derive this equation from Lacan's text? The deduction follows four basic lines of reasoning:

(1) The letter 'belongs' to the Queen as a substitute for the phallus she does not have. It feminizes (castrates) each of its successive holders and is eventually returned to her as its rightful owner.

(2) Poe's description of the position of the letter in the Minister's apartment, expanded upon by the figurative dimensions of Lacan's text, suggests an analogy between the shape of the fireplace, from the centre

of whose mantelpiece the letter is found hanging, and that point on a woman's anatomy from which the phallus is missing.

(3) The letter, says Lacan, cannot be divided: 'But if it is first of all on the materiality of the signifier that we have insisted, that materiality is odd (*singulière*) in many ways, the first of which is not to admit partition' (SPL, p. 53). This indivisibility, says Derrida, is odd indeed, but becomes comprehensible if it is seen as an idealization of the phallus, whose integrity is necessary for the edification of the entire psychoanalytical system. With the phallus safely idealized the so-called 'signifier' acquires the 'unique, living, non-mutilable integrity' of the self-present spoken word, unequivocally pinned down to and by the signified. 'Had the phallus been per(mal)chance divisible or reduced to the status of a partial object, the whole edification would have crumbled down, and this is what has to be avoided at all cost' (PT, pp. 95–6).

(4) Finally, if Poe's story 'illustrates' the 'truth', as Lacan puts it, the last words of the seminar proper seem to reaffirm that truth in no uncertain terms: 'Thus it is that what the "purloined letter" . . . means is that *a letter always arrives at its destination*' (SPL, p. 72, emphasis mine). Now, since it is unlikely that Lacan is talking about the efficiency of the postal service, he must, according to Derrida, be affirming the possibility of unequivocal meaning, the eventual reappropriations of the message, its total equivalence with itself. And since the 'truth' Poe's story illustrates is, in Derrida's eyes, the truth of veiled/unveiled castration and of the transcendental identity of the phallus as the lack that makes the system work, this final sentence in Lacan's seminar seems to affirm both the absolute truth of psychoanalytical theories and the absolute decipherability of the literary text. Poe's message will have been totally, unequivocally understood and explained by the psychoanalytical myth. 'The hermeneutic discovery of meaning (truth), the deciphering (that of Dupin and that of the Seminar), arrives itself at its destination' (PT, p. 66).

Thus, the law of the phallus seems to imply a reappropriating return to the place of true ownership, an indivisible identity functioning beyond the possibility of disintegration or unrecoverable loss, and a totally self-present, unequivocal meaning or truth. The problem with this type of system, counters Derrida, is that it cannot account for the possibility of sheer accident, irreversible loss, unreappropriable residues, and infinite divisibility, which are in fact necessary and inevitable in the system's very elaboration. In order for the circuit of the letter to end up confirming the law of the phallus, it must begin by transgressing it: the letter is a sign of high treason. Phallogocentrism mercilessly represses the uncontrollable multiplicity of ambiguities, the disseminating play of writing, which irreducibly transgresses any unequivocal meaning.

> Not that the letter never arrives at its destination, but part of its structure is that it is always capable of not arriving there. ... Here dissemination threatens the law of the signifier and of castration as a contract of truth. Dissemination mutilates the unity of the signifier, that is, of the phallus. (PT, p. 66)

In contrast to Lacan's *Seminar*, then, Derrida's text would seem to be setting itself up as a *Disseminar*.

From the foregoing remarks, it can easily be seen that the disseminal criticism of Lacan's apparent reduction of the literary text to an unequivocal message depends for its force upon the presupposition of unambiguousness in Lacan's text. And indeed, the statement that a letter always reaches its destination seems straightforward enough. But when that statement is reinserted into its context, things become palpably less certain:

> Is that all, and shall we believe we have deciphered Dupin's real strategy above and beyond the imaginary tricks with which he was obliged to deceive us? No doubt, yes, for if 'any point requiring reflection', as Dupin states at the start, is 'examined to best purpose in the dark', we may now easily read its solution in broad daylight. It was already implicit and easy to derive from the title of our tale, according to the very formula we have long submitted to your discretion: in which the sender, we tell you, receives from the receiver his own message in reverse form. Thus it is that what the 'purloined letter', nay, the 'letter in sufferance' means is that a letter always arrives at its destination. (SPL, p. 72)

The meaning of this last sentence is problematized not so much by its own ambiguity as by a series of reversals in the preceding sentences. If the best examination takes place in darkness, what does 'reading in broad daylight' imply? Could it not be taken as an affirmation not of actual lucidity but of delusions of lucidity? Could it not then move the 'yes, no doubt' as an answer not to the question 'have we deciphered?' but to the question 'shall we believe we have deciphered?' And if this is possible, does it not empty the final affirmation of all unequivocality, leaving it to stand with the force of an assertion, without any definite content? And if the sender receives from the receiver his own message backwards, who is the sender here, who is the receiver, and what is the message? I will take another look at this passage later, but for the moment its ambiguities seem sufficient to problematize, if not subvert, the presupposition of univocality that is the very foundation on which Derrida has edified his interpretation.

Surely such an oversimplification on Derrida's part does not result from mere blindness, oversight, or error. As Paul de Man says of Derrida's similar treatment of Rousseau, 'the pattern is too interesting not to be deliberate'[37]. Derrida's consistent forcing of Lacan's statements into systems and patterns from which they are actually trying to escape must correspond to some strategic necessity different from the attentiveness to the letter of the text that characterizes Derrida's way of reading Poe. And in fact, the more one works with Derrida's analysis, the more convinced one becomes that although the critique of what Derrida calls psychoanalysis is entirely justified, it does not quite apply to what Lacan's text is actually saying. What Derrida is in fact arguing against is therefore not Lacan's text but Lacan's power, or rather, 'Lacan' as the apparent cause of certain effects of power in French discourse today. Whatever Lacan's text may say, it functions, according to Derrida, as if it said what he says it says. The statement that a letter always reaches its destination may be totally undecipherable, but its assertive force is taken all the more seriously as a sign that Lacan himself has everything all figured out. Such an assertion, in fact, gives him an appearance of mastery like that of the Minister in the eyes of the letterless Queen. 'The ascendancy which the Minister derives from the situation,' explains Lacan, 'is attached not to the letter but to the character it makes him into.'

Thus Derrida's seemingly 'blind' reading, whose vagaries we are following here, is not a mistake, but the positioning of what can be called the 'average reading' of Lacan's text, which is the true object of Derrida's deconstruction. Since Lacan's text is read as if it said what Derrida says it says, its actual textual functioning is irrelevant to the agonistic arena in which Derrida's analysis takes place. If Derrida's reading of Lacan's reading of Poe is thus actually the deconstruction of a reading whose status is difficult to determine, does this mean that Lacan's text is completely innocent of the misdemeanors of which it is accused? If Lacan can be shown to be opposed to the same kind of logocentric error that Derrida is opposed to, does that mean that they are both really saying the same thing? These are questions that must be left, at least for the moment, hanging.

But the structure of Derrida's transference of guilt from a certain reading of Lacan onto Lacan's text is not indifferent in itself, in the context of what, after all, started out as a relatively simple crime story. For what it amounts to is nothing less than – a frame. And if Derrida is thus framing Lacan for an interpretative malpractice of which he himself is, at least in part, the author, what can this frame teach us about the nature of the act of reading, in the context of the question of literature and psychoanalysis?

Interestingly enough, one of the major crimes for which Lacan is being framed by Derrida is precisely the psychoanalytical reading's elimination of what Derrida calls the literary text's frame. That frame here consists not only of the two stories that precede 'The Purloined Letter', but of the stratum of narration through which the stories are told, and 'beyond' it, of the text's entire functioning as 'écriture'.

It would seem that Lacan is guilty of several sins of omission: the omission of the narrator, of the non-dialogue parts of the story, and of the other stories in the trilogy. But does this criticism amount to a mere plea for the inclusion of what has been excluded? No, the problem is not simply quantitative. What has been excluded is not homogeneous to what has been included. Lacan, says Derrida, misses the specifically literary dimension of Poe's text by treating it as a 'real drama', a story like the stories a psychoanalyst hears every day from his patients. What has been left out is precisely literature itself.

Does this mean that the 'frame' is what makes a text literary? In a recent issue of 'New Literary History' devoted to the question 'What is Literature?' and totally unrelated to the debate concerning the purloined letter, this is precisely the conclusion to which one of the contributors comes: 'Literature is language, ... but it is language around which we have drawn a frame, a frame that indicates a decision to regard with a particular self-consciousness the resources language has always possessed.[38]

Such a view of literature, however, implies that a text is literary because it remains inside certain definite borders: it is a many-faceted object, perhaps, but still, it is an object. That this is not quite what Derrida has in mind becomes clear from the following remarks:

> By overlooking the narrator's position, the narrator's involvement in the content of what he seems to be recounting, one omits from the scene of writing anything going beyond the two triangular scenes.
>
> And first of all one omits that *what is in question* – with no possible access route or border – is a scene of writing whose boundaries crumble off into an abyss. From the simulacrum of an overture, of a 'first word', the narrator, in narrating himself, advances a few propositions that carry the unity of the 'tale' into an endless drifting off course: a textual drifting not at all taken into account in the Seminar. (PT, pp. 100–1; translation modified)

> These reminders, of which countless other examples could be given, alert us to the effects of the frame, and of the paradoxes in the parergonal logic.

Our purpose is not to prove that 'The Purloined Letter' functions within a frame (omitted by the Seminar, which can thus be assured of its triangular interior by an active, surreptitious limitation starting from a metalinguistic overview), but to prove that the structure of the framing effects is such that no totalization of the border is even possible. Frames are always framed: thus, by part of their content. Pieces without a whole, 'divisions' without a totality – this is what thwarts the dream of a letter without division, allergic to division. (PT, p. 99; translation modified)

Here the argument seems to reverse the previous objection: Lacan has eliminated not the frame but the unframability of the literary text. But what Derrida calls 'parergonal logic' is paradoxical because both of these incompatible (but not totally contradictory) arguments are equally valid. The total inclusion of the 'frame' is both mandatory and impossible. The 'frame' thus becomes not the borderline between the inside and the outside, but precisely what subverts the applicability of the inside/outside polarity to the act of interpretation.

What enables Derrida to problematize the literary text's frame is, as we have seen, what he calls 'the scene of writing'. By this he means two things:

(1) The textual signifier's resistance to being totally transformed into a signified. In spite of Lacan's attentiveness to the path of the letter in Poe's story as an illustration of the functioning of a signifier, says Derrida, the psychoanalytical reading is still blind to the functioning of the signifier in the narration itself. In reading 'The Purloined Letter' as an allegory of the signifier, Lacan, according to Derrida, has made the 'signifier' into the story's truth: 'The displacement of the signifier is analysed as a signified, as the recounted object in a short story' (PT, p. 48). Whereas, counters Derrida, it is precisely the textual signifier that resists being thus totalized into meaning, leaving an irreducible residue: 'The rest, the remnant, would be "The Purloined Letter", the text that bears this title, and whose place, like the once more invisible large letters on the map, is not where one was expecting to find it, in the enclosed content of the "real drama" or in the hidden and sealed interior of Poe's story, but in and as the open letter, the very open letter, which fiction is' (PT, p. 64).

(2) The actual writings – the books, libraries, quotations, and previous tales – that surround 'The Purloined Letter' with a frame of (literary) references. The story begins in 'a little back library, or book-closet' (Poe, p. 199) where the narrator is mulling over a previous conversation on the subject of the two previous instances of Dupin's detective work as told in Poe's two previous tales (the first of which recounted the original meeting between Dupin and the narrator – in a library, of

course, where both were in search of the same rare book). The story's
beginning is thus an infinitely regressing reference to previous writings.
And therefore, says Derrida, 'nothing begins. Simply a drifting or a dis-
orientation from which one never moves away' (PT, p. 101). Dupin
himself is in fact a walking library: books are his 'sole luxuries', and the
narrator is 'astonished' at 'the vast extent of his reading' (Poe, p. 106).
Even Dupin's last, most seemingly personal words – the venomous lines
he leaves in his substitute letter to the Minister – are a quotation; a quotation whose transcription and proper authorship are the last things the
story tells us. 'But,' concludes Derrida, 'beyond the quotation marks
that surround the entire story, Dupin is obliged to quote this last word
in quotation marks, to recount his signature: that is what I wrote to him
and how I signed it. What is a signature within quotation marks? Then,
within these quotation marks, the seal itself is a quotation within quotation marks. This remnant is still literature' (PT, pp. 112–13).

It is by means of these two extra dimensions that Derrida intends to
show the crumbling, abysmal, non-totalizable edges of the story's
frame. Both of these objections, however, are in themselves more problematic and double-edged than they appear. I shall begin with the second. 'Literature,' in Derrida's demonstration, is indeed clearly the
beginning, middle and end – and even the interior – of the purloined
letter. But how was this conclusion reached? To a large extent, by listing the books, libraries, and other writings recounted in the story. That
is, by following the theme, not the functioning, of 'writing' within 'the
content of a representation'. But if the fact that Dupin signs with a quotation, for example, is for Derrida a sign that 'this remnant is still literature', does this not indicate that 'literature' has become not the signifier
but the signified in the story? If the play of the signifier is really to be
followed, doesn't it play beyond the range of the seme 'writing?' And if
Derrida criticizes Lacan for making the 'signifier' into the story's 'signified', is Derrida not here transforming 'writing' into 'the written' in
much the same way? What Derrida calls 'the reconstruction of the
scene of the signifier as a signified' seems indeed to be 'an inevitable
process' in the logic of reading the purloined letter.

Derrida, of course, implicitly counters this objection by protesting –
twice – that the textual drifting for which Lacan does not account
should not be considered 'the real subject of the tale', but rather the
'remarkable ellipsis' of any subject. But the question of the seemingly
inevitable slipping from the signifier to the signified still remains. And it
remains not as an objection to the logic of the frame, but as its fundamental question. For if the 'paradoxes of parergonal logic' are such that
the frame is always being framed by part of its contents, it is precisely

this slippage between signifier and signified (which is acted out by both Derrida and Lacan against their intentions) that best illustrates those paradoxes. If the question of the frame thus problematizes the object of any interpretation by setting it at an angle or fold with itself, then Derrida's analysis errs not in opposing this paradoxical functioning to Lacan's allegorical reading, but in not following the consequences of its own insight far enough.

Another major point in Derrida's critique is that psychoanalysis, wherever it looks, is capable of finding only itself. The first sentence of 'The Purveyor of Truth' is: 'Psychoanalysis, supposing, finds itself' ('La psychanalyse à supposer, se trouve'). In whatever it turns its attention to, psychoanalysis seems to recognize nothing but its own (Oedipal) schemes. Dupin finds the letter because 'he knows that the letter finally *finds itself* where it must be *found* in order to return circularly and adequately to its proper place. This proper place, known to Dupin and to the psychoanalyst who intermittently takes his place, is the place of castration' (PT, p. 60; translation modified). The psychoanalyst's act, then, is one of mere recognition of the expected, a recognition that Derrida finds explicitly stated as such by Lacan in the words he quotes from the Seminar:

> Just so does the purloined letter, like an immense female body, stretch out across the Minister's office when Dupin enters. But just so does he already *expect to find it* [emphasis mine – J. D.] and has only with his eyes veiled by green lenses, to undress that huge body. (PT, pp. 61–2; original emphasis and brackets restored)

But what if the signifier were precisely what puts the polarity 'materiality/ideality' in question? Has it not become obvious that neither Lacan's description ('Tear a letter into little pieces, it remains the letter that it is') nor Derrida's description ('A torn-up letter may be purely and simply destroyed, it happens') can be read literally? Somehow, a rhetorical fold (*pli*) in the text is there to trip us up whichever way we turn. Especially since the expression 'it happens' (*ça arrive*) uses the very word on which the controversy over the letter's arrival at its destination turns.

This study of the readings of 'The Purloined Letter' has thus arrived at the point where the word 'letter' no longer has any literality. But what is a letter that has no literality?

It seems that the letter can only be described as that which poses the question of its own rhetorical status. It moves rhetorically through the two long, minute studies in which it is presumed to be the literal object of analysis, without having any literality. Instead of simply being explained by those analyses, the rhetoric of the letter problematizes the very rhetorical mode of analytical discourse itself.

The letter in the story – and in its readings – acts as a signifier not because its contents are lacking, but because its rhetorical function is not dependent on the identity of those contents. What Lacan means by saying that the letter cannot be divided is thus not that the phallus must remain intact, but that the phallus, the letter, and the signifier are not substances. The letter cannot be divided because it only functions as a division. It is not something with 'an identity to itself inaccessible to dismemberment' as Derrida interprets it; it is a *difference*. It is known only in its effects. The signifier is an articulation in a chain, not an identifiable unit. It cannot be known in itself because it is capable of 'sustaining itself only in a displacement' (SPL, p. 59). It is localized, but only as the nongeneralizable locus of a differential relationship. Derrida, in fact, enacts this law of the signifier in the very act of opposing it:

> Perhaps only one letter need be changed, maybe even less than a letter in the expression: 'missing from its place' ['manque à sa place']. Perhaps we need only introduce a written 'a', i.e. without accent, in order to bring out that if the lack has its place ['le manque a sa place'] in this atomistic topology of the signifier, that is, if it occupies therein a specific place of definite contours, the order would remain undisturbed. (PT, pp. 44–5)

While thus criticizing the hypostasis of a lack – the letter as the substance of an absence – (which is not what Lacan is saying), Derrida is *illustrating* what Lacan is saying about both the materiality and the localizability of the signifier *as the mark of difference* by operating on the letter as a material locus of differentiation: by removing the little signifier '`', an accent mark that has no meaning in itself.[39]

But if recognition is a form of blindness, a form of violence to the otherness of the object, it would seem that, by lying in wait between the brackets of the fireplace to catch the psychoanalyst at his own game, Derrida, too, is 'recognizing' rather than reading. All the more so, since he must correct Lacan's text at another point in order to make it consistent with his critique. For when Lacan notes that the 'question of deciding whether Dupin seizes the letter above the mantelpiece as Baudelaire translates, or beneath it, as in the original text, may be abandoned without harm to the inferences of those whose profession is grilling' (SPL, p. 67), Derrida protests: 'Without harm? On the contrary, the harm would be decisive, within the Seminar itself: on the mantelpiece, the letter could not have been ... "between the legs of the fireplace"' (PT, p. 69). Derrida must thus rectify Lacan's text, eliminate its apparent contradiction, in order to criticize Lacan's enterprise as one of rectification and circular return. What Derrida is doing here, as he himself says, is recognizing a certain classical conception of psychoanalysis: 'From the beginning,' writes Derrida early in his study, '*we recognize* the classical landscape of applied psychoanalysis' (PT, p. 45; emphasis mine). It would seem that the theoretical frame of reference that governs recognition is a constitutive element in the blindness of any interpretative insight. And it is precisely that frame of reference that allows the analyst to frame the author of the text he is reading for practices whose locus is simultaneously beyond the letter of the text and behind the vision of its reader. The reader is framed by his own frame, but he is not even in possession of his own guilt, since it is that guilt that prevents his vision from coinciding with itself. Just as the author of a criminal frame transfers guilt from himself to another by leaving signs that he hopes will be read as insufficiently erased traces or referents left by the other, the author of any critique is himself framed by his own frame of the other, no matter how guilty or innocent the other may be.

What is at stake here is thus the question of the relation between referentiality and interpretation. And here we find an interesting twist: while criticizing Lacan's notion of the phallus as being too referential, Derrida goes on to use referential logic against it. This comes up in connection with the letter's famous 'materiality' that Derrida finds so odd.

> It would be hard to exaggerate here the scope of this proposition on the indivisibility of the letter, or rather on its identity to itself inaccessible to dismemberment, ... as well as on the so-called materiality of the signifier (the letter) intolerant to partition. But where does this idea come from? A torn-up letter may be purely and simply destroyed, it happens. (PT, pp. 86–7; translation modified)

The so-called materiality of the signifier, says Derrida, is nothing but an idealization.

The letter as a signifier is thus not a thing or the absence of a thing, nor a word or the absence of a word, nor an organ or the absence of an organ, but a knot in a structure where words, things, and organs can neither be definably separated nor compatibly combined. This is why the exact representational position of the letter in the Minister's apartment both matters and does not matter. It matters to the extent that sexual anatomical difference creates an irreducible dissymmetry to be accounted for in every human subject. But it does not matter to the extent that the letter is not hidden in geometrical space, where the police are looking for it, or in anatomical space, where a literal understanding of psychoanalysis might look for it. It is located 'in' a symbolic structure, a structure that can only be perceived in its effects and whose effects are perceived as repetition. Dupin finds the letter 'in' the symbolic order not because he knows where to look, but because he knows what to repeat. Dupin's 'analysis' is the repetition of the scene that led to the necessity of analysis. It is not an interpretation or an insight, but an act. An act of untying the knot in the structure by means of the repetition of the act of tying it. The word 'analyse', in fact, etymologically means 'untie', a meaning on which Poe plays in his prefatory remarks on the nature of analysis as 'that moral activity which disentangles' (Poe, p. 102). The analyst does not intervene by giving meaning, but by effecting a dénouement.

But if the act of (psycho) analysis has no identity apart from its status as a repetition of the structure it seeks to analyse (to untie), then Derrida's remarks against psychoanalysis as being always already 'mise en abîme' in the text it studies and as being only capable of finding itself, are not objections to psychoanalysis but in fact a profound insight into its very essence. Psychoanalysis is in fact itself the primal scene it is seeking: it is the first occurrence of what has been repeating itself in the patient without ever having occurred. Psychoanalysis is not itself the interpretation of repetition; it is the repetition of a trauma of interpretation – called 'castration' or 'parental coitus' or 'the Oedipus complex' or even 'sexuality'. It is the traumatic deferred interpretation not of an event, but as an event that never took place as such. The 'primal scene' is not a scene but an interpretative infelicity whose result was to situate the interpreter in an intolerable position. And psychoanalysis is the reconstruction of that interpretative infelicity not as its interpretation, but as its first and last act. Psychoanalysis has content only in so far as it repeats the dis-content of what never took place.

In a way, I have come back to the question of the letter's destination and of the meaning of the enigmatic last words of Lacan's Seminar. 'The sender,' writes Lacan 'receives from the receiver his own message in reverse form. Thus it is that what the "purloined letter", nay, the "letter in sufferance" means is that a letter always arrives at its destination' (SPL, p. 72). What the reversibility of the direction of the letter's movement between sender and receiver has now come to stand for is precisely the fact, underlined by Derrida as if it were an objection to Lacan, that there is no position from which the letter's message can be read as an object: 'no neutralization is possible, no general point of view' (PT, p. 106). This is also precisely the 'discovery' of psychoanalysis – that the analyst is involved (through transference) in the very 'object' of his analysis.

Everyone who has held the letter – or even beheld it – including the narrator, has ended up having the letter addressed to him as its destination. The reader is comprehended by the letter: there is no place from which he can stand back and observe it. Not that the letter's meaning is subjective rather than objective, but that the letter is precisely that which subverts the polarity subjective/objective, that which makes subjectivity into something whose position in a structure is situated by the passage through it of an object. The letter's destination is thus wherever it is read, the place it assigns to its reader as his own partiality. Its destination is not a place, decided a priori by the sender, because the receiver is the sender, and the receiver is whoever receives the letter, including nobody. When Derrida says that a letter can miss its destination and be disseminated, he reads 'destination' as a place that preexists the letter's movement. But if, as Lacan shows, the letter's destination is not its literal addressee, nor even whoever possesses it, but whoever is possessed by it, then the very disagreement over the meaning of 'reaching the destination' is an illustration of the non-objective nature of that 'destination'. The rhetoric of Derrida's differentiation of his own point of view from Lacan's enacts that law:

> Thanks to castration, the phallus always stays in its place in the transcendental topology we spoke of earlier. It is indivisible and indestructible there, like the letter that takes its place. And that is why the *interested* presupposition, never proved, of the letter's materiality as indivisibility was indispensable to this restricted economy, this circulation of propriety.
>
> The difference I am *interested* in here is that, a formula to be read however one wishes, the lack has no place of its own in dissemination. (PT, p. 63; translation modified, emphasis mine)

The play of interest in this expression of difference is quite too interesting not to be deliberate. The opposition between the 'phallus' and 'dissemination' is not between two theoretical objects but between two interested positions. And if sender and receiver are merely the two poles of a reversible message, then Lacan's substitution of 'destin' for 'dessein' in the Crébillon quotation – a misquotation that Derrida finds revealing enough to end his analysis upon – is in fact the quotation's message. The sender (*dessein*) and the receiver (*destin*) of the violence that passes between Atreus and Thyestes are equally subject to the violence the letter is.

The sentence 'a letter always arrives at its destination' can thus either be simply pleonastic or variously paradoxical: it can mean 'the only message I can read is the one I send', 'wherever the letter is, is its destination'; 'when a letter is read, it reads the reader'; 'the repressed always returns'; 'I exist only as a reader of the other'; 'the letter has no destination'; and 'we all die'. It is not any one of these readings, but all of them and others in their very incompatibility, that repeat the letter in its way of reading the act of reading. Far from giving us the Seminar's final truth, these last words, and Derrida's readings of them, can only enact the impossibility of any ultimate analytical metalanguage, the eternal oscillation between unequivocal undecidability and ambiguous certainty.

7 EDMUND WILSON

The Ambiguity of Henry James

A discussion of Henry James's ambiguity may appropriately begin with *The Turn of the Screw*. This story, which seems to have proved more fascinating to the general reading public than anything else of James's except *Daisy Miller*, perhaps conceals another horror behind the ostensible one. I do not know who first suggested this idea; but I believe that Miss Edna Kenton, whose insight into James is profound, was the first to write about it,[40] and the water-colourist Charles Demuth did a set of illustrations for the tale that were evidently based on this interpretation.

The theory is, then, that the governess who is made to tell the story is a neurotic case of sex repression, and that the ghosts are not real ghosts but hallucinations of the governess.

Let us see how the narrative runs. This narrative is supposed to have been written by the governess herself, but it begins with an introduction in which we are told something about her by a man whose sister's governess she had been after the time of the story. The youngest daughter of a poor country parson, she struck him, he explains, as 'awfully clever and nice . . . the most agreeable woman I've ever known in her position' and 'worthy of any whatever'. (Now, it is a not infrequent trick of James's to introduce sinister characters with descriptions that at first sound flattering, so this need not throw us off.) Needing work, she had come up to London to answer an advertisement and had found someone who wanted a governess for an orphaned nephew and niece. 'This prospective patron proved a gentleman, a bachelor in the prime of life, such a figure as had never risen, save in a dream or an old novel, before a fluttered, anxious girl out of a Hampshire vicarage.' It is made clear that the young woman has become thoroughly infatuated with her employer. He is charming to her and lets her have the job on condition that she will take all the responsibility and never bother him about the children; and she goes down to the house in the country where they have been left with a housekeeper and some other servants.

The boy, she finds, has been sent home from school for reasons into which she does not inquire but which she colours, on no evidence at all, with a significance somehow ominous. She learns that her predecessor left, and that the woman has since died, under circumstances which are not explained but which are made in the same way to seem queer. The new governess finds herself alone with the good but illiterate housekeeper and the children, who seem innocent and charming. As she wanders about the estate, she thinks often how delightful it would be if one should come suddenly round the corner and see the Master just arrived from London: there he would stand, handsome, smiling, approving.

She is never to meet her employer again, but what she does meet are the apparitions. One day when his face has been vividly in her mind, she comes out in sight of the house and, looking up, sees the figure of a man on a tower, a figure which is not the master's. Not long afterwards, the figure appears again, towards the end of a rainy Sunday. She sees him at closer range and more clearly: he is wearing smart clothes but is obviously not a gentleman. The housekeeper, meeting the governess immediately afterwards, behaves as if the governess herself were a ghost: 'I wondered why she should be scared.' The governess tells her about the apparition and learns that it answers the description of one of the master's valets, who had stayed down there and who had sometimes stolen his clothes. The valet had been a bad character, had used 'to play with the boy ... to spoil him'; he had finally been found dead, having apparently slipped on the ice coming out of a public house – though one couldn't say he hadn't been murdered. The governess cannot help believing that he has come back to haunt the children.

Not long afterwards, she and the little girl are out on the shore of a lake, the child playing, the governess sewing. The latter becomes aware of a third person on the opposite side of the lake. But she looks first at little Flora, who is turning her back in that direction and who, she notes, has 'picked up a small flat piece of wood, which happened to have in it a little hole that had evidently suggested to her the idea of sticking in another fragment that might figure as a mast and make the thing a boat. This second morsel, as I watched her, she was very markedly and intently attempting to tighten in its place.' This somehow 'sustains' the governess so that she is able to raise her eyes: she sees a woman 'in black, pale and dreadful'. She concludes that it is the former governess.

The housekeeper, questioned, tells her that this woman, although a lady, had had an affair with the valet. The boy had used to go off with the valet and then lie about it afterwards. The governess concludes that the boy must have known about the valet and the woman – the boy and girl have been corrupted by them.

Observe that there is never any reason for supposing that anybody but the governess sees the ghosts. She believes that the children see them, but there is never any proof that they do. The housekeeper insists that she does not see them; it is apparently the governess who frightens her. The children, too, become hysterical; but this is evidently the governess's doing. Observe, also, from the Freudian point of view, the significance of the governess's interest in the little girl's pieces of wood and of the fact that the male apparition first takes shape on a tower and the female apparition on a lake. There seems here to be only a single circumstance which does not fit into the hypothesis that the ghosts are mere fancies of the governess: the fact that her description of the masculine ghost at a time when she knows nothing of the valet should be identifiable as the valet by the housekeeper. And when we look back, we see that even this has perhaps been left open to a double interpretation. The governess has never heard of the valet, but it has been suggested to her in a conversation with the housekeeper that there has been some other male about who 'liked everyone young and pretty', and the idea of this other person has been ambiguously confused with the Master and with the Master's possible interest in her, the present governess. And may she not, in her subconscious imagination, taking her cue from this, have associated herself with her predecessor and conjured up an image who wears the Master's clothes but who (the Freudian 'censor' intervening) looks debased, 'like an actor', she says (would he not have to stoop to love her)? The apparition had 'straight, good features' and his appearance is described in detail. When we look back, we find that the Master's appearance has never been described at all: we have merely been told that he was 'handsome', and it comes out in the talk with the house-keeper that the valet was 'remarkably handsome'. It is impossible for us to know how much the phantom resembles the Master – the governess, certainly, would never tell.

The new apparitions now begin to be seen at night, and the governess becomes convinced that the children get up to meet them, though they are able to give plausible explanations of the behaviour that has seemed suspicious. The housekeeper now says to the governess that, if she is seriously worried about all this, she ought to report it to the Master. The governess, who has promised not to bother him, is afraid he would think her insane; and she imagines 'his derision, his amusement, his contempt for the breakdown of my resignation at being left alone and for the fine machinery I had set in motion to attract his attention to my slighted charms'. The house-keeper, hearing this, threatens to send for the Master herself; the governess threatens to leave if she does. After this, for a considerable period, the visions no longer appear.

But the children become uneasy: they wonder when their uncle is coming, and they try to communicate with him – but the governess suppresses their letters. The boy finally asks her frankly when she is going to send him to school, intimates that if he had not been so fond of her, he would have complained to his uncle long ago, declares that he will do so at once.

This upsets her: she thinks for a moment of leaving, but decides that this would be deserting them. She is now, it seems, in love with the boy. Entering the schoolroom, after her conversation with him, she finds the ghost of the other governess sitting with her head in her hands, looking 'dishonoured and tragic', full of 'unutterable woe'. At this point the new governess feels – the morbid half of her split personality is now getting the upper hand of the other – that it is she who is intruding upon the ghost: 'You terrible miserable woman!' she cries. The apparition disappears. She tells the housekeeper, who looks at her oddly, that the soul of the woman is damned and wants the little girl to share her damnation. She finally agrees to write to the Master, but no sooner has she sat down to the paper than she gets up and goes to the boy's bedroom, where she finds him lying awake. When he demands to go back to school, she embraces him and begs him to tell her why he was sent away; appealing to him with what seems to her desperate tenderness but in a way that disquiets the child, she insists that all she wants is to save him. There is a sudden gust of wind – it is a stormy night outside – the casement rattles, the boy shrieks. She has been kneeling beside the bed: when she gets up, she finds the candle extinguished. 'It was I who blew it, dear!' says the boy. For her, it is the evil spirit disputing her domination. She cannot imagine that the boy may really have blown out the candle in order not to have to tell her with the light on about his disgrace at school. (Here, however, occurs a detail which is less easily susceptible of double explanation: the governess has *felt* a 'gust of frozen air' and yet sees that the window is 'tight'. Are we to suppose she merely fancied that she felt it?)

The next day, the little girl disappears. They find her beside the lake. The young woman for the first time now speaks openly to one of the children about the ghosts. 'Where, my pet, is Miss Jessel?' she demands – and immediately answers herself: 'She's there, she's there!' she cries, pointing across the lake. The housekeeper looks with a 'dazed blink' and asks where she sees anything; the little girl turns upon the governess 'an expression of hard, still gravity, an expression absolutely new and unprecedented and that appeared to read and accuse and judge me'. The governess feels her 'situation horribly crumble' now. The little girl breaks down, becomes feverish, begs to be taken away from the governess; the housekeeper sides with the girl and hints that the governess had better go. But the young woman forces her, instead, to take the little girl away; and she tries to make it impossible, before their departure, for the children to see one another.

She is now left alone with the boy. A strange and dreadful scene ensues. 'We continued silent while the maid was with us – as silent, it whimsically occurred to me, as some young couple who, on their wedding-journey, at the inn, feel shy in the presence of the waiter.' When the maid has gone, and she presses him to tell her the reason for his expulsion from school, the boy seems suddenly afraid of her. He finally confesses that he 'said things' – to 'a few', to 'those he liked'. It all sounds sufficiently harmless: there comes to her out of her 'very pity the appalling alarm of his being perhaps innocent. It was for the instant confounding and bottomless, for if he *were* innocent, what then on earth was I?' The valet appears at the window – it is 'the white face of damnation'. (But is it really the spirits who are damned or the governess who is slipping to damnation herself?) She is aware that the boy does not see it. 'No more, no more, no more!' she shrieks to the apparition. 'Is she *here*?' demands the boy in panic. (He has, in spite of the governess's efforts, succeeded in seeing his sister and has heard from her of the incident at the lake.) No, she says, it is not the woman: 'But it's at the window – straight before us. It's *there*!' ... 'It's *he*?' then whom does he mean by 'he'?

' "Peter Quint – you devil!" His face gave again, round the room, its convulsed supplication. "Where?" ' 'What does he matter now, my own?' she cries. 'What will he *ever* matter? *I* have you, but he has lost you for ever!' Then she shows him that the figure has vanished: 'There, *there*!' she says, pointing towards the window. He looks and gives a cry; she feels that he is dead in her arms. From the governess's point of view, the final disappearance of the spirit has proved too terrible a shock for the child and 'his little heart, dispossessed, has stopped'; but if we study the dialogue from the other point of view, we see that he must have taken her 'There, *there*!' as an answer to his own 'Where?' Instead of persuading him that there is nothing to be frightened of, she has, on the contrary, finally convinced him either that he has actually seen or that he is just about to see some horror. He gives 'the cry of a creature hurled over an abyss'. She has literally frightened him to death.

When one has once got hold of the clue to this meaning of *The Turn of the Screw*, one wonders how one could ever have missed it. There is a very good reason, however, in the fact that nowhere does James unequivocally give the thing away: almost everything from beginning to end can be read equally in either of two senses. In the preface to the collected edition, however, as Miss Kenton has pointed out, James does seem to want to give a hint. He asserts that *The Turn of the Screw* is 'a fairy-tale pure and simple' – but adds that the apparitions are of the order of those involved in witchcraft cases rather than those in cases of psychic research. And he goes on to tell of his reply to one of his readers who objected that he had not characterized the governess sufficiently. At this criticism, he says, 'One's artistic, one's ironic heart shook for the instant almost to breaking'; and he answered: 'It was *"déjà très-joli"* ... please believe, the general proposition of our young woman's keeping crystalline her record of so many intense anomalies and obscurities – *by which I don't of course mean her explanation of them, a different matter* ... She has "authority", which is a good deal to have given her ...' The italics above are mine: these words seem impossible to explain except on the hypothesis of hallucination (though this is hardly consistent with the intention of writing 'a fairy-tale pure and simple') [·] And note too, that in the collected edition James has not included *The Turn of the Screw* in the volume with his other ghost stories but with stories of another kind: between *The Aspern Papers* and *The Liar* – the first a study of a curiosity which becomes a mania and menace (to which we shall revert in a moment), the second a study of a pathological liar, whose wife protects his lies against the world, acting with very much the same sort of 'authority' as the governess in *The Turn of the Screw*.

When we look back in the light of these hints, we are inclined to conclude from analogy that the story is primarily intended as a characterization of the governess: her sombre and guilty visions and the way she behaves about them seem to present, from the moment we examine them from the obverse side of her narrative, an accurate and distressing picture of the poor country parson's daughter, with her English middle-class class-consciousness, her inability to admit to herself her natural sexual impulses, and the relentless English 'authority' which enables her to put over on inferiors even purposes which are totally deluded and not at all in the other people's best interests. Remember, also, in this connexion, the peculiar psychology of governesses, who, by reason of their isolated position between the family and the servants, are likely to become ingrown and morbid. One has heard of actual cases of women who have frightened a household by opening doors or smashing mirrors and who have succeeded in torturing parents by mythical

stories of kidnappers. The traditional 'poltergeist' who breaks crockery
and upsets furniture has been for centuries a recurring phenomenon.
First a figure of demonology, he later became an object of psychic
research, and is now a recognized neurotic type.

Once we arrive at this conception of *The Turn of the Screw*, we can
see in it a new significance in its relation to Henry James's other work.
We find that it is a variation on one of his familiar themes: the thwarted
Anglo-Saxon spinster; and we remember unmistakable cases of women
in James's fiction who deceive themselves and others about the origins
of their aims and emotions.

8 SHOSHANA FELMAN

Turning the Screw of Interpretation

Putting into effect the very title of her function, the 'governess' does
govern: she does indeed clutch at the helm of the boat with the same
kind of violence and forceful determination with which she ultimately
grips the body of little Miles. The textual repetition of the metaphor of
the boat thus serves to illustrate, through the singular gesture of
grasping the rudder-bar, the very enterprise of reading as a political
project of sense-control, the taking over of the very power implied by
meaning.

Curiously enough, the image of the boat recurs in yet another strategic, although apparently unrelated context in the story: in the incident
beside the lake during which the governess comes upon Flora playing
(under the influence, thinks the governess, of Miss Jessel) with two
pieces of wood out of which she is trying to construct a toy boat:

> [Flora] had picked up a small flat piece of wood, which happened to have
> in it a *little hole* that had evidently suggested to her the *idea of sticking in
> another fragment* that might *figure as a mast* and *make the thing a boat*. This
> second morsel, as I watched her, she was very markedly and intently
> attempting to *tighten in its place*.
> (...)
> I got hold of Mrs Grose as soon after this as I could (...)

I still hear myself cry as I fairly threw myself into her arms: '*They know* –
it's too monstrous: they know, they know!'

'And what on earth –? (. . .)

'Why, all that *we*˙ know – and heaven knows what else besides!' (ch. 6–7,
p. 30; ˙ James's italics; other italics mine)

This incident is crucial, not only because it constitutes for the governess
a decisive proof of the children's knowledge, but also because, implicitly but literally, it evokes an image related to the very *title* of the story: in
attempting to fit the stick into the hole as a mast for her little boat,
Flora 'tightens it in its place' with a gesture very like that of *tightening a
screw*.

But what precisely does this gesture mean? The screw – or the mast –
is evidently, in this incident, at least to the governess's eyes, a phallic
symbol, a metaphor connoting sexuality itself. This phallic connotation,
the reader will recall, was pointed out and underlined, indeed, by
Wilson. Wilson's exegesis, however, viewed the sexual reference as an
answer, as the literal, proper meaning which it sufficed to *name* in order
to understand and 'see it all', in order to put an end to all textual questions and ambiguities. As an emblem of the sexual act, Flora's boat was
for Wilson a simple indication of the literal object – the real organ –
desired by the governess without her being able or willing to admit it.
But it is precisely *not* as an unequivocal *answer* that the text here
evokes the phallus, but on the contrary rather as a *question*, as a figure –
itself ambiguous – produced by the enigma of the *double meaning* of
the metaphorical equation: phallus = ship's mast. To say that the mast is
in reality a phallus is no more illuminating or unambiguous than to say
that the phallus is in reality a mast. The question arises not of what the
mast 'really is' but of what a phallus – *or* a mast – might be, if they can
thus so easily be interchangeable, i.e., signify what they are not. What is
the meaning of this movement of *relay* of meaning between the phallus
and the mast? And since the mast, which is a figure of the phallus, is
also a figure of the *screw*, it seems that the crucial question raised by the
text and valorized by its title might be: what is, after all, a *screw* in *The
Turn of the Screw*?

Let us take another look at Flora's boat. It is as a phallic symbol that
the boat disturbs the governess and convinces her of the perversity of
the children: 'They know – it's too monstrous: they know, they know!'
The screw, or the phallic mast, thus constitutes for the governess a *key
to meaning*, a *master-signifier*: the very key to what the Other knows.

In such a context it is no longer possible to be insensitive to the
remarkable phonetical resemblance between the word 'mast' and the
word 'master', which it cannot but bring to mind: indeed, if the mast is a

kind of 'master', i.e., a dominant element determining both the structure and the movement of a boat, the Master is himself a kind of 'mast' which at once determines and supports the structure and the movement of the entire story of *The Turn of the Screw*. As one of the principal elements in a ship, the mast is thus not unrelated to the helm which the governess clutches with the same convulsive grasp as that with which she seizes Miles (who is himself a little Master).[41]

Now, to suggest that all these metaphorical elements – *Miles* in the governess's arms, the tightly gripped *helm* in the uncanny drifting ship, the little *mast* in Flora's boat, and the *screw* in *The Turn of the Screw* – refer alternately to the phallus *and* to the Master (as well as to one another), is to set up a *signifying chain* in which the phallus (or the screw, or the mast, or the Master), far from incarnating the unambiguous literal meaning behind things, symbolizes rather the incessant *sliding* of signification, the very principle of movement and displacement which on the contrary *prevents* the chain (or the text) from ever stopping at a final, literal, fixed meaning. The phallus, far from being a real object, is in fact a *signifier*; a signifier which only appears to become a Master – a key to meaning and a key to the knowledge of the Other – by virtue of its incarnating, like the Master, the very function of the semiotic *bar* – the very principle of imposition of a limit, the principle of censorship and of repression which forever *bars* all access to the signified as such.[42]

> 'The question is,' said Alice, 'whether you can make words mean so many different things.'
> 'The question is,' said Humpty Dumpty, 'which is to be master – that's all.'[43]

In reaching out both for the master and for the mast, in aspiring to *be*, in fact, herself a master and a mast, in clasping Miles as she would clutch at the ship's helm, the governess becomes, indeed, the *Master* of the ship, the Master of the *meaning* of the story (a master-reader) in two different ways: in clutching the helm, she *directs* the ship and thus apparently determines and controls its sense, its meaning; but at the same time, in the very gesture of directing, steering, she also masters meaning in the sense that she represses and limits it, striking out its other senses; in manipulating the rudder bar, she also, paradoxically, *bars* the signified. While the governess thus believes herself to be in a position of command and mastery, her *grasp* of the ship's helm (or of 'the little Master' or of the screw she tightens) is in reality the grasp but of a *fetish*, but of a *simulacrum* of a signified, like the simulacrum of the mast in Flora's toy boat, erected only as a filler, as a stop-gap, designed to fill a hole, to close a gap. The screw, however, by the very gesture of its tightening, while seemingly filling the hole, in reality only makes it deeper.

> I was blind with victory, though even then *the effect that was to have brought him so much nearer* was already that of an *added separation.* (ch. 24, p. 87)

> The grasp with which I recovered him might have been that of catching him in his fall. I caught him, yes, I held him, it may be imagined with what a passion; but at the end of a minute I began to feel *what it truly was that I held*. We were alone with the quiet day, and his little heart, dispossesssed, had stopped. (ch. 24, p. 88)

Even though, within this ultimate blind grip of comprehension, the 'name' has been 'surrendered' and meaning at last *grasped*, the governess's very satisfaction at the successful ending of the reading process is compromised by the radical frustration of a tragic loss: the embrace of meaning turns out to be but the embrace of death; the grasp of the signified turns out to be the grasp but of a corpse. The very enterprise of appropriating meaning is thus revealed to be the strict appropriation of precisely *nothing* – nothing alive, at least: 'le démontage impie de la fiction et conséquemment du mécanisme littéraire,' writes Mallarmé, 'pour étaler la pièce principale ou rien (...) le conscient manque chez nous de ce qui là-haut éclate.'[44]

Literature, suggests thus Mallarmé, like the letters of *The Turn of the Screw*, contains precisely 'nothing'; fiction's mainspring is but 'nothing', because consciousness in us is lacking, and cannot account for, 'that which bursts'. But what, precisely, bursts or splits, if not consciousness itself through the very fact that, possessing *nothing* (as it does in the end of *The Turn of the Screw*), it is dispossessed of its own mastery? What is it that bursts and splits if not consciousness itself to the extent that it remains estranged from that which splits, estranged, in other words, from its own split? When Miles dies, what is once again radically and unredeemably *divided*, is at once the unity of meaning and the unity of its possessor: the governess. The attempt to *master* meaning, which ought to lead to its *unification*, to the *elimination* of its contradictions and its 'splits', can reach its goal only at the cost, through the infliction of a new wound, of an added split or distance, of an irreversible 'separation'. The seizure of the signifier creates an unrecoverable *loss*, a fundamental and irreparable *castration*: the tightened screw, the governed helm, bring about 'the supreme surrender of the name', *surrender* meaning only by *cleaving* the very *power* of their holder. Meaning's *possession* is itself ironically transformed into the radical *dispossession* of its possessor. At its final, climactic point, the attempt at *grasping* meaning and at *closing* the reading process with a *definitive* interpretation in effect discovers = and comprehends – only death.

The Turn of the Screw could thus be read not only as a remarkable *ghost* story but also as a no less remarkable *detective* story: the story of the discovery of a *corpse* and of a singularly redoubtable crime: *the murder of a child*. As in all detective stories, the crime is not uncovered until the end. But in contrast to the classical mystery novel plot, *this* crime is also not *committed* until the end: paradoxically enough, the process of detection here *precedes* the committing of the crime. As a *reader*, the governess plays the role of the detective: from the outset she tries to *detect*, by means of logical inferences and decisive 'proofs', both the *nature of the crime* and the *identity of the criminal*.

> I remember (...) my thrill of joy at having brought on a *proof*. (ch. 20, p. 71)

> I was so determined to have all my *proof*, that I flashed into ice to challenge him. (ch. 24, p. 88)

> It didn't last as *suspense* – it was superseded by horrible *proofs*. (ch. 6, p. 28)

Ironically enough, however, not knowing what the crime really consists of, the governess-detective finally ends up *committing it herself*. This unexpected and uncanny turn given by James's story to the conventions of the mystery novel is also, as it happens, the constitutive narrative peripeteia of one of the best-known detective stories of all time: *Oedipus Rex*. In James's text as well as in Sophocles', the self-proclaimed detective ends up discovering that he himself is the author of the crime he is investigating: that the crime is his, that he is, himself, the criminal he seeks. 'The interest of crime,' writes James, in a discussion of modern mystery dramas, 'is in the fact that it compromises the criminal's personal safety':

> The play is a tragedy, not in virtue of an avenging deity, but in virtue of a preventive system of law; not through the presence of a company of fairies, but through that of an admirable organization of police detectives. Of course, *the nearer the criminal and the detective are brought home to the reader, the more lively his 'sensation'.*[45]

The Turn of the Screw appears indeed to have carried this ideal of proximity or 'nearness' (of the criminal and the detective to the reader) to its ultimate limits, since the criminal himself is here as *close* as possible to the detective, and the detective is only a detective in his (her) function *as a reader*. Incarnated in the governess, the detective and the criminal both are but dramatizations of the *condition of the reader*. Indeed, the governess as at once detective, criminal, and reader is here so intimately 'brought home' to the reader that it is henceforth *our own* search for the mysterious 'evil' or the hidden meaning of *The Turn of the Screw* which becomes, in effect, itself nothing other than a repetition of the crime. The reader of *The Turn of the Screw* is also the detective of a crime which in reality is his, and which 'returns upon himself'. For if it is by the very act of forcing her suspect to confess that the governess ends up committing the crime she is investigating, it is nothing other than the very *process of detection* which *constitutes the crime*. The detection process, or reading process, turns out to be, in other words, nothing less than a peculiarly and uncannily effective *murder weapon*. The story of meaning as such (or of consciousness) thus turns out to be the uncanny story of the crime of its own detection.

Just as, in the end, the *detective* is revealed to be the *criminal*, the doctor-therapist, the would-be *analyst*, herself turns out to be but an analysand. *The Turn of the Screw* in fact deconstructs all these traditional oppositions; the exorcist and the possessed, the doctor and the patient, the sickness and the cure, the symptom and the proposed interpretation of the symptom, become here interchangeable, or at the very least, undecidable. Since the governess's 'remedy' is itself a symptom, since the patient's 'cure' is in effect his murder, nothing could indeed look more like *madness* than the very self-assurance of the project (of the notion) of *therapy* itself. There can be no doubt, indeed, that the ship is really drifting, that the governess is in command but of a 'drunken boat'. Sailing confidently toward shipwreck, the helm that the governess violently 'grasps' and 'clutches' is indeed the helm of a phantom ship.

Notes

1 Elizabeth Wright, *Psychoanalytic Criticism: Theory into Practice* (London: Methuen, 1984), p. 39.
2 John P. Muller and William J. Richardson (eds), 'Preface', *The Purloined Poe: Lacan, Derrida, and Psychoanalytic Reading* (Baltimore: Johns Hopkins University Press, 1988), p. xii.
3 Poe's tale is reprinted and available widely; I have quoted from the version reprinted ibid. Page references are given in the text.
4 See Celia Bertin, *Marie Bonaparte: A Life* (New York: Harcourt Brace Jovanovich, 1982).

5 Norman N. Holland, 'Re-Covering "The Purloined Letter": Reading as a Personal Transaction', in Susan R. Suleiman and Inge Crosman (eds), *The Reader in the Text: Essays on Audience and Interpretation* (Princeton, N J: Princeton University Press, 1980), p. 358.

6 Ibid., p. 369.

7 Shoshana Felman, 'On Reading Poetry: Reflections on the Limits and Possibilities of Psychoanalytic Approaches', in Muller and Richardson (eds), *The Purloined Poe*, p. 147.

8 Just as a symptom acts as the signifier for a signified in the unconscious, so the letter is also the signifier of an unconscious signified.

9 Felman, 'On Reading Poetry', p. 152.

10 David Van Leer, 'Detecting Truth: The World of the Dupin Tales', in Kenneth Silverman (ed.), *New Essays on Poe's Major Tales* (Cambridge: Cambridge University Press, 1993), p. 67. Felman quotes Poe's perspicacious and 'amazingly' prefigural comment on his own tale: ' "the mental features discoursed of as the analytical are, in themselves, but little susceptible of analysis. We appreciate them only in their effects" ' ('On Reading Poetry', p. 149); she adds that this comment has gone unnoticed, perhaps being too obvious, like the letter itself, to be perceived.

11 Quoted from Jacques Lacan, 'Seminar on "The Purloined Letter" ', *French Freud: Structural Studies in Psychoanalysis, Yale French Studies*, 48 (1972), in Muller and Richardson (eds), *The Purloined Poe*, p. 39.

12 Catherine Belsey, *Critical Practice* (London: Methuen, 1980), p. 141.

13 Ibid., p. 142.

14 Ibid.

15 Review in *The Independent*, 5 January 1899, p. 73. Reprinted in Robert Kimbrough (ed.), *The Turn of the Screw* (New York: W. W. Norton, 1966), p. 175.

16 Review in *The Chautauquan*, XXVIII, old series (March 1899), p. 630; in Kimbrough, (ed.), *The Turn of the Screw*, p. 177.

17 Letter to H. G. Wells, (9 December) 1898; in Kimbrough (ed.), *The Turn of the Screw*, p. 111.

18 Letter to F. W. H. Myers, (19 December) 1898; ibid., p. 112.

19 Henry James, preface to *The Aspern Papers; The Turn of the Screw; The Liar; the Two Faces*, vol. XII, *The Novels and Tales of Henry James* (New York: Charles Scribner's Sons, 1908), p. xvi.

20 Edmund Wilson, 'The Ambiguity of Henry James', in *The Triple Thinkers* (New York: Octagon Books, 1977), p. 99.

21 Christine Brooke-Rose, 'The Readerhood of Man', in Susan R. Suleiman and Inge Crosman (eds), *The Reader in the Text: Essays on Audience and Interpretation* (Princeton, NJ: Princeton University Press, 1980), p. 135. See also her three essays 'The Squirm of the True', *Poetics and Theory of Literature*, 1 (1976), 2 (1977).

22 Kimbrough (ed.), *The Turn of the Screw*, p. 181, editorial introduction.

23 See Edna Kenton, 'Henry James to the Ruminant Reader: *The Turn of the Screw*', *The Arts*, VI (November 1924), and Harold C. Goddard, 'A Pre-

Freudian Reading of *The Turn of the Screw'*, *Nineteenth Century Fiction*, XXII (June 1957), both in Kimbrough (ed.), *The Turn of the Screw*.

24 Martina Slaughter, 'Edmund Wilson and *The Turn of the Screw'*, ibid., p. 212.

25 Shoshana Felman, 'Turning the Screw of Interpretation', *Yale French Studies*, 55/56 (1977), p. VII 1977), p. 159; reprinted in Felman, (ed.), *Psychoanalysis and Literature: The Question of Reading: Otherwise* (Baltimore: Johns Hopkins University Press, 1982), p. 174.

26 The governess sees Quint's face at the window: 'yet I believe no woman so overwhelmed ever in so short a time recovered her grasp of the *act*' (Henry James, *The Turn of the Screw and Other Short Novels* (New York: New American Library, 1962), 1st pub. 1898, ch. XXIV, p. 398); she frightens Miles: 'he uttered the cry of a creature hurled over an abyss, and the grasp with which I recovered him might have been that of catching him in his fall' (ibid., p. 403).

27 See Allan Lloyd Smith, 'The Phantom of Child Abuse in *The Turn of the Screw'*, *Diacritics* (forthcoming).

28 Wright, *Psychoanalytic Criticism*, p. 131.

29 Ibid., p. 132.

Reading 6 (Johnson)

30 An extended version of this essay can be found in *Yale French Studies*, 55/6 (1977), special issue entitled 'Literature and Psychoanalysis', pp. 457–505.

31 In Edgar Allan Poe, *Great Tales and Poems of Edgar Allan Poe* (New York: Pocket Books, 1951), pp. 199–219, hereafter designated as Poe.

32 In Jacques Lacan, *Ecrits* (Paris: Seuil, 1966) (reissued in Seuil's 'Collection Points' [no. 5], 1969). Quotations in English are taken, unless otherwise indicated, from the partial translation in *Yale French Studies*, 48 (1973) (special issue entitled 'French Freud'), pp. 38–72, hereafter designated as SPL.

33 This article was published in French in *Poétique*, 21 (1975), pp. 96–147 (reprinted in '*La Carte postale* [1980], pp. 441–524), and, somewhat reduced, in English in *Yale French Studies*, 52 (1975) (special issue entitled 'Graphesis'), pp. 31–113. Unless otherwise indicated, references are to the English version, hereafter designated as PT.

34 'So infamous a scheme/If not worthy of Atreus, is worthy of Thyestes'.

35 'La politique de l'autruiche' combines the policy of the ostrich (autruche), others (autrui), and Austria (Autriche).

36 Lacan, *Ecrits*, p. 57; translation and emphasis Johnson's. Not translated in SPL.

37 Paul de Man, *Blindness and Insight* (New York: Oxford University Press, 1971), p. 140.

38 Stanley E. Fish, 'How Ordinary is Ordinary Language?', *New Literary History*, 5 (Autumn 1973), p. 52.

39 It is perhaps not by chance that the question arises here of whether or not to put the accent on the letter 'a'. The letter 'a' is perhaps the purloined letter *par excellence* in the writings of all three authors. Lacan's 'objet *a*', Derrida's 'différ*a*nce', and Edgar Allan Poe's middle initial, A., taken from his foster father, John Allan.

Reading 7 (Wilson)

40 In *The Arts*, VI (November 1924). This issue also contains photographs of the Demuth illustrations.

Reading 8 (Felman)

41 Cf.: 'At this, with one of the quick *turns* of simple folk, she suddenly flamed up. "*Master* Miles! – *him*' an injury?"' (ch. 2, p. 11). [Felman's references are to Kimbrough (ed.), *The Turn of the Screw*; asterisks indicate original emphasis].

42 Cf. Jacques Lacan, 'The Meaning of the Phallus' ('La Signification du Phallus'): 'In Freudian thought, the phallus is not a fantasy, if a fantasy is understood to be an imaginary effect, nor is it as such an object (partial, internal, good, bad, etc.) if the term is used to designate the reality it symbolizes. It is not without cause that Freud took his reference from the *simulacrum* it was for the ancients. For the phallus is a signifier [...] It can only play its role under a veil, that is, as itself the sign of the latency which strikes the signifiable as soon as it is raised to the function of a signifier [...] It then becomes that which [...] bars the signified' (*Ecrits*, pp. 690–2).

43 Lewis Carroll, *Through the Looking-Glass* (London: Macmillan & Co., 1871) VI.

44 'The impious dismantling of fiction and consequently of the literary mechanism as such in an effort to display the principal part or nothing, [...] the conscious lack(s) within us of what, above, bursts out and splits', Stéphane Mallarmé, *La Musique et les Lettres*, in *Oeuvres Complètes*, (Paris: Pléïade, 1945), p. 647; Felman's translation.

45 From a review of 'Aurora Floyd', by M. E. Braddon, in Kimbrough (ed.), *The Turn of the Screw*, p. 98.

Part IV
Jacques Lacan: the Unconscious Structured as a Language

Jacques Lacan received his doctorate, on paranoid psychosis, in 1932; his thesis was that 'personality' was an element not taken into account by medical treatment of paranoid patients' hallucinations. He opposed formalist approaches to psychoanalytic practice, which he felt failed to utilize the Freudian notion of the unconscious. By the 1950s, his analysis of mental life was taking into account contemporary work on semiotics, and in 1953 he gave the first of the public seminars which continued throughout his life. In 1964 he founded the Ecole Freudienne de Paris, which he dissolved in 1980, a year before his death at the age of eighty.[1]

Lacan may be one of the less immediately accessible psychoanalytic writers – his style, punning and allusive, brings the unconscious dimension of language to the surface, and its shifting pronouns emphasize the fact that language belongs to another.[2] It is an enactment of his own theories in showing that, as Jane Gallop argues, the truth appears 'not in thoughts, but in things, not in the spirit, but in the material, contingent letter', that is, not in the subject him or herself but in the signifier.[3] Lacan's style differentiates itself from the deceptively easy inroad into analysis offered by psychobabble ('the degradation of psychoanalysis consequent on its American transplantation', as Lacan puts it). Gallop suggests that the 'nostalgia' Lacan feels for the uncontaminated past of a psychoanalysis free from American ego psychologists amounts almost to a sense that for him it is no longer phallic but '"degraded", castrated'.[4]

Lacan is currently probably the most influential psychoanalytic writer, with his work cited in or underlying literary theory, art, film studies, social and cultural theory, and feminism. Lacan was the self-styled pioneer of a 'return to Freud' in the 1950s, and he contributed to the Freudian approach, often seen as reductively biologistic,⁵ an interest in semiotics and language: within the 'passion of the signifier', he says, 'it is not only man who speaks, but in man and through man that it [*ça*] speaks, that his nature is woven by effects in which we can find the structure of language, whose material he becomes'.⁶ This quotation draws attention to the nature of Lacanian psychoanalysis as 'above all a practice of speech and a theory of the speaking subject'.⁷ This emphasis differentiates Lacan from Freud, whose theories were based on the idea that biological needs determine culture, rather than language or sign systems in general.

From this point of view, shared by Jacqueline Rose, Lacan's theories have potential for forming part of a feminist psychoanalytic project, but the continuing investment in patriarchal priorities suggested by his essay 'The Meaning of the Phallus' has inspired other writers, such as Elizabeth Grosz, to question the feminist application of Lacan's work. Cynthia Chase summarizes the problematic points at issue in reading Lacan: 'How could the notion of a necessary identification with the phallus or even the mere identification of the phallus as the signifier of desire form part of a feminist understanding of desire and meaning?', and, further, 'How can such conditions for the emergence of the subject be understood as a genuinely *linguistic* predicament?'⁸

'The Meaning of the Phallus'

As Jacqueline Rose's preface to 'The Meaning of the Phallus' says, Lacan's essay is concerned to make clear what he thinks the position of the phallus is in the symbolic realm; and for this reason it has become a much-debated paper in terms of both femininity and feminism. Lacan discusses not only the role of the phallus in the formation of gender, but also the concept of 'masquerade' as the way in which femininity is constructed in relation to the phallus.

Lacan suggests that the unconscious works in the same way that language does, 'along the two axes of metaphor and metonymy which generate the signified', an opposition of two figures first discussed by linguist Roman Jakobson.⁹ Metaphor works by likening two concepts to each other; to call an island 'the pearl of the Antilles', for example, is to speak metaphorically. Metonymy, on the other hand, works by association or closeness rather than likeness, particularly through synecdoche, in which a part is taken to stand for the whole: to call the sovereign 'the crown' is to speak metonymically. Metaphor, Jakobson notes, works by substituting one signifier for another, while metonymy works by accumulation, adding signifiers to each other. In terms of how the unconscious works, its metaphoric structure involves moving from one signifier to another found with it (see, for instance, Elizabeth Grosz's discussion of why a shoe might stand in for the maternal phallus: through contiguity rather than resemblance); metonymically, it slides from one to another which is similar (for instance, from father to husband: as Catherine Belsey puts it,[10] desire itself is constructed metonymically).[11] It is partly in this sense that Lacan suggests the unconscious is structured like a language.

Women and signification

The woman's privileged relation to the mother's body makes signification (at least in theory) difficult. She does not lose the mother's body as the man does (she turns into the mother herself), and as she cannot be castrated either, what of her body can achieve signification? Some writers, including Mary Ann Doane in the essay 'Woman's Stake: Filming the Female Body' reproduced in part VI, have suggested that the 'masquerade', a concept Lacan borrows from Joan Riviere, is a way for women to signify, particularly on screen. Does the apparently difficult relationship between women and signification mean that a different term should be constructed – 'uterus' rather than 'phallus', for instance, or 'thallus', a word invented for the occasion, as Samuel Weber has suggested[12] – or the use of a different logic altogether, such as the hysterical language and bodily symptoms of Dora?[13] Jane Gallop argues for a term like Ernest Jones's 'aphanisis', which means fear of sexual loss, and which he saw as a more deep-rooted and general fear, shared by both sexes, than castration or its female equivalent, penis-envy.[14] She calls 'aphanisis' a 'generalizable, sexually indifferent term [...] which unveils the obscene privilege of the phallus',[15] although of course, as Lacan would be the first to agree, and especially clearly in the case of this term, altering the word itself means the concept alters too.

As Mary Ann Doane has pointed out, attempts to deny the relation between penis and phallus are in a sense 'veils' and 'illusions', since '[t]he phallus, as signifier, may no longer be the penis, but any effort to conceptualize its function is inseparable from an imaging of the body'.[16] Diana J. Fuss amplifies that this means 'that the relation between the penis and the phallus is as much one of association or metonymy as similarity or metaphor'.[17] Jane Gallop acutely points out that it is not so much the pretence that penis and phallus are different, but the act of confusing the two, which causes problems: 'as long as the attribute of power is a phallus which refers to and can be confused (in the imaginary register?) with a penis, this confusion will support a structure in which it seems reasonable that men have power and women do not'.[18] The question reveals the inevitable politicization of psychoanalysis.

Cynthia Chase suggests that Lacan's theories rest on the belief that, 'although it is non-referential, signification takes place according to rules determined by a transcendental structure of meaning', which is substantively the same as the objection Derrida made against Lacan's discussion of Poe: the phallus underlies and guarantees meaning in Lacanian theory. Chase adds that a feminist discussion of identification with the phallus could take place only if it could 'undercut the structuralist conception of signification as ultimately determined' in this way.[19]

Lacanian textual readings

Jane Gallop, in *Reading Lacan*, describes what Lacanian textual readings often look like: they 'show symbolic fathers and signifying chains', in the same way that Freudian ones might show 'anal drives or negative oedipal complexes'.[20] As we saw in relation to Edmund Wilson's and Shoshana Felman's writings on *The Turn of the Screw*, their positions might respectively be termed symbol-oriented versus 'dialectic', one an interpretation, the other teasing out the implications of the transferential situation. Felman concentrates on this distinction in the introduction to her edited volume *Literature and Psychoanalysis*, and Gallop in *Reading Lacan* emphasizes that the central difference between transference and interpretation is that transference is a dialogue, something which takes place between subjects, unlike interpretation, which depends on 'the one who knows' explaining the hidden meanings of an inert text, in a one-way process. As we saw in relation to Dora's case history, transference involves the analysand seeing her or his past history acted out in the person of the analyst, and it is the successful resolution of the analytic relationship which constitutes the cure. At the same time, the analyst may experience 'countertransference', which Freud ignored in his case history of Dora, and which since his time has been increasingly emphasized, to turn analysis into a relationship rather than a treatment. 'Countertransference' refers to the analyst's experience of his or her own unconscious being acted out in the person of the analysand, particularly the analyst's response to the transference.[21]

As a model of reading a text, a transferential approach would do away with the idea of the critic as one with superior knowledge, finding out textual elements unknown to the text's author, and replace it with a way of explaining how certain textual effects work. As in analysis, for instance, the reader's psychic history may predispose him or her to feel particularly engaged with a book: this could be termed an example of successful transference. The potential for the role of the reader to alternate between analyst and analysand also suggests the increased fluidity of this critical approach; in fact countertransference might more often be an accurate description of what goes on in the reading process – the reader listens to the 'case history' of the text and responds to its attitude to that reader (transference). Felman argues that, '[w]ith respect to the text, the literary critic occupies thus at once the place of the psychoanalyst (in the relation of interpretation) *and* the place of the patient (in the relation of transference)'.[22]

As Gallop says, 'A Lacanian reading of literature would have to analyze *something like* a "transference" at play between reader and text, but it would have to be careful to attend to the specificity of that something, to the specific dynamic of the relation of reading';[23] a Lacanian reading 'thus would not be the uncovering of Lacanian concepts – castration or the Name-of-the-Father – in a literary text'.[24]

9 JACQUES LACAN

The Meaning of the Phallus

What follows is the unaltered text of a paper delivered in German on 9 May 1958, at the Max Planck Institute of Munich where Professor Paul Matussek had invited me to speak.

The vaguest idea of the state of mind then prevailing in circles, not for the most part uninformed, will give some measure of the impact of terms such as 'the other scene', to take one example used here, which I was the first to extract from Freud's work.

If 'deferred action' (*Nachtrag*), to rescue another such term from its current affectation, makes this effort unfeasible, it should be realized that they were unheard of at that time.

We know that the unconscious castration complex has the function of a knot:

(1) In the dynamic structuring of symptoms in the analytic sense of the term, meaning that which can be analysed in neuroses, perversions and psychoses;
(2) as the regulator of development giving its *ratio* to this first role: that is, by installing in the subject an unconscious position without which he would be unable to identify with the ideal type of his sex, or to respond without grave risk to the needs of his partner in the sexual relation, or even to receive adequately the needs of the child thus procreated.

What we are dealing with is an antinomy internal to the assumption by man (*Mensch*) of his sex: why must he take up its attributes only by means of a threat, or even in the guise of a privation? As we know, in *Civilization and its Discontents*, Freud went so far as to suggest not a contingent, but an essential disturbance of human sexuality, and one of his last articles turns on the irreducibility for any finite (*endliche*) analysis of the effects following from the castration complex in the masculine unconscious and from *penisneid* (penis envy) in the unconscious of the woman.

This is not the only point of uncertainty, but it is the first that the Freudian experience and its resulting metapsychology introduced into our experience of man. It cannot be solved by any reduction to biological factors, as the mere necessity of the myth underlying the structuring of the Oedipus complex makes sufficiently clear.

Any recourse to an hereditary amnesic given would in this instance be mere artifice, not only because such a factor is in itself disputable, but because it leaves the problem untouched, namely, the link between the murder of the father and the pact of the primordial law, given that it is included in that law that castration should be the punishment for incest.

Only on the basis of the clinical facts can there be any fruitful discussion. These facts go to show that the relation of the subject to the phallus is set up regardless of the anatomical difference between the sexes, which is what makes its interpretation particularly intractable in the case of the woman and in relationship to her, specifically on the four following counts:

(1) as to why the little girl herself considers, if only for a moment, that she is castrated, in the sense of being deprived of the phallus, at the hand of someone who is in the first instance her mother, an important point, and who then becomes her father, but in such a way that we must recognize in this transition a transference in the analytic sense of the term;
(2) as to why, at a more primordial level, the mother is for both sexes considered as provided with a phallus, that is, as a phallic mother;
(3) as to why, correlatively, the meaning of castration only acquires its full (clinically manifest) weight as regards symptom formation when it is discovered as castration of the mother;
(4) these three problems culminate in the question of the reason for the phallic phase in development. We know that Freud used this term to specify the earliest genital maturation – as on the one hand characterized by the imaginary predominance of the phallic attribute and masturbatory pleasure, and on the other by a localizing of this pleasure for the woman in the clitoris, which is thereby raised to the function of the phallus. This would seem to rule out for both sexes, until the end of this phase, that is, until the dissolution of the Oedipus complex, any instinctual awareness of the vagina as the place of genital penetration.

This ignorance smacks of mis-recognition (*méconnaissance*) in the technical sense of the term, especially as it is on occasions disproved. All it agrees with, surely, is Longus's fable in which he depicts the initiation of Daphnis and Chloë as dependent on the revelations of an old woman.

It is for this reason that certain authors have been led to regard the phallic phase as an effect of repression, and the function assumed in it by the phallic object as a symptom. The difficulty starts when we need to know *which* symptom. Phobia, according to one, perversion according to another – or, indeed, to the same one. In this last case, it's not worth speculating: not that interesting transmutations of the object from phobia into fetish do not occur, but their interest resides precisely in the different place which they occupy in the structure. There would be no point in asking these authors to formulate this difference from the perspective of object relations which is currently in favour. This being for lack of any reference on the matter other than the loose notion of the part object, uncriticized since Karl Abraham first introduced it, which is more the pity in view of the easy option which it provides today.

The fact remains that, if one goes back to the surviving texts of the years 1928–32, the now abandoned debate on the phallic phase is a refreshing example of a passion for doctrine, which has been given an additional note of nostalgia by the degradation of psychoanalysis consequent on its American transplantation.

A mere summary of the debate could only distort the genuine diversity of the positions taken by figures such as Helene Deutsch, Karen Horney and Ernest Jones, to mention only the most eminent.

The series of three articles which Jones devoted to the subject is especially suggestive: if only for the starting premise on which he constructs his argument, signalled by the term *aphanisis*, which he himself coined. For by correctly posing the problem of the relationship between castration and desire, he reveals such a proximity to what he cannot quite grasp that the term which will later provide us with the key to the problem seems to emerge out of his very failure.

The amusing thing is the way he manages, on the authority of the very letter of Freud's text, to formulate a position which is directly opposed to it: a true model in a difficult genre.

The problem, however, refuses to go away, seeming to subvert Jones's own case for a re-establishment of the equality of natural rights (which surely gets the better of him in the Biblical 'Man and woman God created them' with which he concludes). What does he actually gain by normalizing the function of the phallus as part object if he has to invoke its presence in the mother's body as internal object, a term which is a function of the fantasies uncovered by Melanie Klein, and if he cannot therefore separate himself from her doctrine which sees these fantasies as a recurrence of the Oedipal formation which is located right back in earliest infancy?

We will not go far wrong if we re-open the question by asking what could have imposed on Freud the obvious paradox of his position. For one has to allow that he was better guided than anyone else in his recognition of the order of unconscious phenomena, which order he had discovered, and that for want of an adequate articulation of the nature of these phenomena his followers were bound to go more or less astray.

It is on the basis of such a wager – laid down by me as the principle of a commentary of Freud's work which I have been pursuing for seven years – that I have been led to certain conclusions: above all, to argue, as necessary to any articulation of analytic phenomena, for the notion of the signifier, in the sense in which it is opposed to that of the signified in modern linguistic analysis. The latter, born since Freud, could not be taken into account by him, but it is my contention that Freud's discovery stands out precisely for having had to anticipate its formulas, even while setting out from a domain in which one could hardly expect to recognize its sway. Conversely, it is Freud's discovery that gives to the opposition of signifier to signified the full weight which it should imply: namely, that the signifier has an active function in determining the effects in which the signifiable appears as submitting to its mark, becoming through that passion the signified.

This passion of the signifier then becomes a new dimension of the human condition, in that it is not only man who speaks, but in man and through man that it (*ça*) speaks, that his nature is woven by effects in which we can find the structure of language, whose material he becomes, and that consequently there resounds in him, beyond anything ever conceived of by the psychology of ideas, the relation of speech.

It is in this sense that one can say that the consequences of the discovery of the unconscious have not been so much as glimpsed in the theory, although its repercussions have been felt in the praxis to a much greater extent than we are as yet aware of, even if only translated into effects of retreat.

Let me make clear that to argue for man's relation to the signifier as such has nothing to do with a 'culturalist' position in the ordinary sense of the term, such as that which Karen Horney found herself anticipating in the dispute over the phallus and which Freud himself characterized as feminist. The issue is not man's relation to language as a social phe-nomenon, since the question does not even arise of anything resembling that all too familiar ideological psychogenesis, not superseded by a peremptory recourse to the entirely metaphysical notion, underlying the mandatory appeal to the concrete, which is so pathetically conveyed by the term 'affect'.

It is a question of rediscovering in the laws governing that other scene (*eine andere Schauplatz*) which Freud designated, in relation to dreams, as that of the unconscious, the effects discovered at the level of the materially unstable elements which constitute the chain of language: effects determined by the double play of combination and substitution in the signifier, along the two axes of metaphor and metonymy which generate the signified; effects which are determinant in the institution of the subject. What emerges from this attempt is a topology in the mathe-matical sense of the term, without which, as soon becomes clear, it is impossible even to register the structure of a symptom in the analytic sense of the term.

It speaks in the Other, I say, designating by this Other the very place called upon by a recourse to speech in any relation where it intervenes. If it speaks in the Other, whether or not the subject hears it with his own ears, it is because it is there that the subject, according to a logic prior to any awakening of the signified, finds his signifying place. The discovery of what he articulates in that place, that is, in the unconscious, enables us to grasp the price of the division (*Spaltung*) through which he is thus constituted.

The phallus is elucidated in its function here. In Freudian doctrine, the phallus is not a fantasy, if what is understood by that is an imaginary effect. Nor is it as such an object (part, internal, good, bad, etc. . . .) in so far as this term tends to accentuate the reality involved in a relation-ship. It is even less the organ, penis or clitoris, which it symbolizes. And it is not incidental that Freud took his reference for it from the simu-lacrum which it represented for the Ancients.

For the phallus is a signifier, a signifier whose function in the intra-subjective economy of analysis might lift the veil from that which it served in the mysteries. For it is to this signifier that it is given to desig-nate as a whole the effect of there being a signified, inasmuch as it con-ditions any such effect by its presence as signifier.

Let us examine, then, the effects of this presence. First, they follow from the deviation of man's needs by the fact that he speaks, in the sense that as long as his needs are subjected to demand they return to him alienated. This is not the effect of his real dependency (one should not expect to find here the parasitic conception represented by the notion of dependency in the theory of neuroses) but precisely of the putting into signifying form as such and of the fact that it is from the place of the Other that his message is emitted.

What is thus alienated in needs constitutes an *Urverdrängung* (primal repression) because it cannot, by definition, be articulated in demand. But it reappears in a residue which then presents itself in man as desire (*das Begehren*). The phenomenology which emerges from analytic experience is certainly such as to demonstrate the paradoxical, deviant, erratic, excentric and even scandalous character by which desire is distinguished from need. A fact too strongly attested not to have always won the recognition of moralists worthy of the name. It does seem that early Freudianism had to give this fact its due status. Yet paradoxically psychoanalysis finds itself at the head of an age-old obscurantism, all the more wearisome for its denial of the fact through the ideal of a theoretical and practical reduction of desire to need.

Hence the necessity for us to articulate that status here, starting with demand whose proper characteristics are eluded in the notion of frustration (which was never employed by Freud).

Demand in itself bears on something other than the satisfactions which it calls for. It is demand for a presence or an absence. This is manifest in the primordial relation to the mother, pregnant as it is with that Other to be situated *some way short of* any needs which it might gratify. Demand constitutes this Other as already possessing the 'privilege' of satisfying needs, that is, the power to deprive them of the one thing by which they are satisfied. This privilege of the Other thus sketches out the radical form of the gift of something which it does not have, namely, what is called its love.

Hence it is that demand cancels out (*aufhebt*) the particularity of anything which might be granted by transmuting it into a proof of love, and the very satisfactions of need which it obtains are degraded (*sich erniedrigt*) as being no more than a crushing of the demand for love (all of which is palpable in the psychology of early child-care to which our nurse-analysts are so dedicated).

There is, then, a necessity for the particularity thus abolished to reappear *beyond* demand. Where it does indeed reappear, but preserving the structure harbouring within the unconditional character of the demand for love. In a reversal which is not a simple negation of negation, the force of pure loss arises from the relic of an obliteration. In place of the unconditional aspect of demand, desire substitutes the 'absolute' condition: in effect this condition releases that part of the proof of love which is resistant to the satisfaction of a need. Thus desire is neither the appetite for satisfaction, nor the demand for love, but the difference resulting from the subtraction of the first from the second, the very phenomenon of their splitting (*Spaltung*).

One can see how the sexual relation occupies this closed field of desire in which it will come to play out its fate. For this field is constituted so as to produce the enigma which this relation provokes in the subject, by 'signifying' it to him twice over: as a return of the demand it arouses in the form of a demand made on the subject of need, and as an ambiguity cast on to the Other who is involved, in the proof of love demanded. The gap in this enigma betrays what determines it, conveyed at its simplest in this formula: that for each partner in the relation, the subject and the Other, it is not enough to be the subjects of need, nor objects of love, but they must stand as the cause of desire.

This truth is at the heart of all the mishaps of sexual life which belong in the field of psychoanalysis.

It is also the precondition in analysis for the subject's happiness: and to disguise this gap by relying on the virtue of the 'genital' to resolve it through the maturation of tenderness (that is by a recourse to the Other solely as reality), however piously intended, is none the less a fraud. Admittedly it was French psychoanalysts with their hypocritical notion of genital oblativity who started up the moralizing trend which, to the tune of Salvationist choirs, is now followed everywhere.

In any case man cannot aim at being whole (the 'total personality' being another premise where modern psychotherapy goes off course) once the play of displacement and condensation, to which he is committed in the exercise of his functions, marks his relation as subject to the signifier.

The phallus is the privileged signifier of that mark where the share of the logos is wedded to the advent of desire. One might say that this signifier is chosen as what stands out as most easily seized upon in the real of sexual copulation, and also as the most symbolic in the literal (typographical) sense of the term, since it is the equivalent in that relation of the (logical) copula. One might also say that by virtue of its turgidity, it is the image of the vital flow as it is transmitted in generation.

All these propositions merely veil over the fact that the phallus can only play its role as veiled, that is, as in itself the sign of the latency with which everything signifiable is struck as soon as it is raised (*aufgehoben*) to the function of signifier.

The phallus is the signifier of this *Aufhebung* itself which it inaugurates (initiates) by its own disappearance. This is why the demon of Αἰδώς (*Scham*, shame) in the ancient mysteries rises up exactly at the moment when the phallus is unveiled (cf. the famous painting of the Villa of Pompei).

It then becomes the bar which, at the hands of this demon, strikes the signified, branding it as the bastard offspring of its signifying concatenation.

In this way a condition of complementarity is produced by the signifier in the founding of the subject: which explains his *Spaltung* as well as the intervening movement through which this is effected. Namely:

(1) that the subject designates his being only by crossing through everything which it signifies, as can be seen in the fact that he wishes to be loved for himself, a mirage not dispelled merely by being denounced as grammatical (since it abolishes discourse);
(2) that the living part of that being in the *urverdrängt* (primary repressed) finds its signifier by receiving the mark of the *Verdrängung* (repression) of the phallus (whereby the unconscious is language).

The phallus as signifier gives the ratio of desire (in the musical sense of the term as the 'mean and extreme' ratio of harmonic division).

It is, therefore, as an algorithm that I am going to use it now, relying – necessarily if I am to avoid drawing out my account indefinitely – on the echoes of the experience which unites us to give you the sense of this usage.

If the phallus is a signifier then it is in the place of the Other that the subject gains access to it. But in that the signifier is only there veiled and as the ratio of the Other's desire, so it is this *desire of the Other* as such which the subject has to recognize, meaning, the Other as itself a subject divided by the signifying *Spaltung*.

What can be seen to emerge in psychological genesis confirms this signifying function of the phallus.

Thus, to begin with, we can formulate more correctly the Kleinian fact that the child apprehends from the outset that the mother 'contains' the phallus.

But it is the dialectic of the demand for love and the test of desire which dictates the order of development.

The demand for love can only suffer from a desire whose signifier is alien to it. If the desire of the mother *is* the phallus, then the child wishes to be the phallus so as to satisfy this desire. Thus the division immanent to desire already makes itself felt in the desire of the Other, since it stops the subject from being satisfied with presenting to the Other anything real it might *have* which corresponds to this phallus – what he has being worth no more than what he does not have as far as his demand for love is concerned, which requires that he *be* the phallus.

Clinical practice demonstrates that this test of the desire of the Other is not decisive in the sense that the subject learns from it whether or not he has a real phallus, but inasmuch as he learns that the mother does not. This is the moment of experience without which no symptomatic or structural consequence (that is, phobia or *penisneid*) referring to the castration complex can take effect. It is here that the conjunction is signed between desire, in so far as the phallic signifier is its mark, and the threat or the nostalgia of lack-in-having.

It is, of course, the law introduced into this sequence by the father which will decide its future.

But simply by keeping to the function of the phallus, we can pinpoint the structures which will govern the relations between the sexes.

Let us say that these relations will revolve around a being and a having which, because they refer to a signifier, the phallus, have the contradictory effect of on the one hand lending reality to the subject in that signifier, and on the other making unreal the relations to be signified.

This follows from the intervention of an 'appearing' which gets substituted for the 'having' so as to protect it on one side and to mask its lack on the other, with the effect that the ideal or typical manifestations of behaviour in both sexes, up to and including the act of sexual copulation, are entirely propelled into comedy.

These ideals gain new strength from the demand which it is in their power to satisfy, which is always the demand for love, with its complement of reducing desire to demand.

Paradoxical as this formulation might seem, I would say that it is in order to be the phallus, that is to say, the signifier of the desire of the Other, that the woman will reject an essential part of her femininity, notably all its attributes through masquerade. It is for what she is not that she expects to be desired as well as loved. But she finds the signifier of her own desire in the body of the one to whom she addresses her demand for love. Certainly we should not forget that the organ actually invested with this signifying function takes on the value of a fetish. But for the woman the result is still a convergence onto the same object of an experience of love which as such (cf. above) ideally deprives her of that which it gives, and a desire which finds in that same experience its signifier. Which is why it can be observed that the lack of satisfaction proper to sexual need, in other words, frigidity, is relatively well tolerated in women, whereas the *Verdrängung* inherent to desire is lesser in her case than in the case of the man.

In men, on the other hand, the dialectic of demand and desire gives rise to effects, whose exact point of connection Freud situated with a sureness which we must once again admire, under the rubric of a specific depreciation (*Erniedrigung*) of love.

If it is the case that the man manages to satisfy his demand for love in his relationship to the woman to the extent that the signifier of the phallus constitutes her precisely as giving in love what she does not have – conversely, his own desire for the phallus will throw up its signifier in the form of a persistent divergence towards 'another woman' who can signify this phallus under various guises, whether as a virgin or a prostitute. The result is a centrifugal tendency of the genital drive in the sexual life of the man which makes impotence much harder for him to bear, at the same time as the *Verdrängung* inherent to desire is greater.

We should not, however, think that the type of infidelity which then appears to be constitutive of the masculine function is exclusive to the man. For if one looks more closely, the same redoubling is to be found in the woman, except that in her case, the Other of love as such, that is to say, the Other as deprived of that which he gives, is hard to perceive in the withdrawal whereby it is substituted for the being of the man whose attributes she cherishes.

One might add here that masculine homosexuality, in accordance with the phallic mark which constitutes desire, is constituted on its axis, whereas the orientation of feminine homosexuality, as observation shows, follows from a disappointment which reinforces the side of the demand for love. These remarks should be qualified by going back to the function of the mask inasmuch as this function dominates the identifications through which refusals of love are resolved.

The fact that femininity takes refuge in this mask, because of the *Verdrängung* inherent to the phallic mark of desire, has the strange consequence that, in the human being, virile display itself appears as feminine.

Correlatively, one can glimpse the reason for a feature which has never been elucidated and which again gives a measure of the depth of Freud's intuition: namely, why he advances the view that there is only one libido, his text clearly indicating that he conceives of it as masculine in nature. The function of the signifier here touches on its most profound relation: by way of which the Ancients embodied in it both the Νονς (*Nous*, sense) and the Λογος (*Logos*, reason).

10 JACQUELINE ROSE

Feminine Sexuality: Introduction

Addressing Melanie Klein, Lacan makes it clear that the argument for a reintroduction of the concept of desire into the definition of human sexuality is a return to, and a reformulation of, the law and the place of the father as it was originally defined by Freud ('a dimension ... increasingly evaded since Freud'[25]):

> Melanie Klein describes the relationship to the mother as a mirrored relationship: the maternal body becomes the receptacle of the drives which the child projects onto it, drives motivated by aggression born of a fundamental disappointment. This is to neglect the fact that the outside is given for the subject as the place where the desire of the Other is situated, and where he or she will encounter the third term, the father.[26]

Lacan argued, therefore, for a return to the concept of the father, but this concept is now defined in relation to that of desire. What matters is that the relationship of the child to the mother is not simply based on 'frustration and satisfaction' ('the notion of frustration (which was never employed by Freud))',[27] but on the recognition of her desire. The mother is refused to the child in so far as a prohibition falls on the child's desire to be what the mother desires (not the same, note, as a desire to possess or enjoy the mother in the sense normally understood):

> What we meet as an accident in the child's development is linked to the fact that the child does not find himself or herself alone in front of the mother, and that the phallus forbids the child the satisfaction of his or her own desire, which is the desire to be the exclusive desire of the mother.[28]

The duality of the relation between mother and child must be broken, just as the analytic relation must be thrown onto the axis of desire. In Lacan's account, the phallus stands for that moment of rupture. It refers mother and child to the dimension of the symbolic which is figured by the father's place. The mother is taken to desire the phallus not because she contains it (Klein), but precisely because she does not. The phallus therefore belongs somewhere else; it breaks the two-term relation and initiates the order of exchange. For Lacan, it takes on this value as a function of the androcentric nature of the symbolic order itself. But its status is in itself false, and must be recognized by the child as such. Castration means first of all this – that the child's desire for the mother does not refer *to* her but *beyond* her, to an object, the phallus, whose status is first imaginary (the object presumed to satisfy her desire) and then symbolic (recognition that desire cannot be satisfied).

The place of the phallus in the account, therefore, follows from Lacan's return to the position and law of the father, but this concept has been reformulated in relation to that of desire. Lacan uses the term 'paternal metaphor', metaphor having a very specific meaning here. First, as a reference to the act of substitution (substitution is the very law of metaphoric operation), whereby the prohibition of the father takes up the place originally figured by the absence of the mother. Secondly, as a reference to the status of paternity itself which can only ever logically be *inferred*. And thirdly, as part of an insistence that the father stands for a place and a function which is not reducible to the presence or absence of the real father as such:

> To speak of the Name of the Father is by no means the same thing as invoking paternal deficiency (which is often done). We know today that an Oedipus complex can be constituted perfectly well even if the father is not there, while originally it was the excessive presence of the father which was held responsible for all dramas. But it is not in an environmental perspective that the answer to these questions can be found. So as to make the link between the Name of the Father, in so far as he can at times be missing, and the father whose effective presence is not always necessary for him not to be missing, I will introduce the expression *paternal metaphor*.[29]

Finally, the concept is used to separate the father's function from the idealized or imaginary father with which it is so easily confused and which is exactly the figure to be got round, or past: 'Any discourse on the Oedipus complex which fails to bring out this figure will be inscribed within the very effects of the complex'.[30]

Thus when Lacan calls for a return to the place of the father he is crucially distinguishing himself from any sociological conception of role. The father is a function and refers to a law, the place outside the imaginary dyad and against which it breaks. To make of him a referent is to fall into an ideological trap: the 'prejudice which falsifies the conception of the Oedipus complex from the start, by making it define as natural, rather than normative, the predominance of the paternal figure'.[31]

There is, therefore, no assumption about the ways in which the places come to be fulfilled (it is this very assumption which is questioned). This is why, in talking of the genetic link between the mother and child, Lacan could refer to the 'vast social connivance' which *makes* of her the 'privileged site of prohibitions'.[32] And why Safouan, in an article on the function of the real father, recognizes that it is the intervention of the third term which counts, and that nothing of itself requires that this should be embodied by the father as such.[33] Lacan's position should be read against two alternative emphases – on the actual behaviour of the mother alone (adequacy and inadequacy), and on a literally present or absent father (his idealization and/or deficiency).

The concept of the phallus and the castration complex can only be understood in terms of this reference to prohibition and the law, just as rejection of these concepts tends to lose sight of this reference. The phallus needs to be placed on the axis of desire before it can be understood, or questioned, as the differential mark of sexual identification (boy or girl, having or not having the phallus). By breaking the imaginary dyad, the phallus represents a moment of division (Lacan calls this the subject's 'lack-in-being') which re-enacts the fundamental splitting of subjectivity itself. And by jarring against any naturalist account of sexuality ('phallocentrism ... strictly impossible to deduce from any pre-established harmony of the said psyche to the nature it expresses'),[34] the phallus relegates sexuality to a strictly other dimension – the order of the symbolic outside of which, for Lacan, sexuality cannot be understood. The importance of the phallus is that its status in the development of human sexuality is something which nature *cannot* account for.

When Lacan is reproached with phallocentrism at the level of his theory, what is most often missed is that the subject's entry into the symbolic order is equally an exposure of the value of the phallus itself. The subject has to recognize that there is desire, or lack in the place of the Other, that there is no ultimate certainty or truth, and that the status of the phallus is a fraud (this is, for Lacan, the meaning of castration). The phallus can only take up its place by indicating the precariousness of any identity assumed by the subject on the basis of its token. Thus the phallus stands for that moment when prohibition must function, in the sense of whom may be assigned to whom in the triangle made up of mother, father and child, but at that same moment it signals to the subject that 'having' only functions at the price of a loss and 'being' as an effect of division. Only if this is dropped from the account can the phallus be taken to represent an unproblematic assertion of male privilege, or else lead to reformulations intended to guarantee the continuity of sexual development for both sexes.[35]

It is that very continuity which is challenged in the account given here. The concept of the phallus and the castration complex testify above all to the problematic nature of the subject's insertion into his or her sexual identity, to an impossibility writ large over that insertion at the point where it might be taken to coincide with the genital drive.

Looking back at Jones's answer to Freud, it is clear that his opposition to Freud's concept of the phallic phase involves a rejection of the dimension of desire, of the loss of the object, of the difficulty inherent in subjectivity itself (the argument of the first article from *Scilicet* translated [in *Feminine Sexuality*]).[36] Just as it was Freud's failure to apply the concept of castration literally to the girl child which brought him up against the concept of desire (the argument of the second article).[37]

The subject then takes up his or her identity with reference to the phallus, but that identity is thereby designated symbolic (it is something enjoined on the subject). Lacan inverts Saussure's formula for the linguistic sign (the opposition between signifier and signified), giving primacy to the signifier over that which it signifies (or rather creates in that act of signification). For it is essential to his argument that sexual difference is a legislative divide which creates and reproduces its categories. Thus Lacan replaces Saussure's model for the arbitrary nature of the linguistic sign:

TREE

(which is indeed open to the objection that it seems to reflect a theory of language based on a correspondence between words and things), with this model.[38] 'Any speaking being whatever' must line up on one or other side of the divide.[39]

Sexual difference is then assigned according to whether individual subjects do or do not possess the phallus, which means not that anatomical difference *is* sexual difference (the one as strictly deducible from the other), but that anatomical difference comes to *figure* sexual difference, that is, it becomes the sole representative of what that difference is allowed to be. It thus covers over the complexity of the child's early

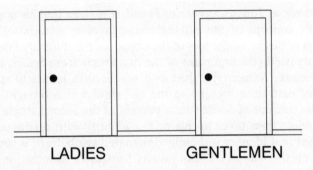

LADIES   GENTLEMEN

sexual life with a crude opposition in which that very complexity is
refused or repressed. The phallus thus indicates the reduction of difference to an instance of visible perception, a *seeming* value.

Freud gave the moment when boy and girl child saw that they were
different the status of a trauma in which the girl is seen to be lacking
(the objections often start here). But something can only be *seen* to be
missing according to a pre-existing hierarchy of values ('there is nothing
missing in the real').[40] What counts is not the perception but its already
assigned meaning – the moment therefore belongs in the symbolic. And
if Lacan states that the symbolic usage of the phallus stems from its visi-
bility (something for which he was often criticized), it is only in so far as
the order of the visible, the apparent, the seeming is the object of his
attack. In fact he constantly refused any crude identification of the phallus with the order of the visible or real ('one might say that this signifier
is chosen as what stands out as most easily seized upon in the real of
sexual copulation'),[41] and he referred it instead to that function of 'veiling' in which he locates the fundamental duplicity of the linguistic sign:

> All these propositions merely veil over the fact that the phallus can only
> play its role as veiled, that is, as in itself the sign of the latency with which
> everything signifiable is struck as soon as it is raised to the function of
> signifier.[42]

Meaning is only ever erected, it is set up and fixed. The phallus symbolizes the effects of the signifier in that having no value in itself, it can
represent that to which value *accrues*.

Lacan's statements on language need to be taken in two directions –
towards the fixing of meaning itself (that which is enjoined on the subject), and away from that very fixing to the point of its constant slippage, the risk or vanishing-point which it always contains (the
unconscious). Sexuality is placed on both these dimensions at once. The
difficulty is to hold these two emphases together – sexuality in the symbolic (an ordering), sexuality as that which constantly fails. Once the

relationship between these two aspects of psychoanalysis can be seen, then the terms in which feminine sexuality can be described undergo a radical shift. The concept of the symbolic states that the woman's sexuality is inseparable from the representations through which it is produced ('images and symbols *for* the woman cannot be isolated from images and symbols *of* the woman [...] it is the representation of sexuality which conditions how it comes into play'),[43] but those very representations will reveal the splitting through which they are constituted as such. The question of what a woman is in this account always stalls on the crucial acknowledgement that there is absolutely no guarantee that she *is* at all. But if she takes up her place according to the process described, then her sexuality will betray, necessarily, the impasses of its history.

Sexuality belongs for Lacan in the realm of masquerade. The term comes from Joan Riviere,[44] for whom it indicated a failed femininity. For Lacan, masquerade is the very definition of 'femininity' precisely because it is constructed with reference to a male sign. The question of frigidity (on which, Lacan recognized, psychoanalysis 'gave up'),[45] also belongs here, and it is described in 'The Meaning of the Phallus' as the effect of the status of the phallic term. But this does not imply that there is a physiology to which women could somehow be returned, or into which they could be freed. Rather the term 'frigidity' stands, on the side of the woman, for the difficulty inherent in sexuality itself, the disjunction laid over the body by desire, at the point where it is inscribed into the genital relation. Psychoanalysis now recognizes that any simple criterion of femininity in terms of a shift of pleasure from clitoris to vagina is a travesty, but what matters is the fantasies implicated in either (or both). For both sexes, sexuality will necessarily touch on the duplicity which underpins its fundamental divide. As for 'normal' vaginal femininity, which might be taken as the recognition of the value of the male sign (a 'coming to' that recognition), it will always evoke the splitting on which its value is erected ('why not acknowledge that if there is no virility which castration does not consecrate, then for the woman it is a castrated lover or a dead man ... who hides behind the veil where he calls on her adoration').[46]

The description of feminine sexuality is, therefore, an exposure of the terms of its definition, the very opposite of a demand as to what that sexuality should be. Where such a definition is given – 'identification with her mother as desiring and a recognition of the phallus in the real father'[47] – it involves precisely a collapse of the phallus into the real and of desire into recognition – giving the lie, we could say, to the whole problem outlined.

11 ELIZABETH GROSZ

The Penis and the Phallus

The processes by which the phallus, a signifier, becomes associated with the penis, an organ, involves the procedures by which women are systematically excluded from positive-self-definition and a potential autonomy. The relations each sex has to the phallus *qua* signifier map the position(s) each occupies as a feminine or masculine subject in the patriarchal symbolic order. Moreover, it defines the structure of romantic relations between them.

The misappropriation of the penis by the phallus is delineated step-by-step in the relations between need, demand, and desire outlined earlier. The penis is removed from its merely anatomical and functional role within ('natural') need, (where its organic role for the little boy lies in urination in the first instance, and insemination, in the second), to the role of object, the *objet a*, in a circuit of demand addressed to the (m)other. It is then capable of taking on the symbolic role of signifier at the level of desire, an object of unconscious phantasy.

As the successive 'object' of need, demand, and desire, the phallus is the valorized signifier around which both men and women define themselves as complementary or even supplementary subjects.[48] Because the penis and the phallus are (albeit illusorily) identified, women are regarded as castrated. By its presence or absence, the penis becomes the defining characteristic of both sexes. Lacan himself concedes that this equation is illusory or misrecognized, but claims that nevertheless the equation is constitutive of human desire, and of the symbolic order.

> Castration may derive support from privation, that is to say, from the apprehension in the Real of the absence of the penis in women – but even this implies a symbolization of the object, since the Real is full and 'lacks' nothing. In so far as one finds castration in the genesis of the neuroses, it is never Real but symbolic and aimed at an imaginary object.[49]

The phallus functions to enable the penis to define all (socially recognized) forms of human sexuality. The *differences* between genitals becomes expressed in terms of the presence or absence of a single (male) term.[50] The Real, where the vagina, clitoris, or vulva have the same ontological status and functional utility as the penis and testicles, must be displaced and recoded if women's bodies are to be categorized as *necessarily* incomplete. The narcissistic imaginary order mediates between the Real, in which there is no lack, and the symbolic, where women represent *for men* a lack men have disavowed. It is during the identificatory blurring of self and other that (from the boy's point of view, at least), the penis becomes regarded as a 'detachable' organ, along the lines of the fantasy of the body in bits-and-pieces. The detachable penis, the penis that the mother once had, prefigures the function of the phallus. It produces the penis as an object of signification, rather than a biological organ. It represents what some 'possess' and others have lost, becoming the term through which the child comes to recognize sexual difference.

The imaginary object – the detachable penis – becomes an element in the symbolic circuit of exchange when it comes to stand as the link or bridge between the two sexes, a form of linguistic *copula*. It becomes a signifier within a signifying system, and cannot thus be possessed or owned by anyone.

The phallus is both the signifier of the differences between the sexes and the signifier which effaces lack and thus difference. It is the term with respect to which the two sexes are defined as different, and the term which functions to bring them together, the term of their union: 'It is a copula, a hyphen – in the evanescence of its erection – the signifier par excellence of impossible identity.'[51] For both sexes, though in quite different ways, the phallus serves as a means of access to the 'domain of the Other'. The Other is understood here in two senses: as a socio-symbolic network regulated according to language-like rules; and as a psychical structure, representative of this social Other, internalized in the form of the unconscious. According to Lacan, the signifier orders and organizes the radically heteronomous drives and impulses from the raw data of the unconscious. He follows Freud here in seeing the unconscious as a consequence of primal repression, where the phallus is the preserved infantile nucleus of the unconscious, a residue of the child's primal repression of its maternal desire.

If the penis assumes the function of the phallus this is because female sexuality is considered a mutilation or castration. Because of its erectile form and 'preference' for penetration, the phallus serves to 'fill' the lack. This function can only be 'performed' in so far as the phallus can also be regarded, in addition to being the sign of sexual difference, as the signifier of the object of the other's desire. As a signifier, the phallus works its effects on the subject only through the mediation of the other.

Even in Lacan's terms, the penis can only ever approximate the function of the phallus. 'Having' a penis, i.e. being a man, is no guarantee of warding off lack. On the contrary, rendering them equivalent has problems of its own, manifested in anxieties about sexual performance (impotence fears) as well as a sometimes desperate search for the other through whom the man can have his position as the possessor of the valued/desired organ confirmed. Without circulation, without the mediation of the other and the Other, no one has access to it. As a signifier, no one has a privileged or unique relation to it, for it exists only by virtue of the entire signifying chain and an intersubjective, multi-subjective, symbolically regulated social order. It functions only through the Other and the other, and this makes clear its divergence from the male biological organ.

The fetishist's relation to the phallus makes clear the sociolinguistic/symbolic investment in the phallus. The fetishist demands that there be such a thing as the maternal phallus. By this demand, he falsifies or disavows his perception of female genitals. Disavowal is the simultaneous affirmation and denial of perception. It is a common mode of defence against undesired perceptions (e.g. the oedipal boy disavows women's castration by simply refusing to believe what he sees). The fetishist is the adult who, because of his attachment to the fetish, is 'saved' from psychosis (which is the more typical consequence of disavowal in adults). The fetishist demands that the mother have a genital organ the same as his own. His disavowal functions to ward off threats to his own organ, threats which force him to acknowledge the possibility of its loss. In place of the missing maternal phallus, he will position the fetish (shoe, raincoat, underwear, etc.). The substitutability of the fetish for the maternal phallus is not the effect of a simple coincidence in reality (there is little or no resemblance between the maternal phallus and, say, the raincoat), but is always an effect of signification in so far as the phallus is *already* a signifier. The link between the fetish and the phallus is always already a signifying relation.

> The whole problem of the perversions [incidentally, fetishism is the only perversion for which there is no corresponding neurosis] consists in conceiving how the child, in his relation to the mother, a relation constituted in analysis not by his vital dependence on her but by his dependence on her love, that is to say, by the desire for her desire, identifies himself with the imaginary object of this desire in so far as the mother herself symbolizes it in the phallus.
>
> The phallocentrism produced by this dialectic is all that need concern us here. It is, of course, entirely conditioned by the intrusion of the signifier in man's psyche and is strictly impossible to deduce from any pre-established harmony of this psyche with the nature that it expresses.[52]

The paternal metaphor is the threshold permitting access to the symbolic. It does not presume a Real castration but an acknowledgement by the boy of his willingness to give up his most powerful desires to accept the Law. His 'reward' is the preservation of the penis as a narcissistic organ, and its (provisional) elevation to the position of object of desire for the other. Through the (castrated) other's desire, the penis approximates (even if only on loan, as it were) the phallus. By means of the desire of the other, the male comes to be affirmed as possessing or *having* the phallus.

Women, the mother in particular, must therefore be construed as *not having*, that is, as *lacking* the phallus in order for men to be regarded as having it. Women desire the penis as castrated subjects; men can offer them the sexual organ, object of desire, as a means of secondary access to phallic status. The (imaginary, detachable), penis is not a *representation* or sign of the phallus. For one thing, this would relegate the phallic signifier to the barred position of signified; for another, it would create two parallel orders – organic and symbolic – that are only externally, not constitutively, connected. The signifier is active in giving meaning and value to the organ, i.e., in constituting it as an organ with particular attributes and values. The penis, in other words, does not have the sole right of alignment with the phallus. Not only does the penis act as if it were the 'meaning of the phallus', a series of substitute objects are also capable of taking on this function; a baby (in the equation of penis = baby);[53] the whole of a woman's body;[54] and parts of her body (in hysteria).[55] The penis, as imaginary object, is *already* bound up with signification. It is itself already a signifier, and as such, can function as a *metonymic displacement* of the phallus.

If we take the case of Little Harry, cited by Lacan in his detailed discussion of fetishism,[56] the boy has had ample pre-Oedipal access to the mother's body, having slept in the same bed as her until he was over three.[57] He knew that she had no penis or organ similar to his own. It is also clear that the boy occupied the role of the object of her desire. He takes on the role of phallus *for her*. He disavows any knowledge of genital differences in order to stave off the threat of castration directed towards his own organ, thereby being able to continue his special relationship with the mother. His desire is the desire of the other. He functions as the phallus for her, and for himself.

Harry develops a fondness for caressing shoes, especially those belonging to women he likes. His other symptoms are also relevant to understanding the role of representation in the function of the phallus: he develops a phobia about pendulum clocks (which reminded him of the doctor's surgery when he had an operation for phimosis at the age of two); he impulsively, almost obsessively cuts locks of his own hair without knowing why;[58] and particularly, he develops a mortal dread and fear of amputees:

> a relative came in to visit the family, a man with one leg amputated. Harry could not be induced to enter the room; the moment he had heard the voice of the man outside the door he ran screaming into the bedroom.[59]

Harry thus both affirms and denies, both acknowledges and refuses to accept, the possibility of his own castration:

> To stress the point: if the strength of repression (of the affect) is to be founded in the *interest* of the successor of the feminine phallus, it is the denegation of its absence which will have constructed the memorial. The fetish will become the vehicle both of denying and asseverating the castration.[60]

Shoes, in Harry's case, or shiny noses in the case discussed by Freud,[61] do not function as signs by virtue of their resemblance to the penis. The penis *already* functions as a signifier, an imaginary object, from the moment the boy attributes it to the mother. The fetish is thus not based on a one-to-one representation of the penis, any more than, in Freud's example, a pore of the skin can represent a vagina.[62] The relation is not one of visual resemblance, analogy, nor even contiguity or simultaneity. The child's perception of the mother's lack, and his symbolic use of the last object seen before witnessing the mother's 'absence', including shoes, stockings, underwear, fur, etc. – (those objects the child is likely to see when looking up at his mother) does not adequately explain fetishism. The relation between the maternal phallus and the fetish is not Real. As Freud saw in his analysis of the fetishist who was attracted to shiny noses, the connection is purely verbal, a relation entirely within signification:

> Indeed, if a slipper were, strictly speaking, a displacement of the female organ and no other elements were present to elaborate the primary data, we would consider ourselves faced with a primitive perversion completely beyond the reach of analysis.[63]

The penis takes on the function of the phallus only because it is a mark or trace that is able to signify, indeed, produce, the exclusion of half the population. From being a Real organ, the penis becomes an imaginary object dividing the sexes according to its presence or absence, possessed by some, desired by others; it then functions as a symbolic object (an object of exchange or union) between the sexes. Because the phallus is the term signifying both division and union, the penis is not the only 'object' that is able to serve as its metonym. In different socio-political structures, the phallus seems to function as the signifier of the presence and absence of access to power and self-definition. In spite of Lacan's otherwise universalist claims, he acknowledges at some points in his work that the chain of signifiers in which the phallus finds its context varies historically:

> the phallus is not a question of a form or of an image, or of a phantasy, but rather a signifier, the signifier of desire. In Greek antiquity, the phallus is *not represented by an organ but as an insignia.*[64]

The phallus thus distributes access to the social categories invested with various power relations. In Greece, the family insignia, which served to differentiate one class from another through the exclusion of slaves from access to the family name, functioned as the phallus. In our culture, the presence and absence of the penis serves to differentiate one sex from another, according to the interests of one of them. It can thus, if interpreted socio-politically, be seen to represent some of the ways in which subjects are positioned in different locations within a hierarchized social geography.

For Lacan, the phallus is the 'signifier of signifiers',[65] the term which defines each subject's access to the symbolic order. It is an emblem of the structure of language: the gap in language which makes the sliding of the signifier over the signified and the regulation of the polyvalence and play within language possible. This gap or lack is also the founding trace of the unconscious, constituted as such by the repressed signifier: 'It is the ultimately significative object which appears when all the veils are lifted. Everything related to it is an object of amputations and interdictions ...' When the veils are lifted, there is only the Medusa – woman's castrated genitals, lacking, incomplete, horrifying (for men). Salomé's dance, like strip-tease, can only seduce when at least one veil remains, alluring yet hiding the *nothing* of woman's sex.

> the phallus, that is, *the image of the penis*, is negativity in its place in the specular image. It is what predestines the phallus to embody *jouissance* in the dialectic of desire.

> ... the specular image is the channel taken by the transfusion of the body's libido towards the object. But even though part of it remains preserved from this immersion, concentrating within it the most intimate aspects of auto-eroticism, its position at the 'tip' of the form predisposes it to the phantasy of decrepitude in which is completed its exclusion from the specular image and from the prototype that it constitutes for the world of objects,

> Thus the erectile organ comes to symbolize the place of *jouissance* not in itself, or even in the form of an image, but as a part lacking in the desired image ...[66]

The phallus and power

The phallus and penis can only be aligned if there are those who lack it. It is assumed only on the basis of division and dichotomy, represented by the lack attributed to women. The penis can only enhance one's narcissism if it is somehow distinguished from other organs and parts of the body. It enhances men's narcissism because it constitutes their corporeal unity in relation to women's incompleteness. The penis comes to represent tangibly the differences between the sexes as other organs, in our culture, do not, enabling it to function on an imaginary level to signify presence and absence or fullness and privation.

In spite of Lacan's claims, the phallus is not a 'neutral' term functioning equally for both sexes, positioning them both in the symbolic order. As the word suggests, it is a term privileging masculinity, or rather, the penis. The valorization of the penis and the relegation of female sexual organs to the castrated category are effects of a socio-political system that also enables the phallus to function as the 'signifier or signifiers', giving the child access to a (sexual) identity and speaking position within culture. Its position as a threshold signifier is symptomatic of the assumed patriarchal context in Freud's and Lacan's work.

The phallus cannot be merely a signifier like any other. In Saussure's understanding, the materiality of the signifier is irrelevant to its signifying capacities. For Saussure, only the relations between the signifier and the signified, or relations between signs confer meaning and value on any term. Yet, if the relation between signifier and signified is arbitrary, Saussure describes one relation between signifier and signified as relatively motivated, motivated, that is, by the already existing structure of language. The symbolic function of the phallus envelops the penis as the tangible sign of a privileged masculinity, thus in effect naturalizing male dominance.

In this context, it is significant that although Lacan is at least partially responsible for feminist rereadings of the Freudian concept of penis-envy in terms of the socio-symbolic meaning of the organ, he is also responsible for positing a metonymic relation between an organ and a signifier which may turn out to be just as problematic in feminist terms as Freud's biologism. The penis comes to function as the signified for the phallic signifier.

Lacan's distinction between the penis and the phallus enables Freud's biologistic account of male superiority and women's penis-envy to be explained in linguistic and symbolic, and thus historical terms. This had the major advantage of enabling the possibility of change to be articulated. Yet although Lacan's account is directed to the phallus as signifier, not to the penis as an organ, it is committed to an *a priori* privilege of the masculine that is difficult, if not impossible, to dislodge. It is unclear if Lacan does distinguish his position from Freud's as sharply as I have suggested, when one reads passages like the following:

> the fact that the penis is dominant in the shaping of the body-image is evidence of [an autonomous, non-biological imaginary anatomy]. Though this may shock the champions of the autonomy of female sexuality, such dominance *is a fact* and one moreover which *cannot be put down to cultural influences alone.*[67]

Lacan has been avidly defended by a number of feminists for his use of the phallic signifier in place of the male sexual organ. Ellie Ragland-Sullivan, for example, argues that:

> the phallic signifier is intrinsically neutral, meaningless in its own right, and only takes its power from association catalyzed in the Oedipal drama ... Lacan is describing first causes, not approving them.[68]

Her defence of Lacan is strongly reminiscent of Juliet Mitchell's justification of Freud's phallocentrism a decade earlier in *Psychoanalysis and Feminism*. Mitchell's defence of Freud consisted in claiming that psychoanalysis merely provides a description of patriarchal power relations. It explains the transmission and reproduction of sex roles and their different social values. Both claim the structural neutrality of oedipal or phallic law in positioning the two sexes as subjects:

> Sexual difference can only be the consequence of a division; *without this division it would cease to exist.* But it must exist because no human being can become a subject outside the division into two sexes. One must take up a position as either a man or a woman. Such a position is by no means identical with one's biological sexual characteristics, nor is it a position of which one can be very confident ...[69]

Mitchell's coeditor, Jacqueline Rose, acknowledges that the phallic signifier should remain arbitrary and purely conventional in its relations to the penis and the attributes of masculinity. She asks 'why that necessary symbolization and the privileged status of the phallus appear as interdependent in the structuring and securing (never secure) of human subjectivity?'[70] This is a crucial question. It locates the key differences between Lacan's feminist defenders and critics. Given that his work *does* provide a description of our culture in its past and present forms, the question remains as to how relevant and useful or constricting and precommitting his understanding is for conceptualizing a non-patriarchal future. Contrary to Mitchell, Ragland-Sullivan and others, I will claim that the phallic signifier is *not* a neutral 'third' term against which both sexes are analogously or symmetrically positioned. The relation between the penis and phallus is not arbitrary, but socially and politically motivated. The two sexes come to occupy the positive and negative positions not for arbitrary reasons, or with arbitrary effects. It is motivated by the already existing structure of patriarchal power, and its effects guarantee the reproduction of this particular form of social organization and no other. They are distinguished *not* on the basis of (Saussurian 'pure') difference, but in terms of dichotomous opposition or distinction; not, that is, as contraries ('A' and 'B'), but as contradictories ('A' and 'not-A'). In relations governed by pure difference, *each* term is defined by all the others; there can be no privileged term which somehow dispenses with its (constitutive) structuring and value in relations to other terms. Distinctions, binary oppositions, are relations based on one rather than many terms, the one term generating a non-reciprocal definition of the other as its negative. The presence and absence of *one* term defines *both* positions in the dichotomy.[71] Mitchell believes that the subject must occupy a symbolic position as either male or female. Yet it is surely arbitrary, in the sense of social or conventional, that the continuum of differences between gradations of sexual difference along a continuum is divided into categories only according to the presence or absence of the one, male, organ.

Lacan, as usual, is ambiguous. If he blurs the boundary between the biological and the symbolic, he also helps to undo the certainty that many men have about their phallic position:

> It can be said that this signifier is chosen because it is the most tangible element in the real of sexual copulation and also the most symbolic in the literal (typographical) sense of the term, since it is equivalent there to the (logical) copula.[72]

As the logical or grammatical copula, it serves to connect two terms together while disappearing or evacuating itself of any identity of its own. It functions to unite (and disappear) or to separate and divide. This fundamental ambiguity or duplicity in the term will provide a vulnerable, contradictory point within male relations and sexual domination. As signifier, the phallus is not an object to be acquired or an identity to be achieved. It is only through the desire of the other that one's own position – as either being or having – the phallus is possible.

To summarize in point form:

(1) the phallus is the crucial signifier in the distribution of power, authority and a speaking position, a kind of mark or badge of a social position;

(2) the phallus is the signifier of lack marking castration. As such, it also signifies presence or possession, for only in opposition to the absence of the term does its presence have any meaning or value. It thus signifies what men (think they) *have* and what women (are considered to) *lack*;

(3) the phallus is the 'signifier of signifiers', the representative of signification and language. By means of the phallus, the subject comes to occupy the position of 'I' in discourse; by means of its signification as lack, the subject can use language in place of a direct or unmediated relation to the Real, a relation that it must relinquish;

(4) as a signifier, the phallus has no given content or signified; it is 'filled in' only in concrete contexts, in momentary alignments with other signifiers. For this reason, it is capable of enveloping many objects or bodily organs – the child, the woman's body, the penis, the hysterogenic zone have all functioned as phallic for subjects Freud analysed;

(5) the phallus designates the object of desire. It is the heir to the role of the *objet a*. It signifies the desire of the other, which is always organized with reference to the Other;

(6) the phallus is the condition of symbolic exchange relations which Lévi-Strauss:[73] saw as the condition of culture. The phallus is both the object circulated in ritually inscribed networks of social exchange, and in the rules which govern the direction and flow of the object;[74]

(7) the phallus represents the name-of-the-father, through which the subject is positioned in culture;

(8) the phallus is the signifier which established the subject's unconscious, an internalized locus of the Other and the repository of repressed desire.

It is thus simultaneously and indissolubly the mark of sexual difference (and identity), the signifier of the speaking position in language, and the order governing exchange relations.

Notes

1 See the chronology in Madan Sarup, *Jacques Lacan* (Hemel Hempstead: Harvester, 1992); Elizabeth Wright (ed.), *Feminism and Psychoanalysis: A Critical Dictionary* (Oxford: Blackwell, 1992), p. 201ff.

2 See Robert Con Davis's discussion of this issue in terms suggested by George Steiner, *Lacan and Narration* (Baltimore and London: Johns Hopkins University Press, 1983), pp. 855–6.

3 Jane Gallop, *Feminism and Psychoanalysis: The Daughter's Seduction* (London: Macmillan, 1982).

4 Jane Gallop, *Reading Lacan* (Ithaca and London: Cornell University Press, 1985), p. 147; see also her discussion of Lacan's decisive paper the 'Rapport de Rome' (published as 'The Function and Field of Speech and Language in Psychoanalysis', *Ecrits: A Selection*, trans. Alan Sheridan (New York: W. W. Norton, 1977), which divided him from the American establishment and helped create his distinctive approach and style (*Reading Lacan*, pp. 55–6).

5 See Teresa Brennan (ed.), 'Introduction', *Between Feminism and Psychoanalysis* (London: Routledge, 1989), pp. 9, 18.

6 Samuel Weber, *Return to Freud: Jacques Lacan's Dislocation of Psychoanalysis*, trans. Michael Levine (Cambridge: Cambridge University Press, 1991) gives the history of Freud's thought on castration and its influence on Lacan's theory (p. 140ff.).

7 Gallop, *Reading Lacan*, p. 55.

8 Cynthia Chase, 'Desire and Identification in Lacan and Kristeva', in Richard Feldstein and Judith Roof (eds), *Feminism and Psychoanalysis* (Ithaca and London: Cornell University Press, 1989), pp. 66–7.

9 See Steven Connor, *Theory and Cultural Value* (Oxford: Blackwell, 1992), p. 44; Margaret Whitford, *Luce Irigaray: Philosophy in the Feminine* (London: Routledge, 1991), p. 178ff.; and Gallop, *Feminism and Psychoanalysis*, p. 20: Gallop suggests that metonymy can also be phallic, in contrast to Whitford (and Irigaray), who suggest that it is a feminine mode.

10 Catherine Belsey, *Critical Practice* (London: Methuen, 1980), p. 65.

11 See Elizabeth Wright, *Psychoanalytic Criticism: Theory into Practice* (London: Methuen, 1984), p. 111.

12 Charles Levin, 'Lacanian Psychoanalysis and Feminist Metatheory', in A. and M. Kroker (eds), *The Hysterical Male: New Feminist Theory* (London: Macmillan, 1991), p. 245; Chase, 'Desire and Identification in Lacan and Kristeva', p. 72.

13 Juliet Mitchell and Jacqueline Rose (eds), *Feminine Sexuality: Jacques Lacan and the 'Ecole Freudienne'* (London: Macmillan, 1982), p. 56.

14 Gallop, *Feminism and Psychoanalysis*, pp. 18–20.

15 Ibid., p. 20.

16 See Mary Ann Doane, 'Woman's Stake: Filming the Female Body', reproduced here in Part VI.

17 Diana J. Fuss, ' "Essentially Speaking": Luce Irigaray's Language of Essence', in Nancy Fraser and Sandra Lee Bartky (eds), *Revaluing French Feminism: Critical Essays on Difference, Agency, and Culture* (Bloomington: Indiana University Press, 1992), p. 104.

18 Gallop, *Feminism and Psychoanalysis*, p. 97.

19 Chase, 'Desire and Identification in Lacan and Kristeva', p. 77. Weber is not of this opinion: he says that the phallus is 'a *specific*, determinate signifier, not a transcendental one' (*Return to Freud*, p. 149).

20 Gallop, *Reading Lacan*, p. 26.

21 See also J. Laplanche and J. P. Pontalis, *The Language of Psychoanalysis*

(London: Karnac Books, 1988), p. 455ff. (on transference) and pp. 92–3 (on countertransference).

22 Shoshana Felman (ed.), *Literature and Psychoanalysis: The Question of Reading: Otherwise* (Baltimore and London: Johns Hopkins University Press, 1982), p. 7.

23 Gallop, *Reading Lacan*, p. 30; see the essays in Con Davis, *Lacan and Narration*, and his edited volume, *Fictional Fathers: Lacanian Readings of the Text* (Amherst: University of Massachusetts Press, 1981); and, one of various essays which do just what Gallop says a Lacanian reading ought not, Earl G. Ingersoll's 'Lacan, Browning, and the Murderous Voyeur: "Porphyria's Lover" and "My Last Duchess"', *Victorian Poetry* (Summer 1990).

24 Gallop, *Reading Lacan*, p. 30.

Reading 10 (Rose)

25 Lacan, 'The Phallic Phase and the Subjective Import of the Castration Complex', in Mitchell and Rose (eds), *Feminine Sexuality*, p. 117.

26 Lacan, 'Les formations de l'inconscient', *Bulletin de Psychologie*, II (1857–8), p. 13.

27 Lacan, 'The Meaning of the Phallus', in Mitchell and Rose (eds), *Feminine Sexuality*, p. 80.

28 Lacan, 'Les formations de l'inconscient', p. 14.

29 Ibid., p. 8.

30 M. Safouan, *Etudes sur l'Oedipe (le champ freudien)* (Paris: Seuil, 1974), p. 9.

31 Lacan, 'Intervention on Transference', in Mitchell and Rose (eds), *Feminine Sexuality*, p. 69.

32 Lacan, 'L'envers de la psychanalyse': Le séminaire XVIII, 1969–70 (unpublished typescript).

33 Safouan, *Etudes sur l'Oedipe*, p. 127.

34 Lacan, 'D'une question préliminaire à tout traitement possible de la psychose', *Ecrits* (Paris: Seuil, 1966), pp. 554–5, and in *Ecrits: A Selection*, trans. Alan Sheridan (London: Tavistock, 1977), p. 198.

35 Ernest Jones, 'The Phallic Phase', *International Journal of Psychoanalysis*, XXIV (1933), pp. 1–33.

36 Lacan, 'The Phallic Phase and the Subjective Import of the Castration Complex'; *Scilicet*, review of Lacan's series, *le champ freudien*, nos 1–VII (Paris: Seuil, 1968–76).

37 Lacan, 'Feminine Sexuality in Psychoanalytic Doctrine', in Mitchell and Rose (eds), *Feminine Sexuality*.

38 Lacan, 'L'instance de la lettre dans l'inconscient ou la raison depuis Freud', *Ecrits*, p. 499; *Ecrits: A Selection*, p. 151.

39 Lacan, *Encore*: Le séminaire XX (Paris: Seuil, 1975), p. 150; it is not, therefore, a question of philology and *then* the phallus, as John Forrester argues,

but of sexuality/the phallus *as* language (John Forrester, 'Philology and the Phallus', in C. MacCabe (ed.), *The Talking Cure: Essays in Psychoanalysis and Language* (London: Macmillan, 1981).

40 Lacan, 'The Phallic Phase and the Subjective Import of the Castration Complex', p. 113.

41 Lacan, 'The Meaning of the Phallus', p. 82.

42 Ibid., p. 82.

43 Lacan, 'Guiding Remarks for a Congress on Feminine Sexuality', in Mitchell and Rose (eds), *Feminine Sexuality*, p. 90.

44 Joan Riviere, 'Womanliness as a Masquerade', *International Journal of Psychoanalysis* X (1929).

45 Lacan, 'Guiding Remarks for a Congress on Feminine Sexuality', in Mitchell and Rose (eds), *Feminine Sexuality*, p. 89.

46 Ibid., p. 95.

47 M. Safouan, *La sexualité féminine dans la doctrine freudienne* (*le champ freudien*) (Paris: Seuil, 1976), p. 110.

Reading 11 (Grosz)

48 To avoid charges of naturalism, or the assumption of a natural harmony between the sexes, Lacan refuses to describe female sexuality as complementary to male sexuality; instead he describes it as 'supplementary', excessive, or 'beyond' the phallus (see Lacan, 'God and the Jouissance of The Woman', in Mitchell and Rose (eds), *Feminine Sexuality*, p. 144). Derrida also uses the notion of the supplement to confound or unhinge the (phallogocentric) binary opposition between lack and excess (Jacques Derrida, *Dissemination*, trans. B. Johnson, Chicago: University of Chicago Press, 1981). Yet if we assume that a supplementarity describes the relation between female and male sexuality, even if Lacan sees female pleasure as a reserve largely untapped by the phallus – in this case, by its degree of distance from phallic sexuality – the phallus remains the fixed point of reference for all sexualities, as far as psychoanalysis is concerned.

49 Lacan, 'L'instance de la lettre dans l'inconscient ou la raison depuis Freud', *Ecrits*, pp. 851–2.

50 As Nancy Jay, in her paper, 'Gender and Dichotomy' (*Feminist Studies*, 7 (1) Spring 1981) points out, relations of difference, described in logical symbols as a relation between A and B, are reduced to an oppositional form in phallocentric discourses, which take the form of relations between A and not-A. The presence and absence of a single term defines the oppositional pair; while relations of difference, by contrast, are based on the presence of different attributes for the terms in the pair.

51 S. Leclaire quoted in A. Lemaire, *Jacques Lacan* (London: Routledge & Kegan Paul, London, 1977), p. 86.

52 Lacan, *Ecrits: A Selection*, pp. 197–8.

53 See Freud, 'On the Transformation of Instinct as Exemplified in Anal Eroticism', *SE*, vol. 17 (1918), pp. 128–9 and 132–3.

54 Freud, 'On Narcissism: An Introduction', *SE*, vol. 14 (1915).

55 Freud, *The Interpretation of Dreams*, *SE*, vols. 4 and 5 (1900), pp. 387, 390.

56 J. Lacan and W. Granoff, 'Fetishism: The Symbolic, the Imaginary, and the Real', in M. Balint (ed.), *Perversions, Psychodynamics and Therapy* (London: Tavistock, 1956).

57 A. Lorand, 'Fetishism in *Statu Nascendi*', *International Journal of Psychoanalysis*, 2 (1930), p. 423.

58 Ibid., p. 422.

59 Ibid.

60 Lacan and Granoff, 'Fetishism', p. 268.

61 Freud, 'Fetishism', *SE*, vol. 19 (1919).

62 Freud, 'The Unconscious', *SE*, vol. 14 (1914).

63 Lacan and Granoff, 'Fetishism', p. 268.

64 Lacan, quoted in Anthony Wilden, *Speech and Language in Psychoanalysis* (Baltimore: Johns Hopkins University Press, 1981), p. 187; emphasis added.

65 The phallus signifies the act of signification itself, seeing that it is the signifier which constitutes both lack, and functions to fill the lack, just as the sign does in the absence of the thing. The Sanskrit noun, *lakshana* (Lacan, 'The Function and Field of Speech and Language', *Ecrits: A Selection*, p. 104 and fn. 108) is both the mark, token, sign, or rather, signifier, and the 'sign or organ of virility' (Wilden, *Speech and Language*, p. 151).

66 Lacan, *Ecrits: A Selection*, pp. 319–20; emphasis added.

67 Lacan, 'Some Reflections on the Ego', *International Journal of Psychoanalysis*, 34 (1953), p. 13; emphasis added.

68 Ellie Ragland-Sullivan, 'Jacques Lacan: Feminism and the Problem of Gender Identity', *Sub-Stance*, 36 (1982), p. 10.

69 Mitchell, in Mitchell and Rose (eds), *Feminine Sexuality*, p. 6; emphasis added.

70 Ibid., p. 56.

71 Along with Nancy Jay ('Gender and Dichotomy'), Anthony Wilden will posit a difference between difference and distinction. Difference is a term capable of defining *analog* or continuous relations between terms, while distinction or (binary) opposition refers to *digital* relations between discontinuous terms. Distinctions rely on an empty space, a lack, dividing its two terms, which philosophers have described as the 'excluded middle'. Difference, by contrast, implies no necessary gap or boundary separating one term from another. See Wilden, *System and Structure: Essays in Communication and Exchange* (London: Tavistock, 1972), ch. 7, 'Analog and Digital Communication: On Negation, Signification and Meaning'.

72 Lacan, *Ecrits: A Selection*, p. 287.

73 Claude Lévi-Strauss, *Structural Anthropology* (New York; Basic Books, 1961).

74 Wilden refers to Malinowski's analysis, in *Argonauts of the Western Pacific*, of the ritualized circulation of 'gifts' in relations of exchange in Kula society. This serves as an illustration of the circulation of an order that can only be seen as the exchange of the signifier, not a trade governed by economic or

biological imperatives. The objects exchanged are not just particularly use-ful; often they cannot be used – bracelets which can't be worn or used as ornaments, shells which have no use value: 'the circuit of exchange consists in two vast circles of channels along which "bits" of one type are constantly substituted for "bits" of the other type. Thousands of partners are provided with dyadic links through the exchange, but the dyads are a function of the circuit as a whole, not of any individual connections ... This highly complex network of relations is governed by strict communicational rules as regards the flow of the "Symbolic object" (bracelets move from left hand to right hand and from north-west to south-west and never in the other direction) but the "value" of the object "owed" is a matter of unarticulated reciprocity not of convention' (Wilden, *System and Structure*, p. 256).

Part V
Julia Kristeva: the Abject and the Semiotic

Julia Kristeva transforms Lacan's categories of Imaginary and Symbolic into, respectively, the semiotic and the symbolic. Her innovation is to suggest that the semiotic continues to make itself felt even when the subject has acceded to the symbolic, and that signification itself comes about through the interaction of the two realms.

Kristeva arrived in Paris in 1966, from Bulgaria, where, as Toril Moi describes, she quickly became a central figure in Left Bank intellectual life. Her intellectual background – Marxist, formalist and philosophical – formed a fruitful conjunction with the structuralist and psychoanalytic thought she encountered in France, as a woman and as a 'stranger', factors which combined to influence her own project. The philosophical group *Tel Quel* to which she belonged espoused Maoist Marxism for a time, until a visit to China in 1974 and increasing information about the repressive aspects of the regime suggested that this enthusiasm was misplaced; to some extent, a (qualified) interest in the USA then replaced the Chinese one. More recently, Kristeva has published two novels.[1]

The Kristevan subject

What Kristeva describes as 'the semiotic' is the pre-Oedipal realm where the infant exists in the 'chora',[2] a state characterized by the pulsions of the mother's body and the infant's own drives. When experienced from the standpoint of the symbolic, the semiotic takes the form of a disruptive pressure on ordered language, as word-play, concentration on colour and negativity (death), gaps in sense, laughter, even tending towards meaninglessness. As Elizabeth Grosz says,

> In animating the child's body, the semiotic transfers its particular characteristics onto signifying elements: phonemic units are produced from the energies and impulses of the drives, creating repetition, allusion, rhyme, intonation, rhythm and the other specifically and irreducibly material elements of representation.[3]

Such tendencies in language are most clearly seen in poetry and avant-garde texts, which, as Kristeva puts it, operate by 'cracking the socio-symbolic order, splitting it open, changing vocabulary, syntax, the word itself'.[4]

Abjection

This coinage of Kristeva's refers to the state the subject falls into when it is threatened with a return to the pre-symbolic, maternal realm. The relationship between abjection and the semiotic is not absolutely clear, and Kristeva has been criticized for moving from the philosophical and aesthetic of the semiotic to the moral realm of the abject.[5] It seems that the abject is one way of reacting to the threatened encroachment of the semiotic, perhaps constituting its borderline in the symbolic. Paul Smith, however, contrasts the abject unfavourably with the dialectic of semiotic and symbolic, suggesting that the abject displaces the object in psychoanalytic theory, according to Kristeva, as it is not objects at all against which subjects define themselves. As if it were similar to the Lacanian phallus, Smith describes the abject as 'a term of transcendence', without a dialectical other.[6]

As the child is socialized, it progressively learns to reject the mother through rituals of toilet training, cleanliness and eating habits; it is as if the mother gives the child all the skills needed in order to leave her behind. What Kristeva calls 'the rite of defilement'[7] maintains the distance between the corporeal maternal realm and the paternal symbolic by allowing them 'to brush lightly against each other'; however, when order and identity are disturbed in the symbolic, the subject is threatened with a return to the maternal which was supposed to be abandoned. Kristeva describes the symbolic, and its implications for the subject's attitude to her/his body, as 'a totally different universe of socially signifying performances where embarrassment, shame, guilt, desire, etc. come into play – the order of the phallus'.[8]

As with the semiotic, what is excluded to form the 'clean and proper' body constantly exerts pressure on the symbolic order, threatening disruption and reminding the subject of the impossibility of transcending the corporeal origins of subjectivity. As Elizabeth Grosz says,

> Understanding abjection involves examining the ways in which the inside and outside of the body are constituted, the spaces between the self and the other, and the means by which the child's body comes to be a bounded, unified whole [... and] gains access to symbolization.[9]

Thus the abject marks the site of both the genesis and the obliteration of the subject, which may – and in the end must – slip back into the non-sentience and chaos it came from. In her essay '*Alien* and the Monstrous Feminine', Barbara Creed analyses horror films about, in particular, death-dealing reproductive bodies as centring on an 'abject' fear of the reproductive powers of the archaic mother and her body. She suggests that such films are our version of the 'defilement rites' which mark the boundary between clean and proper symbolic order, and abyssal, impure abject.[10]

As Kristeva vividly describes in the extract reproduced here, occurrences of abjection are marked by the subject's disgust, nausea and retching: in her case, at the skin on milk. Maud Ellmann, in an essay on the abjection of T. S. Eliot's *The Waste Land*, links this episode of self-expulsion from *Powers of Horror* with the '*fort-da*' scene in Freud's 'Beyond the Pleasure Principle', similarly about expelling the self. She argues that the child is fascinated by the 'drama' of casting the bobbin away, not by the bobbin itself, and to show this is the case experiments with his own person: he hides from his reflection in the mirror and says, 'Baby o-o-o-o!' [Baby gone!]. Just as Kristeva describes the process of abjection here – 'I expel *myself*' – so the child, by casting '*himself* out, founds his subjectivity by rehearsing his annihilation in a game that can only end in death'.[11]

Virginia Woolf

Makiko Minow-Pinkney's book, *Virginia Woolf and the Problem of the Subject: Feminine Writing in the Major Novels*, is an attempt to read Woolf in the light of Kristeva, and in a close textual manner which is often uncommon in discussions of Kristevan or Lacanian theory. Minow-Pinkney puts her reading of Woolf into the context of Woolf's harsh treatment at the hands of certain feminist critics (Elaine Showalter,[12] Sidney Janet Kaplan, and, as a representative of the

Marxist camp, Terry Eagleton), and notes that more recently other critics such as Jane Marcus (as well as Toril Mol and Rachel Bowlby) have
aimed to 'retrieve the radical political dimension of Woolf's writing'.[13]
Minow-Pinkney's reading of Woolf's novels emphasizes the elements of
semiotic slippage and threatened irruption of repressed material which
feature in Kristeva's theory of art's revolutionary potential. She claims
that Woolf's experimental novels do not, as has been argued, retreat
into effete modernism, but can 'best be seen as a feminist subversion of
the deepest formal principles – of the very definitions of narrative, writing, the subject – of a patriarchal social order'.[14] This is especially the
case in view of Woolf's own writings on patriarchy and gender, her conviction that cultural training (or lack of it) was at the root of women's
social role,[15] and her interest in androgyny as a position from which to
write: 'a dialectic of symbolic and semiotic,' as Minow-Pinkney puts it.[16]

Minow-Pinkney shows that Kristeva's concept of subjectivity, the
'subject in process', and of the semiotic modality, both contribute to the
disruption in Woolf's texts of narrative form,[17] without doing away with
such a form (in a total surrender to the semiotic) altogether. In this
Woolf conforms to Kristeva's own definition of poetic language, as
'poised over the tension between thetic and semiotic practices'.[18] As
Kristeva says, 'no signifying practice can be without [the thetic subject,
but ...] the semiotic, which also precedes it, constantly tears it open,
and this transgression brings about all the various transformations of
the signifying practice that are called "creation" '.[19]

In the extract reproduced here, from Minow-Pinkney's chapter on
Woolf's novel *Mrs Dalloway*, a meticulous analysis of one passage
shows the construction of a Kristevan 'subjective haziness', while another discusses Woolf's ability to make chronology ambiguous, and to
make a 'radically heterogeneous' text look at first sight quite conventional. It is characteristic of Woolf's style that '[w]henever we try to pinpoint the locus of the subject, we get lost in a discursive mist', and
although this is an effect of Woolf's style which other critics have noted,
the Kristevan framework links it to a political rather than simply an aesthetic dissidence. In her book *Reconstructing Desire*, for instance, Jean
Wyatt analyses such texts as Kate Chopin's *The Awakening* in a
Kristevan framework, but sees this element simply as something to be
noted for its own sake.[20] However, as Minow-Pinkney says later in the
chapter on *Mrs Dalloway*, within Woolf's apparent conformism 'her
writing tries to give voice to the specificity of a female subject who is
outside any principle of identity-to-self, which can identify with multiple scenes without fully integrating herself into them'.[21]

12 JULIA KRISTEVA

Approaching Abjection

No Beast is there without glimmer of infinity,
No eye so vile nor abject that brushes not
Against lightning from on high, now tender, now fierce.
                                    Victor Hugo, *La Légende des siècles*

Neither subject nor object

There looms, within abjection, one of those violent, dark revolts of
being, directed against a threat that seems to emanate from an exorbi-
tant outside or inside rejected beyond the scope of the possible, the tol-
erable, the thinkable. It lies there, quite close, but it cannot be
assimilated. It beseeches, worries, and fascinates desire, which, nevertheless, does not let itself be seduced. Apprehensive, desire turns aside;
sickened, it rejects. A certainty protects it from the shameful – a certainty of which it is proud holds on to it. But simultaneously, just the
same, that impetus, that spasm, that leap is drawn toward an elsewhere
as tempting as it is condemned. Unflaggingly, like an inescapable
boomerang, a vortex of summons and repulsion places the one haunted
by it, literally beside himself.

When I am beset by abjection, the twisted braid of affects and
thoughts I call by such a name does not have, properly speaking, a
definable *object*. The abject is not an ob-ject facing me, which I name or
imagine. Nor is it an ob-jest, an otherness ceaselessly fleeing in a systematic quest of desire. What is abject is not my correlative, which, providing me with someone or something else as support, would allow me
to be more or less detached and autonomous. The abject has only one

quality of the object – that of being opposed to *I*. If the object, however, through its opposition, settles me within the fragile texture of a desire for meaning, which, as a matter of fact, makes me ceaselessly and infinitely homologous to it, what is *abject*, on the contrary, the jettisoned object, is radically excluded and draws me toward the place where meaning collapses. A certain 'ego' that merged with its master, a superego, has flatly driven it away. It lies outside, beyond the set, and does not seem to agree to the latter's rules of the game. And yet, from its place of banishment, the abject does not cease challenging its master. Without a sign (for him), it beseeches a discharge, a convulsion, a crying out. To each ego its object, to each superego its abject. It is not the white expanse or slack boredom of repression, not the translations and transformations of desire that wrench bodies, nights, and discourse; rather it is a brutish suffering that 'I' puts up with, sublime and devastated, for 'I' deposits it to the father's account [*verse au père – père-version*]: I endure it, for I imagine that such is the desire of the other. A massive and sudden emergence of uncanniness, which, familiar as it might have been in an opaque and forgotten life, now harries me as radically separate, loathsome. Not me. Not that. But not nothing, either. A 'something' that I do not recognize as a thing. A weight of meaninglessness, about which there is nothing insignificant, and which crushes me. On the edge of non-existence and hallucination, of a reality that, if I acknowledge it, annihilates me. There, abject and abjection are my safeguards. The primers of my culture.

The improper/unclean

Loathing an item of food, a piece of filth, waste, or dung. The spasms and vomiting that protect me. The repugnance, the retching that thrusts me to the side and turns me away from defilement, sewage, and muck. The shame of compromise, of being in the middle of treachery. The fascinated start that leads me toward and separates me from them.

Food loathing is perhaps the most elementary and most archaic form of abjection. When the eyes see or the lips touch that skin on the surface of milk – harmless, thin as a sheet of cigarette paper, pitiful as a nail paring – I experience a gagging sensation and, still farther down, spasms in the stomach, the belly; and all the organs shrivel up the body, provoke tears and bile, increase heartbeat, cause forehead and hands to perspire. Along with sight-clouding dizziness, *nausea* makes me balk at that milk cream, separates me from the mother and father who proffer it. 'I' want none of that element, sign of their desire; 'I' do not want to listen, 'I' do not assimilate it, 'I' expel it. But since the food is not an 'other' for 'me', who am only in their desire, I expel *myself*, I spit *myself* out, I abject *myself* within the same motion through which 'I' claim to establish *myself*. That detail, perhaps an insignificant one, but one that they ferret out, emphasize, evaluate, that trifle turns me inside out, guts sprawling; it is thus that *they* see that 'I' am in the process of becoming an other at the expense of my own death. During that course in which 'I' become, I give birth to myself amid the violence of sobs, of vomit. Mute protest of the symptom, shattering violence of a convulsion that, to be sure, is inscribed in a symbolic system, but in which, without either wanting or being able to become integrated in order to answer to it, it reacts, it abreacts. It abjects.

The corpse (or cadaver: *cadere*, to fall), that which has irremediably come a cropper, is cesspool, and death; it upsets even more violently the one who confronts it as fragile and fallacious chance. A wound with blood and pus, or the sickly, acrid smell of sweat, of decay, does not *signify* death. In the presence of signified death – a flat encephalograph, for instance – I would understand, react, or accept. No, as in true theater, without makeup or masks, refuse and corpses *show me* what I permanently thrust aside in order to live. These body fluids, this defilement, this shit are what life withstands, hardly and with difficulty, on the part of death. There, I am at the border of my condition as a living being. My body extricates itself, as being alive, from that border. Such wastes drop so that I might live, until, from loss to loss, nothing remains in me and my entire body falls beyond the limit – *cadere*, cadaver. If dung signifies the other side of the border, the place where I am not and which permits me to be, the corpse, the most sickening of wastes, is a border that has encroached upon everything. It is no longer I who expel, 'I' is expelled. The border has become an object. How can I be without border? That elsewhere that I imagine beyond the present, or that I hallucinate so that I might, in a present time, speak to you, conceive of you – it is now here, jetted, abjected, into 'my' world. Deprived of world, therefore, I *fall in a faint*. In that compelling, raw, insolent thing in the morgue's full sunlight, in that thing that no longer matches and therefore no longer signifies anything, I behold the breaking down of a world that has erased its borders: fainting away. The corpse, seen without God and outside of science, is the utmost of abjection. It is death infecting life. Abject. It is something rejected from which one does not part, from which one does not protect oneself as from an object. Imaginary uncanniness and real threat, it beckons to us and ends up engulfing us.

It is thus not lack of cleanliness or health that causes abjection but what disturbs identity, system, order. What does not respect borders, positions, rules. The in-between, the ambiguous, the composite. The traitor, the liar, the criminal with a good conscience, the shameless rapist, the killer who claims he is a savior. ... Any crime, because it draws attention to the fragility of the law, is abject, but premeditated crime, cunning murder, hypocritical revenge are even more so because they heighten the display of such fragility. He who denies morality is not abject; there can be grandeur in amorality and even in crime that flaunts its disrespect for the law – rebellious, liberating, and suicidal crime. Abjection, on the other hand, is immoral, sinister, scheming, and shady: a terror that dissembles, a hatred that smiles, a passion that uses the body for barter instead of inflaming it, a debtor who sells you up, a friend who stabs you ....

In the dark halls of the museum that is now what remains of Auschwitz, I see a heap of children's shoes, or something like that, something I have already seen elsewhere, under a Christmas tree, for instance, dolls I believe. The abjection of Nazi crime reaches its apex when death, which, in any case, kills me, interferes with what, in my living universe, is supposed to save me from death: childhood, science, among other things.

13 TORIL MOI

Language, Femininity, Revolution

The acquisition of language

We have seen how Kristevan semiotics emphasizes the marginal and the heterogeneous as that which can subvert the central structures of traditional linguistics. In order to show how Kristeva can posit language as being at once structured and heterogeneous, and why this view presupposes an emphasis on language as discourse uttered by a speaking subject, it is necessary to study her theory of the acquisition of language as it appears in her monumental doctoral thesis *La Révolution du lan-*

gage poétique, published in Paris in 1974. Philip E. Lewis has pointed out that all of Kristeva's work up to 1974 constitutes an extensive attempt to define or apprehend what she calls the *procès de signifiance* or the 'signifying process'.[22] In order to approach this problem, she displaces Lacan's distinction between the Imaginary and the Symbolic into a distinction between the *semiotic* and the *symbolic*.[23] The interaction between these two terms then constitutes the signifying process.

The semiotic is linked to the pre-Oedipal primary processes, the basic pulsions of which Kristeva sees as predominantly anal and oral; and as simultaneously dichotomous (life v. death, expulsion v. introjection) and heterogeneous. The endless flow of pulsions is gathered up in the *chora* (from the Greek word for enclosed space, womb), which Plato in the *Timaeus* defines as 'an invisible and formless being which receives all things and in some mysterious way partakes of the intelligible, and is most incomprehensible'.[24] Kristeva appropriates and redefines Plato's concept and concludes that the *chora* is neither a sign nor a position, but 'a wholly provisional articulation that is essentially mobile and con-stituted of movements and their ephemeral stases. ... Neither model nor copy, it is anterior to and underlies figuration and therefore also specularization, and only admits analogy with vocal or kinetic rhythm' (*Révolution*, p. 24).[25]

For Kristeva, *signifiance* is a question of positioning. The semiotic continuum must be split if signification is to be produced. This splitting (*coupure*) of the semiotic *chora* is the *thetic* phase (from *thesis*) and it enables the subject to attribute differences and thus signification to what was the ceaseless heterogeneity of the *chora*. Kristeva follows Lacan in positing the mirror phase as the first step that 'opens the way for the constitution of all objects which from now on will be detached from the semiotic *chora*' (*Révolution*, p. 44), and the Oedipal phase with its threat of castration as the moment in which the process of sepa-ration or splitting is fully achieved. Once the subject has entered into the Symbolic Order, the *chora* will be more or less successfully repressed and can be perceived only as pulsional *pressure* on symbolic language: as contradictions, meaninglessness, disruption, silences and absences in the symbolic language. The *chora* is a rhythmic pulsion rather than a new language. It constitutes, in other words, the hetero-geneous, disruptive dimension of language, that which can never be caught up in the closure of traditional linguistic theory.

Kristeva is acutely aware of the contradictions involved in trying to theorize the untheorizable *chora*, a contradiction located at the centre of the semiotic enterprise. She writes:

Being, because of its explanatory metalinguistic force, an agent of social
cohesion, semiotics contributes to the formation of that reassuring image
which every society offers itself when it understands everything, down to
and including the practices which voluntarily expend it.[26]

If Kristeva nevertheless argues that semiotics should replace linguistics,
it is in the belief that although this new science is always already caught
up in the multiple networks of conflicting ideologies, it can still *unsettle*
these frameworks:

Semanalysis carries on the semiotic discovery ... it places itself at the service of the social law which requires systematization, communication,
exchange. But if it is to do this, it must inevitably respect a further, more
recent requirement – and one which neutralizes the phantom of 'pure science': the subject of the semiotic metalanguage must, however briefly, call
himself in question, must emerge from the protective shell of a transcendental ego within a logical system, and so restore his condition with that
negativity – drive-governed, but also social, political and historical – which
rends and renews the social code.[27]

It is already possible to distinguish here the theme of revolution within
Kristeva's linguistic theory. Before we approach this question, however,
we must take a closer look at her views of the relationship between language and femininity.

Femininity as marginality

Kristeva flatly refuses to define 'woman': 'To believe that one "is a
woman" is almost as absurd and obscurantist as to believe that one "is a
man"', she states in an interview with women from the 'psychanalyse et
politique' group published in 1974.[28] Though political reality (the fact
that patriarchy defines women and oppresses them accordingly) still
makes it necessary to campaign in the name of women, it is important
to recognize that in this struggle a woman cannot *be*: she can only exist
negatively, as it were, through her refusal of that which is given: 'I
therefore understand by "woman"', she continues, 'that which cannot
be represented, that which is not spoken, that which remains outside
naming and ideologies'.[29] Though this is reminiscent of Irigaray's image
of woman, Kristeva, unlike Irigaray, sees her proposed 'definition' as
entirely relational and strategic. It is an attempt to locate the negativity
and refusal pertaining to the marginal in 'woman', in order to undermine the phallocentric order that defines woman as marginal in the first
place. Thus the ethics of subversion that dominate Kristeva's linguistic
theory here feed into her feminism as well. Her deep suspicion of

identity ('What can "identity", even "sexual identity", mean in a new theoretical scientific space where the very notion of identity is challenged?')[30] leads her to reject any idea of an *écriture féminine* or a *parler femme* that would be inherently feminine or female: 'Nothing in women's past or present publications seems to allow us to affirm that there is a feminine writing (*écriture féminine*)', she claims in an interview published in 1977 ('A partir de', p. 496).[31] It is possible, Kristeva admits, to distinguish various recurrent stylistic and thematic peculiarities in writing by women; but it is not possible to say whether these characteristics should be ascribed to a 'truly feminine specificity, sociocultural marginality or more simply to a certain structure (for instance hysteric) which the present market favours and selects among the totality of feminine potentiality'.[32]

In a sense, then, Kristeva does not have a theory of 'femininity', and even less of 'femaleness'. What she does have is a theory of marginality, subversion and dissidence.[33] In so far as women are defined as marginal by patriarchy, their struggle can be theorized in the same way as any other struggle against a centralized power structure. Thus Kristeva uses exactly the same terms to describe dissident intellectuals, certain *avantgarde* writers and the working class;

> As long as it has not analysed their relation to the instances of power, and has not given up the belief in its own identity, any libertarian movement (including feminism) can be recuperated by that power and by a spirituality that may be laicized or openly religious. The solution? ... Who knows? It will in any case pass through that which is repressed in discourse and in the relations of production. Call it 'woman' or 'oppressed classes of society', it is the same struggle, and never the one without the other.[34]

The strength of this approach is its uncompromising anti-essentialism; its principal weakness the somewhat glib homologization of quite distinct and specific struggles, a problem that will be further discussed in the last section of this chapter.

The anti-essentialist approach is carried over into her theorization of sexual difference. So far, we have seen that her theory of the constitution of the subject and the signifying process is mostly concerned with developments in the pre-Oedipal phase where sexual difference does not exist (the *chora* is a pre-Oedipal phenomenon). The question of difference only becomes relevant at the point of entry into the symbolic order, and Kristeva discusses the situation for little girls at this point in her book *Des Chinoises* (translated as *About Chinese Women*), published in France in the same year as *La Révolution du langage poétique*. She points out that since the semiotic *chora* is pre-Oedipal, it is linked to the mother, whereas the symbolic, as we know, is dominated by the Law of the Father. Faced with this situation, the little girl has to make a choice: 'either she identifies with her mother, or she raises herself to the symbolic stature of her father. In the first case, the pre-Oedipal phases (oral and anal eroticism) are intensified'.[35] If on the other hand the little girl identifies with her father, 'the access she gains to the symbolic dominance [will] censor the pre-Oedipal phase and wipe out the last traces of dependence on the body of the mother'.[36]

Kristeva thus delineates two different options for women: mother-identification, which will intensify the pre-Oedipal components of the woman's psyche and render her marginal to the symbolic order, or father-identification, which will create a woman who will derive her identity from the same symbolic order. It should be clear from these passages that Kristeva does not define femininity as a pre-Oedipal and revolutionary essence. Far from it, femininity for Kristeva comes about as the result of a series of options that are also presented to the little boy. This is surely why at the beginning of *About Chinese Women* she repeats her contention that '*woman as such* does not exist'.[37]

The claim advanced by the Marxist-Feminist Literature Collective and by Beverly Brown and Parveen Adams that Kristeva associates the semiotic with the feminine is thus based on a misreading.[38] The fluid motility of the semiotic is indeed associated with the pre-Oedipal phase, and therefore with the pre-Oedipal mother, but Kristeva makes it quite clear that like Freud and Klein she sees the pre-Oedipal mother as a figure that encompasses both masculinity and femininity. This fantasmatic figure, which looms as large for baby boys as for baby girls, cannot, as Brown and Adams are well aware,[39] be reduced to an example of 'femininity', for the simple reason that the opposition between feminine and masculine does not exist in pre-Oedipality. And Kristeva knows this as well as anybody. Any strengthening of the semiotic, which knows no sexual difference, must therefore lead to a weakening of traditional gender divisions, and not at all to a reinforcement of traditional notions of 'femininity'. This is why Kristeva insists so strongly on the necessary refusal of any theory or politics based on the belief in any absolute form of identity. Femininity and the semiotic do, however, have one thing in common: their marginality. As the feminine is defined as marginal under patriarchy, so the semiotic is marginal to language. This is why the two categories, along with other forms of 'dissidence', can be theorized in roughly the same way in Kristeva's work.

It is difficult, then, to maintain that Kristeva holds an essentialist or even biologistic notion of femininity.[40] It is certainly true that she

believes with Freud that the body forms the material basis for the constitution of the subject. But this in no way entails a simplistic equation
of desire with physical needs, as Jean Laplanche has shown. For
Laplanche 'oral' and 'anal' drives are 'oral' and 'anal' because they are
first produced as a spin-off to (as 'anaclitic' to) the satisfaction of the
purely physical needs linked to the mouth and anus, although they in no
way are reducible to or identical with those needs.

If 'femininity' has a definition at all in Kristevan terms, it is simply, as
we have seen, as 'that which is marginalized by the patriarchal symbolic
order'. This relational 'definition' is as shifting as the various forms of
patriarchy itself, and allows her to argue that men can also be constructed as marginal by the symbolic order, as her analyses of male avant-
garde artists (Joyce, Céline, Artaud, Mallarmé, Lautréamont) have
shown. In *La Révolution du langage poétique*, for instance, she claims
that Artaud, among others, strongly stresses the fluidity of sexual identification for the artist when he states that 'the "author" becomes at
once his "father", "mother" and "himself"'.[41]

Kristeva's emphasis on femininity as a patriarchal construct enables
feminists to counter all forms of biologistic attacks from the defenders
of phallocentrism. To posit all women as necessarily feminine and all
men as necessarily masculine is precisely the move that enables the
patriarchal powers to define, not femininity, but all *women* as marginal
to the symbolic order and to society. If, as Cixous and Irigaray have
shown, femininity is defined as lack, negativity, absence of meaning,
irrationality, chaos, darkness – in short, as non-Being – Kristeva's
emphasis on marginality allows us to view this repression of the feminine in terms of *positionality* rather than of essences. What is perceived
as marginal at any given time depends on the position one occupies. A
brief example will illustrate this shift from essence to position: if patriarchy sees women as occupying a marginal position within the symbolic
order, then it can construe them as the *limit* or borderline of that order.
From a phallocentric point of view, women will then come to represent
the necessary frontier between man and chaos; but because of their
very marginality they will also always seem to recede into and merge
with the chaos of the outside. Women seen as the limit of the symbolic
order will in other words share in the disconcerting properties of *all*
frontiers: they will be neither inside nor outside, neither known nor
unknown. It is this position that has enabled male culture sometimes to
vilify women as representing darkness and chaos, to view them as Lilith
or the Whore of Babylon, and sometimes to elevate them as the repre-
sentatives of a higher and purer nature, to venerate them as Virgins and
Mothers of God. In the first instance the borderline is seen as part of

the chaotic wilderness outside, and in the second it is seen as an inherent part of the inside: the part that protects and shields the symbolic
order from the imaginary chaos. Needless to say, neither position corresponds to any essential truth of woman, much as the patriarchal powers
would like us to believe that they did.

14 MAKIKO MINOW-PINKNEY

Mrs Dalloway

In *Mrs Dalloway* Woolf comes close to the view of life recommended in
'Modern Fiction': 'not a series of gig-lamps symmetrically arranged' but a
'luminous halo'.[42] While writing the novel she had discussed the problems
of her work in correspondence with Jacques Raverat. Himself a painter,
Raverat discussed with her the dilemmas posed by the essentially linear
nature of writing. He proposed an anti-linear account of the effect of a
word, which is like casting a pebble into a pond: 'There are splashes in the
outer air in every direction, and under the surface waves that follow one
another into dark and forgotten corners'. This phenomenon, he argued,
can only be represented by some graphic expedient such as placing the
word in the middle of the page and surrounding it radially with associated
ideas. Woolf replied that it was precisely to this that she aspired, 'to catch
and consolidate and consummate . . . those splashes of yours'.[43]

I wish to consider the novelistic techniques which enabled Woolf to
claim that she had exorcised the spell which Middleton Murry and others said she had laid herself under with *Jacob's Room*.[44] The disjointed
fragmentation of that novel is transcended in *Mrs Dalloway* by the systematic use of 'represented speech' (free indirect speech) which generates an effect of subjective haziness – a 'semi-transparent envelope' –
across the whole text.[45] The so-called 'stream of consciousness' or 'indirect interior monologue' based on represented speech allows the novelist's discourse to move from a character's interior world to the exterior
world (or vice versa) in a homogeneous medium, which produces a continuous indeterminacy. The subject of any apparently seamless passage
is constantly shifting:

Remember my party, remember my party, said Peter Walsh as he stepped down the street, speaking to himself rhythmically, in time with the flow of the sound, the direct downright sound of Big Ben striking the half-hour. (The leaden circles dissolved in the air.) Oh these parties, he thought; Clarissa's parties. Why does she give these parties? he thought. Not that he blamed her or this effigy of a man in a tail-coat with a carnation in his but-ton-hole coming towards him. Only one person in the world could be as he was, in love. And there he was, this fortunate man, himself, reflected in the plate-glass window of a motor-car manufacturer in Victoria Street. All India lay behind him; plains, mountains; epidemics of cholera; a district twice as big as Ireland; decisions he had come to alone – he, Peter Walsh; who was now really for the first time in his life in love. Clarissa had grown hard, he thought; and a trifle sentimental into the bargain, he suspected, looking at the great motor cars capable of doing – how many miles on how many gallons? For he had a turn for mechanics; had invented a plough in his district, had ordered wheel-barrows from England, but the coolies wouldn't use them, all of which Clarissa knew nothing whatever about.[46]

The paragraph opens with Peter echoing Clarissa's cry and proceeds in conventional narrative style (not entirely straightforwardly, however – Peter projects on to Big Ben qualities he believes himself to possess, 'direct, downright'). After the parenthetic refrain describing Big Ben, Peter's interior monologue is presented, in this case in 'direct speech' without quotation marks: 'Why does she give these parties, he thought ...' But his thoughts and perceptions are now presented in the third-person past tense ('represented speech'). However, at certain moments it becomes unclear whether this is interior monologue or narrative description. 'Looking at the great motor cars capable of doing ...' might be a simple description of an action, but 'how many miles on how many gallons?' confirms that it is a transcription of Peter's perceptions. Nor is one sure whose logic is represented by the immediately following 'For ...', a connective used recurrently throughout the book. The sen-tence is ambivalently poised between a straightforward statement about Peter and the contents of his consciousness, though as it proceeds it becomes more and more like his own monologue.

Another important formal development in *Mrs Dalloway* is what Woolf terms the 'tunnelling process' – 'by which I tell the past by instal-ments, as I have need of it'.[47] During the course of the day Clarissa, Peter and Sally all delve into their common past, their youthful days at Bourton. The tense system of these scenes from the past is inconsistent. Since the characters' present is given, in traditional narrative style, in the past tense, their past should presumably be in the pluperfect, but this is not the case. After recalling a painful encounter with Clarissa at

Bourton, Peter protests, 'No, no, no! He was not in love with her any more!' (*MD*, p. 85) The discourse returns to his present, but the tense remains the same as that used in the remembered scene; from a formal point of view, past and present are indistinguishable. In fact, within Peter's memory-image, though it is initially clear that the scene occurred in the past ('She came into a room; she stood ...'), matters become gradually ambiguous; present and past are fused. In the last few lines the Clarissa resurrected from the past is no longer merely the young girl at Bourton but the latter-day Clarissa as well.

The text presents itself as a homogeneous unity in the conventional narrative guise of third-person past tense, but is in fact radically heterogeneous. Subjects of sentences are continually shifting, and writing is made 'porous' by the tunnelling process. One is suddenly pitched into a 'cave' of the past, for Woolf records her 'discovery: how I dig out beautiful caves behind my characters'.[48] An early paragraph of the novel epitomizes these characteristics:

> What a lark! What a plunge! For so it had always seemed to her when, with a little squeak of the hinges, which she could hear now, she had burst open the French windows and plunged at Bourton into the open air. How fresh, how calm, stiller than this of course, the air was in the early morning; like the flap of a wave; the kiss of a wave; chill and sharp and yet (for a girl of eighteen as she then was) solemn, feeling as she did, standing there at the open window, that something awful was about to happen; looking at the flowers, at the trees with the smoke winding off them and the rooks rising, falling; standing and looking until Peter Walsh said, 'Musing among the vegetables?' – was that it? (*MD*, p. 5)

The 'hinges' of Woolf's transitions don't usually 'squeak' as noticeably as here. One technical means of oiling them is the conjunction 'for', which as in the above passage often connects slightly different planes of discourse in a very loose, characteristically 'half-logical' way.[49] A profuse use of present participles, another characteristic of Woolf's writing, loosens the binding function of syntax. Its effect is to attenuate human energy: contrast 'she looked at the flowers' with 'looking at the flowers', where activity is reduced to contemplative stasis. The present participles begin as supplements to a main clause, but generate an autonomous energy; they meander lyrically on until disrupted by Peter's brusque comment. Transformed into a present-participle phrase, an action composed of subject-verb becomes an adverbial or adjectival phrase, and as a result the sentence gives a sense of the simultaneity of several acts and states. Thus writing can to a certain extent go beyond its essential linearity. Woolf diagnosed this effect, somewhat anxiously, in her diary: 'It is a disgrace that I ... write sloppily, using nothing but present participles. I find them very useful in the last lap of *Mrs D*'.[50]

A further fine example of her transcendence of narrative linearity is the scene in Regent's Park with its aleatory method of composition. As one character strolls beside another who had till then been the focus of narrative attention, so the 'fickle' narrative abandons its object to follow the newcomer. A sense of the coexisting currents and eddies in the park is thereby created. In its nimble manoeuvring between individuals and groups, the narrative in Regent's Park is behaving like a hostess at a party, and this is no accident. Parks and parties are privileged symbols for Woolf because they are protected enclaves outside the normal run of social life. They are places of a libidinal indulgence that must be repressed elsewhere, mini-utopias of the senses. Every time Clarissa gives a party she has a 'feeling of being something not herself, and that everyone was unreal in one way: much more real in another'. 'Unreal' because detached from everyday occupations but 'more real' because in touch with libidinal energies the social ego represses. Hence 'it was possible to say things you couldn't say anyhow else ... to go much deeper' (*MD*, pp. 187–8). Bourton, with its spacious grounds and continuous social gatherings, derives its resonance in the novel from being both park and party at once.

In his famous discussion of *To the Lighthouse* in *Mimesis*, Erich Auerbach asks, 'Who is speaking in this paragraph?' He sees its narrator as 'spirits between heaven and earth, nameless spirits capable of penetrating the depths of the human soul ... but not of attaining clarity as to what is in process there, with the result that what they report has a doubtful ring'.[51] This unidentifiable narrative voice is achieved by 'represented speech' suspending the location of the subject between character and author. This ambiguous 'between-ness' produces at once an intimate internalized tone and a certain indirectness; we are so near to, yet somehow distant from, the process of the character's mind. The reader's sense of distance is confused in a mode of writing 'all crepuscular ... as bright as fire in the mist'.[52] 'Who is speaking?' asks Auerbach, and in the case of the conjunction 'for' one might well ask 'who is reasoning?'. Or again: 'It was quite different here from Westminster, she thought, getting off at Chancery Lane. It was so serious; it was so busy. In short, she would like to have a profession. She would become a doctor, a farmer ...' (*MD*, pp. 150–1). With the phrase 'in short', one senses a narrative voice which judges and sums up for the reader, but the discourse glides quickly back into the flow of Elizabeth's consciousness. Whenever we try to pinpoint the locus of the subject, we get lost in a discursive mist. Consider Holmes's visit to Septimus: 'When the damned fool came again, Septimus refused to see him. Did he indeed? said Dr Holmes, smiling agreeably. Really he had to give that charming little lady, Mrs Smith, a friendly push before he could get past her into her husband's bedroom' (*MD*, p. 102). 'The damned fool' is of course Septimus's language, though the whole sentence is straightforward narrative. 'Charming little lady' is Holmes's phrase, but 'smiling agreeably' and 'a friendly push' are neither simply an objective narrative account nor straightforwardly Holmes's own point of view. 'Agreeable' and 'friendly' are corroded by Septimus's 'damned fool', which is backed up by the context of the whole passage; they acquire an ironic edge which satirizes Holmes's self-complacency. The narrative voice is fractured, wavering, multiple, closer to Auerbach's 'spirits' in the plural than to J. Hillis Miller's 'omniscient narrator'.[53] In terms of feminist theory, what Woolf's writing effects is a denial of the unified subject which supports all discourse and is necessarily 'masculine', since the symbolic order is established with the phallus as its fundamental signifier. The narrative consciousness in her writing, if indeed there is one, has stopped judging, interpreting, explaining; it has no single identity or position. It is not, in Kristeva's terms, a 'thetic' subject. Or if that is strictly impossible, since the symbolic is sustained by the thetic subject, at least the latter's control is minimized and the other modality of signifying practice – the semiotic realm – is granted as much autonomy as possible.

The extent to which Woolf is playing with the conventions of novelistic interpretation is revealed as the aeroplane flies over London forming letters of smoke, presumably as an advertisement. 'Only for a moment did they [the letters] lie still; then they moved and melted and were rubbed out up in the sky, and the aeroplane shot further away and again, in a fresh space of sky, began writing a K, and E, a Y perhaps?' (*MD*, pp. 23–4). For this 'key' to all mythologies is doubtless the transcendental signifier or solution to the hermeneutic riddle of the novel. Woolf tantalizes us with its possibility only to withdraw it at once. As narrator, she refuses an 'authoritarian' relation to her own novel. Rejecting the thetic self of keys and master-codes, Woolf once declared: 'when I write I'm merely a sensibility'.[54] This practice of writing as an asocial 'sensibility' aroused much hostile criticism in the 1930s, especially from *Scrutiny*. Its argument that her work is mere subjectivism to be rejected by the mature adult with a responsible life in society is summed up in Leavis's article of 1942.[55] But a more positive assessment of Woolf must rather emphasize that her writing makes the fixed 'I' or K-E-Y recede. It loosens the ligatures of the unifying subject so as to produce a style whose characteristics are simultaneity and fluidity. Yet she never destroys the thetic 'I' completely, which is after all impossible as long as one wants to remain within language (and sane). Nor does she ever go as near to shattering language as James Joyce. Her work is not a drastic demolition but a subtle and elegant infraction of syntactic laws in order to undermine the protocols of writing. It loosens the relations of subject and object (which the thetic subject sustains) by present-participles or intrusive phrases between subject and predicate, or by breaking up noun–verb or subject–object relations into a mere listing of nouns, and thus disrupting the logical relations which language produces for a human subject by its syntactic order. 'Looseness' is a term that indicates for Woolf that her writing is going well: 'I feel as if I had loosened the bonds, pretty completely and could pour everything in. If so – good'. Or again, 'the diary writing has greatly helped my style; loosened the ligatures'.[56]

In Kristevan terms, Woolf's texts disperse the transcendental unified subject that underpins male rationality and narrative, and open new possibilities for subjective activity. Her writing subverts this positionality and tries to adumbrate the area anterior to the logical, judging, naming subjectivity, to bring in the semiotic as the domain of rhythm, sounds, intonation, colour and shape. In her writing rhythm is always very conspicuously at work. Moreover, colours often come into the foreground, detached from their objects, as in such curious intense sketches as 'Blue and Green' and 'Kew Gardens':

> Yellow and black, pink and snow white, shapes of all these colours, men, women, and children were spotted for a second upon the horizon, and then, seeing the breadth of yellow that lay upon the grass, they wavered and sought shade beneath the trees, dissolving like drops of water in the yellow and green atmosphere, staining it faintly with red and blue.[57]

Woolf was criticized by her contemporaries for her failure to create 'characters', but clearly she seeks a state of human being prior to its consolidation into personality. Her work thus undercuts

> the masculine point of view which governs our lives, which sets the standard, which established Whitaker's Table of Precedency, which has become, I suppose, since the war, half a phantom to many men and women, which soon, one may hope, will be laughed into the dustbin where the phantoms go, the mahogany sideboards and the Landseer prints, God and Devils, Hell and so forth, leaving us all with an intoxicating sense of illegitimate freedom.[58]

It is only 'reality' or 'character' as defined by this deeply compromised perspective that Woolf is 'unable' to create. 'I dare say it's true, however, that I don't have that "reality" gift. I insubstantiate, wilfully to some extent, distrusting reality – its cheapness. But to get further. Have I the power of conveying the true reality?'.[59] The 'true reality' is reality for women; but Woolf is nervous of the censorship and condemnation of men. Julia Kristeva writes: 'In women's writing, language seems to be seen from a foreign land. ... Estranged from language, women are visionaries, dancers who suffer as they speak'.[60] In a foreign land, one is naturally more cautious about infractions of the law because of the danger of expulsion. So Woolf would never go to extremes as Joyce did, and throughout her career kept a conventional form of narrative writing in the third-person past tense, for 'writing must be formal. The art must be respected'.[61] Her literary affirmation of 'true reality' remains well protected by an apparent formality as it subtly undermines the fixed positionality of the subject in language. Her natural descriptions often emit a lateral message about the process of the novel's own construction, as in this self-reflexive description of a London cloudscape.

> Fixed though they seem to be at their posts, at rest in perfect unanimity, nothing could be fresher, freer, more sensitive superficially than the snow-white or gold-kindled surface; to change, to go, to dismantle the solemn assemblage was immediately possible; and in spite of the grave fixity, the accumulated robustness and solidity, now they struck light to the earth, now darkness. (*MD*, p. 153)

In a similar way, the apparently ordered 'assemblage' of Woolf's own prose may be dismantled in a flash by some disorientating slippage of narrative voice or some 'tunnelling' and mining of the present by the past.

By disrupting linearity and achieving simultaneity, she modifies the status of the subject. For the unified self is only one stage of a 'subject in process/on trial' (as Auerbach seems to have realized instinctively in his reference to 'what is in process' in the depths of the Woolfian 'soul'). The true subject is not a linear 'series of gig-lamps symmetrically arranged', but is evoked by the more spatial image of 'a luminous halo'. Though the phrase 'from the beginning of consciousness to the end' implies some kind of temporality, yet the image of 'envelope' does not really coincide with the concept of linear continuity. In this image of 'this varying, this unknown and uncircumscribed spirit' with its 'aberration' and 'complexity', Woolf offers us a subject which has no simple unity, no clear boundary between itself and other. The 'envelope' is 'semi-transparent' and therefore not a clear-cut distinction between spirit and world. Woolf's idea of self denies homogeneity: 'she [Nature] let creep instincts and desires which are utterly at variance with his [man's] main being, so that we are streaked, variegated, all of a mixture'.[62]

Notes

1 See Toril Moi (ed.), 'Introduction', *The Kristeva Reader* (Oxford: Blackwell, 1986); Kristeva's novels are *Les Samouraïs* (Paris: Fayard, 1990), and *Le vieil homme et les loups* (Paris: Fayard, 1991).

2 See Julia Kristeva, *Powers of Horror: An Essay on Abjection*, trans. Leon S. Roudiez (New York: Columbia University Press, 1982, first published 1980), p. 14.

3 Elizabeth Grosz, *Sexual Subversions: Three French Feminists* (Sydney: Allen and Unwin, 1989), p. 50.

4 Julia Kristeva, *Revolution in Poetic Language*, trans. Margaret Waller (New York: Columbia University Press, 1984), p. 80.

5 Jennifer Stone, 'The Horrors of Power: A Critique of "Kristeva"', in Francis Barker, et al., (eds), *The Politics of Theory: Proceedings of the Essex Conference on the Sociology of Literature: Proceedings* (Colchester: University of Essex Press, 1983), p. 42.

6 Paul Smith, 'Julia Kristeva Et Al., or, Take Three More', in R. Feldstein and J. Roof (eds), *Feminism and Psychoanalysis* (Ithaca: Cornell University Press, 1989), p. 90.

7 Kristeva, *Powers of Horror*, p. 74.

8 Ibid., p. 74.

9 Elizabeth Grosz, *Sexual Subversions*, p. 71.

10 Barbara Creed, '*Alien* and the Monstrous-Feminine', *Screen*, 27 (1) (1986). See also her full-length study, *The Monstrous-Feminine: Film, Feminism, Psychoanalysis* (London: Routledge, 1993).

11 Maud Ellmann, 'Eliot's Abjection', in John Fletcher and A. Benjamin, (eds), *Abjection, Melancholia and Love: The Work of Julia Kristeva* (London: Routledge, 1990), p. 191.

12 Showalter, however, interestingly analyses Septimus Smith's shellshock in *Mrs Dalloway* in terms of hysteria: *The English Malady: Women, Madness and English Culture, 1830–1980* (London: Virago, 1985).

13 Minow-Pinkney, *Virginia Woolf and the Problem of the Subject*, pp. ix, x.

14 Ibid., p. x.

15 Ibid., pp. 6, 11.

16 Ibid., p. 189.

17 Ibid., p. 17

18 Ibid., p. 23

19 Kristeva, *Revolution in Poetic Language*, p. 62.

20 Jean Wyatt, *Reconstructing Desire: The Role of the Unconscious in Women's Reading and Writing* (Chapel Hill: University of North Carolina Press, 1990), pp. 72–3.

21 Minow-Pinkney, *Virginia Woolf and the Problem of the Subject*, p. 83.

Reading 13 (Moi)

22 Philip E. Lewis, 'Revolutionary semiotics', *Diacritics*, 4 (3), (Fall, 1974), pp. 28–32.

23 For an introduction to these concepts in Lacan see Toril Moi, *Sexual/Textual Politics* (London: Methuen, 1985), pp. 99–101; and this volume, Part IV.

24 Léon S. Roudiez, 'Introduction', in Julia Kristeva, *Desire in Language: A Semiotic Approach to Literature and Art* (Oxford: Blackwell, 1980), p. 6.

25 Throughout this section, when no English translation is cited, all quotations from Kristeva's work are translated by me [Toril Moi]. All further page references are in the text.

26 Kristeva, 'The system and the speaking subject', in Thomas A. Seboek (ed.), *The Tell-Tale Sign: A Survey of Semiotics* (Lisse, Netherlands: The Peter de Ridder Press, 1975), p. 53.

27 Ibid., pp. 54–5.

28 Kristeva, 'La femme, ce n'est jamais ça', *Tel Quel*, 59 (Autumn 1974), p. 20.

29 Ibid., p. 21.

30 Kristeva, 'Woman's time', trans. Alice Jardine and Harry Blake, *Signs*, 7 (1), p. 34.

31 Kristeva, 'A partir de *Polylogue*', *Revue des sciences humaines*, 168 (December 1977), p. 496.

32 Ibid., p. 496.

33 See Kristeva's article on dissidence, 'Un nouveau type d'intellectuel: le dissident', *Tel Quel*, 74 (Winter 1977).

34 Kristeva, 'La femme', p. 24.

35 Kristeva, *About Chinese Women*, trans. A. Barrows (London: Boyars, 1977), p. 28.

36 Ibid., p. 29.

37 Ibid., p. 16.

38 Marxist-Feminist Literature Collective, 'Women's Writing: *Jane Eyre, Shirley, Villette, Aurora Leigh*', *Ideology and Consciousness* 1 (3) (Spring 1978) p. 30; Beverly Brown and Parveen Adams, 'The feminine body and feminist politics', *m/f* 3 (1979).

39 Brown and Adams, 'The feminine body', p. 40.

40 For a discussion of this problem from a somewhat different angle see Claire Pajaczkowska, 'Introduction to Kristeva', *m/f* 5 and 6, (1981).

41 Kristeva, *La Révolution du langage poétique* (Paris: Seuil, 1974), p. 606.

Reading 14 (Minow-Pinkney)

42 Virginia Woolf, *Collected Essays*, vol. 2, ed. Leonard Woolf (London: Hogarth Press, 1966), p. 106.

43 Quentin Bell, *Virginia Woolf: A Biography*, vol. 2 (London: Hogarth Press, 1972), p. 106; and Nigel Nicolson and Joanne Trautmann (eds), *The Letters of Virginia Woolf* (London: Hogarth Press, 1975–80), vol. 3, p. 136.

44 Virginia Woolf, *A Writer's Diary*, ed. Leonard Woolf (London: Hogarth Press, 1969), p. 68.

45 See Otto Jespersen, *The Philosophy of Grammar* (London, 1924), G. Allen and Unwin, pp. 291–2.

46 Virginia Woolf, *Mrs Dalloway*, first pub. 1925 (London: Hogarth Press, 1980), pp. 54–5. All further page references are in the text.

47 Woolf, *A Writer's Diary*, p. 61.

48 Ibid., p. 60.

49 David Daiches argues that 'for' is 'a word which does not indicate a strict logical sequence, at least not in its popular usage, but does suggest a relationship which is at least half-logical', *Virginia Woolf*, revised edn (New York: New Directions, 1963), p. 72.

50 Woolf, *A Writer's Diary*, p. 66.

51 Erich Auerbach, *Mimesis: The Representation of Reality in Western Literature*, trans. Willard R. Trask (Princeton: Princeton University Press, 1968), p. 532.

52 Woolf, *A Writer's Diary*, p. 23.

53 J. Hillis Miller, 'Virginia Woolf's All Souls' Day: The Omniscient Narrator in *Mrs Dalloway*' in Melvin Friedman and John B. Vickery (eds), *The Shaken Realist: Essays in Modern Literature in Honour of F. J. Hoffman* (Louisiana: Louisiana State University Press, 1982), pp. 100–27.

54 Woolf, *A Writer's Diary*, p. 48.

55 'After "To the Lighthouse"' in F. R. Leavis (ed.), *A Selection from Scrutiny* (Cambridge: Cambridge University Press, 1968), vol. 2, pp. 97–100.

56 Woolf, *A Writer's Diary*, pp. 62, 69.

57 Woolf, *A Haunted House and Other Stories*, first pub. 1944 (London: Hogarth Press, 1962).

58 Ibid., p. 44.

59 Woolf, *A Writer's Diary*, p. 57.

60 Kristeva, 'Oscillation between Power and Denial', in Elaine Marks and Isabelle de Courtivron (eds), *New French Feminisms* (Brighton: Harvester 1981), p. 166.

61 Woolf, *A Writer's Diary*, p. 69.

62 Woolf, *Collected Essays*, vol. 4, p. 161.

Part VI
Luce Irigaray: Femininity, Film and the Masquerade

Joan Riviere's 1929 essay, 'Womanliness as a Masquerade',[1] has had a significant influence on writers concerned with the nature of femininity and with representations of femininity – if the two can be separated. The essay's importance lies in its denial of any fixed, essential feminine nature, and it has also been influential for studies of transvestism, dressing up and the subversion of unchanging, sartorially coded gender identities in general.[2] Opponents of claims that the idea of masquerade is liberatory point to its apolitical implications; Stephen Heath, for instance, suggests that in Riviere's reading of her analysand's predicament 'protest becomes merely sadism – sexual politics gives way to a psychology of sex'.[3] Judith Butler asks whether masquerade necessarily transforms aggression and fear of reprisal into seduction and flirtation, as it appears to in Riviere's essay.[4]

In her essay, Riviere discusses three different case studies, which have in common the fact that, according to Riviere, 'women who wish for masculinity may put on a mask of womanliness to avert anxiety and the retribution feared from men' (p. 210). There is the woman who has problems with authoritative men (p. 214), and the one who becomes inappropriately flippant and jokey after evidence of academic success (p. 215). The most extensively treated case is that of a successful American woman who none the less has a problematic relation to public speaking and language. Riviere describes this woman's habit of seeking reassurance after a public lecture from 'unmistakable father-figures', often through the sexualized activity of flirtation, in an act of 'propitiation' which was, however, merely an act of 'masquerading as guiltless and innocent' (p. 213). This behaviour marks the woman's anxiety in relation to both her parents: she identifies with the father and 'takes his place, so she can "restore" him' (p. 217) as an appeasing gift to the mother who is both feared and hated. The father also needs appeasing in case he tries to extract punishment for his daughter's hatred (and perhaps destruction) of the mother, by a counter-masquerade as, again, feminine.

It is as if the (feminine) daughter first assumes a masculine, and then on top of that a further feminine, mask. By this means the daughter feels superior and safe from harm by either parent. She fears that her illicit possession of the penis – her 'masculine' supremacy and success – will be found out, an apprehension allayed if the father acknowledges her possession and thus legitimizes it (p. 219).

Masquerade and Film

The concept and language of masquerade have often been used to discuss the position of the female film spectator, whose gaze is not accommodated, according to some theorists, within classical cinema (Christine Holmlund draws attention to the gendered dichotomy between mainstream and avant-garde cinema in her article 'I love Luce: The Lesbian, Mimesis and Masquerade in Irigaray, Freud, and Mainstream Film'[5]). Laura Mulvey's essay 'Visual Pleasure and Narrative Cinema' suggests that the three gazes – of audience, camera and characters – in film are all masculine, and therefore the only position a female spectator can take up is a masochistic one.[6] Some critics have suggested rather that the exclusion of the female gaze means that the female spectator (that is, the spectator in a feminine position) has a greater gender mobility than the male.[7] In order to be the voyeur which film constructs the spectator as, the woman 'puts on the sexual guise of the male, effecting a trans-sex identification', as Jane Gaines puts it;[8] this is a transvestite spectatorship, rather than a masochistic or non-existent one.

Other critics have similarly attempted to account for the possibility of female spectatorship. Mulvey has revised her argument in 'Visual Pleasure';[9] Paul Willemen has posited a 'fourth look', amplifying Mulvey's tripartite system with a unisex look directed back at 'the viewer, surprising the voyeur in his or her activities and generating shame'.[10] Constance Penley discusses both Janet Bergstrom's and Mary Ann Doane's arguments against 'the theoretical assumption that the spectator is implicitly male and against the accompanying stress on psychical mechanisms related primarily to the male spectator – voyeurism, fetishism, and even identification'.[11] Again, it looks as if femininity does have its own positionality and 'authenticity', but not one which is based on a biological substratum.

Masquerade has also been used to analyse not just the female spectator, but the very possibility of the representation of the female body on screen. Using the theories of Riviere, Irigaray and Michèle Montrelay, Mary Ann Doane points out that woman is evicted equally from psychoanalysis and cinema, two discourses 'purportedly about her', and that 'historically, there has always been a certain imbrication of the cinematic image and the representation of women'.[12] This is even true of film theorist Christian Metz's description of the cinematic discourse operating through 'imaginary signifiers':[13] the phrase seems equally applicable to the female body, which, like the cinematic image, is the site of representation, most itself when covered or veiled, and possesses no hidden secret or signified behind the mask. As Doane puts it, 'For the female spectator there is a certain overpresence of the image – she *is* the image'.[14]

Doane suggests that the relationship between femininity and signification is usually represented as problematic or non-existent, because the woman is too close to her own body for the distance needed for representation – 'the boy's body provides an access to the processes of representation while the girl's body does not'.[15] The woman may, however, be the *object* of representation, a signified without a signifying system: cinema is 'a writing in images of the woman but not *for* her'.[16] Masquerade, especially on screen, can provide women with the necessary distance – the ironic awareness of the pose and clothes – for signification. Judith Butler points out that, in Riviere's essay, this desire for access to sign-production may underlie the fact that the woman in the case history experiences Oedipal rivalry with the father not over the love of the mother, but with the father as a public speaker, 'that is, as a user of signs rather than a sign-object, an item of exchange'. The desire to castrate which Riviere both documents and enacts may be 'understood as the desire to relinquish the status of woman-as-sign in order to appear as a subject within language'.[17]

Luce Irigaray, 'Women, the Sacred and Money'

Luce Irigaray, a Belgian-born analyst who is currently Director of Research at the Centre National de Recherche Scientifique in Paris, was expelled from her job in the Department of Psychoanalysis at Vincennes after the publication of her second book, *Speculum of the*

Other Woman,[18] in 1974, as it was judged to be too critical and too 'politically engaged' for serious psychoanalytic work.[19]

Like Julia Kristeva, Irigaray is concerned with sexual difference, especially the feminine and the maternal; unlike Kristeva, however, Irigaray does not see her aim as to deconstruct sexual difference, which Kristeva does in her essay 'Women's Time',[20] but to point the way for women to gain access to signification in combination with men, thus preserving gender difference. Irigaray sees her project as attempting to bring into existence the unsymbolized – the feminine – by breaking up the 'hom(m)osexual' society in which the masculine is the single valorized gender, and by discussing the possibility of a different, feminine form of representation in which women would not simply be defined in relation to men – as virgin, mother, prostitute – but in their own terms.[21] Irigaray ends her essay 'Women on the Market' by sketching what these terms might look like: changes to the social order would operate '[n]ot by reproducing, by copying, the "phallocratic" models that have the force of law today, but by socializing in a different way the relation to nature, matter, the body, language, and desire'.[22]

Essentialism and mimicry

Adherence to essentialism is the main criticism made of Irigaray, that by trying to bring into being a female symbolic, she is basing her theory on an ahistorical, biological perception of the female body.[23] Irigaray appears to offer as an alternative to the phallus a representational image of the female genitalia instead. Far from getting away from imagery based on the body, Irigaray seems to be doing exactly what the male philosophers she criticizes do, but simply reversing the terms. Irigaray's critics point particularly to her essay 'When Our Lips Speak Together', in which she posits a feminine doubleness, or at least non-unitariness: 'One is never separable from the other. You/I: we are always several at once. And how could one dominate the other? [...] One cannot be distinguished from the other; which does not mean that they are indistinct'. This is in contrast to phallic integrity, using the image of both oral and genital lips: 'Long before your birth, you touched yourself, innocently. Your/my body doesn't acquire its sex through an operation'.[24]

However, it is clear even from this extract that there is more going on than a simple prioritizing of female labia. The 'doubleness' which interests Irigaray applies equally to the feminine speaking subject, a 'we' which alternates between 'I' and 'you'. This represents a relationship which is between subjects, not between a subject and an object; each speaker can take up either position. Ahistoricism might be seen to lurk in the phrase, 'Long before your birth [...]', as if femininity is an innate state, rather than something which is acquired, the product of language and division in the symbolic order: 'Prior to any representation, we are two',[25] but again the issue is more complex than it may seem at first.

Margaret Whitford points out that Irigaray is drawing upon the way in which women are symbolized in western culture, precisely as natural and ahistorical, in order to combat it, making it particularly ironic that she is accused of doing exactly what she is criticizing.[26] What looks essentialist is a 'ruse' to expose philosophy's essentialism, and the maternal-feminine on which it depends.[27]

Irigaray has a particular angle on the idea of impersonation which we examined in relation to Joan Riviere, concentrating on how women can make themselves heard in a culture which recognizes only one sex and its voice. For Irigaray, mimicry is the way out of the alienation of masquerade; the latter is the way in which women construct themselves in relation to male desire, rather than for themselves, while mimicry involves taking masquerade to an extreme in order to defamiliarize and expose the mechanisms by which 'the realm of discourse (where the speaking subject is posited as masculine) [...] exploits her'.[28] Mimicry thus seems exactly the strategy adopted by Irigaray in her own writing: a taking to the extreme of oppressive discourses of the natural, non-transcendence, irrationality and so on which are supposed to constitute femininity. By over-emphasizing these discourses she exposes them, as an interim strategy before being able to discard them in favour of a *parler-femme*.

Women and money

Irigaray uses the relationship of women to money, or currency, in both a rhetorical and a material way, as is suggested in her essay reproduced here. In *Speculum*, she discusses the economic infrastructure of Freud's writing.[29] In *This Sex*, she describes hom(m)osexuality in monetary terms, describing psychoanalysis as 'caught up in phallocentrism, which it claims to make into a universal and eternal value'.[30] In this value system, women are the unit of currency, what enables the system to work – as the (feminizing) letter did in Poe's tale 'The Purloined Letter'. In this argument Irigaray follows anthropologist Claude Lévi-Strauss' analysis of kinship structures, in which women are never the agents but the objects of exchange.[31]

As Steven Connor points out, Irigaray argues that women 'function universally as the objects of every kind of exchange, economic, familial, sexual, psychic, aesthetic, religious, linguistic':[32] in all these areas they are objects but not agents, represented but not representing. The distinctive features of the hom(m)osexual economy arise from this fact. 'Commerce' between men and women is not allowed,[33] as that can only take place between owners and buyers: 'Men make commerce *of* them, but they do not enter into any exchanges *with* them'.[34] Male homosexuality is also forbidden, as it would entail men perhaps becoming commodities rather than exchangers. Women circulate like signs, undifferentiated facilitators of meaning without any fixed meaning of their own, as the impossibility of women's genealogy suggests: the economic and the linguistic meet in the 'proper name', as women are named with the father's name and exchanged in terms of the husband's, without any name, and therefore also without any history, of their own.[35] Irigaray puts it in 'Women on the Market', 'The production of women, signs and commodities is always referred back to men (when a man buys a girl, he "pays" the father or the brother, not the mother [. . .]) and they always pass from one man to another, from one group of men to another.'[36]

One possible way of establishing an alternative feminine economy is lesbianism, as Christine Holmlund points out, which offers the 'discursive potential',[37] Irigaray argues in *This Sex*, of evading the subject–object structure of hom(m)osexuality and its exchange mechanism: 'Exchanges without identifiable terms, without accounts, without end [. . .] Without standard or yardstick'.[38]

Specula(riza)tion

The use of parentheses in the English rendering of this Irigarayan concept suggests how closely linked she sees the economic analysis of hom(m)osexual culture and its prioritization of the visual, something we have come across in both Freud's and Lacan's work. Irigaray expands on the prioritizing of the visual in psychoanalysis to suggest that social life is constructed in such a way that men see around them reflections of themselves, having projected their ego onto the world.[39] She claims that this specularization is apparent in male writings, even – or especially – in those which deny their sexual specificity. Women fit into this structure as part of the mirroring, as Whitford puts it: 'Women as body/matter are the material of which the mirror is made, that part of the mirror which cannot be reflected, the tain of the mirror for example, and so never see reflections of themselves.'[40]

This argument has something in common with Mary Ann Doane's observation that cinema is full of representations of women but not about women;[41] again, the question of whether what women see on screen is themselves, or someone's view of them, or if they are reflected at all, suggests the potential for an Irigarayan approach to film. In 'Women on the Market', Irigaray points out that commodities and women are 'mirrors' of value for man,

> the supporting material of specularization, of speculation. They yield to him their natural and social value as a locus of imprints, marks, and mirage of his activity [...] the relation of commodities among themselves is a projection through which producers-exchangers make [commodities] reenact before their eyes their operations of specula(riza)tion.[42]

The vocabulary Irigaray chooses here is particularly suggestive for film theory, in that she likens the male construction of women to what sounds like the cinematic apparatus itself, its screen (the mirror of value), images (imprints), projective equipment, and the resulting film (mirage). This is particularly apt as the phrase 'cinematic apparatus' itself no longer simply refers to the instrumental base of camera, projector and screen, but also to the spectator and the ways in which this 'desiring subject' fits in with the (psychic and economic) demands of the cinematic institution.[43] De Lauretis points out that approaching cinema as 'a social technology, as a "cinematic apparatus,"'[44] signals terminologically a debt to Lacan, and to Louis Althusser, whose essay 'Ideology and Ideological State Apparatuses' she also quotes. Again, Irigaray is gaining mileage out of the interface between referential and rhetorical language, recognizing, as de Lauretis puts it, that cinema and the cinematic apparatus are 'a technology of gender'.[45]

Mary Ann Doane, 'Woman's Stake: Filming the Female Body'

In this essay, Mary Ann Doane examines 'the material specificity of film in relation to the female body and its syntax'. Film has often been a means simply of reproducing and reinforcing women's reduction to the bodily, to being the object of the gaze, and Doane explores ways in which women might appropriate cinema's significatory potential for themselves. She argues that the body permits but does not demand sexual differentiation – that is, it is there if you look for (and construct) it – and that the male body comes 'fully equipped with a binary opposition'.

It can be castrated or not, represent absence or presence and phonemic opposition, while the female body, at least according to this logic, is undifferentiated and unrepresentable. The female body's nearness to itself, however, is not a comment on its 'essential' nature but of its positionality, 'the delineation of a place culturally assigned to the woman'.[46]

As Doane paraphrases Michèle Montrelay, 'something must be threatened' if the incest prohibition is to separate the desiring subject from the object, and as the little girl's body has no morphology by means of which to suffer the prohibition, and far from losing the mother's body, she turns into it herself, making her body narcissistic, erotic and maternal, but not representable. The woman is 'haunted by the loss of a loss, the lack of that lack so essential for the realization of the ideals of the semiotic system'.[47]

Doane concludes that in order to discuss how the female body may be represented on the screen, and how femininity might be theorized, it is necessary to break away from the essentialist/anti-essentialist debate, and shift the terminological terrain instead towards outlining a feminine 'specificity'. Unlike Holmlund's essay on an Irigarayan analysis of film, which concentrated principally on content, Doane proposes the working out of form, 'a new syntax', a new way of speaking the female body, not simply displayed for the camera in the way much mainstream cinema does. This concern with form extends to narrative order, which might also, Doane suggests, operate as 'a parodic "mime" that distorts, undoes the structure of the classical narrative's'.[48] The element that might be 'threatened' for woman to enter the symbolic could be patriarchal representative clichés themselves.

Montrelay emphasizes the 'anxiety' produced by the overly present female body, which cannot just be looked at but demands response in other registers, including smell, a fact which, as Jane Gallop puts it, threatens 'the stability of the psychic economy, that stability which is achieved by means of representations'.[49] Finally, however, it is the masquerade itself which can offer the woman distance, a gap approximating loss and permitting signification: 'The theorization of femininity as masquerade is a way of appropriating this necessary distance or gap, in the operation of semiotic systems, of deploying it for women, of reading femininity differently.'[50]

15 LUCE IRIGARAY

Women, the Sacred and Money

For the colloquium 'Women and Money', organized by the CEFUP [Centre for Women's Studies] on 15–17 November 1984 at the University of Provence (Aix-Marseille I), I developed a number of questions concerning the function of women in what I consider to be our sacrificial societies. These I have reduced, provisionally, to five points:

(1) What is the meaning of sacrifice in relation to the cosmic time scale and its rhythms?
(2) What rites and what systems of exchange might be appropriate amongst women? At the moment? In the future?
(3) Is there not a collusion between women's unpaid work and the sacrificial?
(4) Doesn't the fact that the mother isn't paid for giving birth and caring for children turn the child into an object of exchange amongst women?
(5) What sort of imbalance is created in our societies as an effect of non-payment or under-payment of their natural and cultural infrastructure: women, mothers and (female) theoreticians?

I

The exclusion or suppression of the religious dimension seems to be impossible. It re-emerges in various and frequently degraded guises: sectarianism, religiosity ... We do, however, need to rethink the religious question, particularly its scope, its categories and its utopias, all of which have been male for centuries and remain so.

Most of our societies are founded upon a sacrifice – an immolation that brings the social space into being. René Girard offers many examples of this,[51] and they apply to numerous social phenomena. But he has little to say about the question viewed from the angle of women. Except perhaps in the chapter of *La violence et le sacré* which he devotes to Dionysus' female companions.[52] In my opinion the example is too simple and hardly relevant. It seems to me more pertinent to wonder whether, under the sacrificial victim, there isn't always another one hidden? And in what place, under what subjective and objective conditions, the *practice of substitution was first staged*? At what point the divine or the human are consecrated not only through words but through an act? At what point cosmic time gives way to a ritual organization of time? Why haven't men regulated their meetings, their communities and their prayers according to natural cycles like morning, noon and evening, the different seasons, the phases of the sun and moon, the various positions of the earth and the other planets? Something of the sort has dominated certain eras, and is trying to emerge in our own, without, however, being conceived as a reworking or an abolition of the sacrificial. It seems that each new discovery is, or becomes, thought of in terms of a sacrifice (who will win or lose? who will be the strongest or the weakest? who is to be feared? . . .), rather than with a view to installing a new rhythm, and a new sociality, sexuality, or covenant which wouldn't depend on a scapegoat. The community could meet together in the morning, at midday and in the evening without need for recourse to some sacrifice. The meeting itself would constitute the rite, with its greetings and with the joy of seeing each other again. Why shouldn't a community be formed at the meeting point of cosmic and social necessities without some such supplement as offering a sacrifice, eating the sacrificial object, etc.? Wouldn't speech then finally find its rightful place, the other rites having provided the substitutes? Speech wouldn't be a substitute for the rite but *vice versa*, or at least the rite would be what takes place in the absence of speech.

Why did speech fail? What was missing? Why kill, cut up and eat as a sign of covenant? To abolish some sort of violence? What sort? Where does it originate? And isn't it possible to analyse why speech was so inadequate that such an act became necessary? Was it, for instance, because of a lack of harmony between words, acts and bodies? Are cultures sacrificial if they manage to unite acts, words, microcosmic and macrocosmic nature and the gods? In that case how are systems of exchange and sexual difference articulated?

Take certain Far Eastern countries where religious rites and individual or collective prayer involve active personal participation (yoga, *tai-chi*, karate, song, dance, tea ceremony, flower arranging), rather than a sacrifice of the other – the spiritual (not simply procreative) richness of eroticism seems to be more in evidence. Even if the impact of the West on these practices is effacing it to some degree, sexual difference has been honoured in the postures of the body, in the rhythm of the seasons, in the representations of the gods (usually copulating), and so on. The organs of the body are viewed and situated according to their qualities and their circuits of energy – more or less male or female – following seasonal cycles, the hours of the day, etc. The sacred consists in honouring nature rather than immolating it. Life in all its dimensions is seen as a discipline, a culture of health insofar as it is spiritual and divine. A community should organize a space-time which is in harmony with micro- and macrocosmic needs.

To be ethical, social and religious means then to be attentive to the season, the hour, the moment, and to see to it that the living order is respected and not destroyed, except where destruction is inherent in the great natural cycles. Besides, this sort of destruction often corresponds to a growth or rebirth in a different form.

Is this a utopia? Can a society live without sacrifice, without aggression? Perhaps it can if it subjects itself to the present moment of the cosmic timescale. The order of the sacrificial superimposes upon natural rhythms a different, cumulative timescale which makes it unnecessary or impossible to be attentive to the present. When that happens, ritual observance becomes increasingly slack [*les inexactitudes s'accumulent*] to the point where a *catharsis* is needed.

Attentiveness to the present might be an adequate catharsis? Physiological, cosmic and social metabolisms can be harmonized. To achieve this harmony, there's no need for a sacrifice to regulate the collective order. Again, is this a utopia? Isn't it rather our sacrificial societies which live or outlive their time on the basis of a delusion which they actually foster? With the result that the sacrificial is virtually the only part we retain of certain religious traditions. In places of worship, Christ is usually represented on the cross. Feast-days, miracles, the Christian mystery, the supernatural are rarely figured. Now, the cross seems to me to be a non-Christian accident (cf. *Amante marine*, 'Epistle to the last Christians').[53] Taken on by Christ, the cross isn't part of his own message – it's part of the refusal by certain powers of this message: a God made man. Christ's role in this event is his fidelity to his incarnation.

Other events are more specifically Christian. And certain rites, such as the eucharist, which is not exclusively Christian in the sacred character of the shared meal. I would attribute the following meaning to the eucharist: I am going to be sacrificed, I am giving you something other than my flesh (namely the fruits of the earth, which I have consecrated), to share out before the sacrifice so that my body can enter into glory and not, once dead, be eaten by you in my absence. In that case the 'sin' would be to perpetuate the sacrificial where sharing with the divine could and should take place.

Something else which is obvious: in sacrificial religions, religious and social rites are almost universally in the hands of men. Men alone carry out the rite, not women or children (male children can occasionally assist with it). In most traditions women are never allowed to celebrate the religious rite, even though this rite provides both the foundation and the structure of society.

If this is the case, doesn't the founding sacrifice precisely correspond to this *extradition* from the celebration of religion, this exile from the places where the ultimate social decisions are taken? As long as we live in sacrificial societies, the choice of who will be victim and of the form of the rite are essential, both during the rite and afterwards. Now women aren't allowed to have anything to do with it. They shouldn't want to? Perhaps not. But they don't have any other societies, at least not yet. They are therefore *reinserted into a form of sociality that has been determined by sacrifice*. They haven't been included in it and they're still excluded from it. At this level they remain an inert body, paralysed in and through cultural bonds which aren't their own. *Minus one* in a society which would like to be (more) *one* [Moins un *d'une société qui se veut (plus)* une],[54] the goal, their goal, is taken away from them. Sublimation (in Freud's terms) would be an impossibility for them since they don't have their own order. They would remain in chaos, formless. Which amounts, in our traditions, to the *profane*. If women are to accede to a different sort of social organization, they need a religion, a language, and either a currency of their own or a non-market economy.[55] These three conditions go hand in hand.

Either we must totally reorganize present-day culture, particularly its spatial and temporal co-ordinates, or we must institute an alternative society more in line with the rites of cultures which are not sacrificial ones. This would mean restoring a form of sociality attentive to the cosmos and regulated by its laws, not just the cycles of the moon but the rhythms of the entire macrocosm. Wouldn't restricting ourselves to the moon mean restricting ourselves to what is traditionally – physiologically – said to be our allotted share? In the West, at least. Some women who attack Freud violently for his biologism declare their allegiance to the moon quite as virulently. Perhaps these two courses of action have something in common?

Of course we have a relation to the moon, but what is it exactly? We also have a relation to the sun. Some cultures link women to the sun, and men to the moon. Any interpretation of a link with a heavenly body should therefore be handled with considerable care. Even in our own culture, the ancient Greek goddesses of the fertility of the earth, like Demeter, are associated with the solar seasons, particularly in their relationships with their daughters: Persephone, carried off by the god of the underworld – of the shadows – is returned to her mother for spring and summer so that the earth can remain fertile. The mother agrees to be fertile *with her daughter*, and this fertility takes place *during the solar periods*. These periods will later come under the rule of Apollo. Even then, this god still makes way for these ancient goddesses in his sanctuary. A strange way it's true!

II

The desire to institute a new form of sociality doesn't alter the fact that we still live in the one that exists at present: a sacrificial, technological, technocratic society set up and managed by men alone. It's still true. More than ever.

How can we inaugurate amongst ourselves rites of some sort which would permit us to live in it and to become women in all our dimensions? How can we set up systems of exchange *amongst ourselves*? I don't know of any societies that have lived on and in exchange *amongst women*. Perhaps such a society existed a very long time ago? Perhaps it still exists somewhere far away. But where are the traces of a *currency* amongst women? Of a god *amongst* women? We can name examples of women's rites or of rites between women: healing rites often defined as witchcraft (even if they anticipate certain modern medical practices which return to older traditions), sabbatical rites close to the cosmic. These rites are often associated with the moon, at least in recent times. And even today, this is often the only part of themselves to which women lay claim, despite such divine goddesses of fertility as Gaea, Demeter ... Most of the gods of the *universe* start out as goddesses. The latter are hidden beneath the sacrificial? Silently. These goddesses are *solar*. They rule over spring and summer. They are only fertile through the affection and proximity of their daughters. When their daughters are taken away from them by male gods they make the earth sterile.

A fertile earth and a high-priced commodity are not the same thing. It often happens that these two forms of produce stand in economic opposition to each other and that the second solution is preferred to the first. But the suppression of the goddesses of cosmic fertility in the process of forming so-called wealthy societies has not been without problems. Each time that man, men, try to build an economic order that disregards the earth, this order becomes sterile, repressive, destructive.

Isn't the sacrifice of natural fertility the primordial sacrifice? The result is an economic superstructure (wrongly called an infrastructure), which fails to respect the infrastructure of natural fertility. This order produces a number of economic aberrations: some lands aren't cultivated, part of the earth's produce is thrown away, part of the world goes hungry even in industrialized countries or an industrialized universe. For what currency? For it is clearly a case of a discrepancy between a currency standard and use value: the products of the earth which are necessary for food, clothing and housing. Today the produce and productive capacity of the earth may be destroyed in order to inflate a currency without reserves.

Sacrificial societies, unconsciously or consciously, perpetuate (or reveal?) the thoughtless destruction of the earth's produce and the potential of that produce. Yet this is what constitutes the initial and final guarantee of an exchange value; not sophisticated arms and the most up-to-date technology. Indeed, what is the point of consolidating the power of countries if their populations are dying of hunger and have no habitable space left? Beneath the animal or human sacrifice is hidden perhaps the vegetable sacrifice and the disappearance of the goddesses of natural fertility.

Nevertheless, there is no question of us simply returning to the earth goddesses, even if that were possible. A return to them would require that they be upheld, and that we establish (or re-establish?) a form of sociality based on those values and that fertility. It's not enough to restore myths if we can't celebrate them and use them as the basis of a social order. Is that possible?

Let's grant that it is possible: will Gaea or Demeter be enough? What will we do with Core? And Persephone? And Diana? And Aphrodite? Aren't we always at least two?[56] How can we unite the two within us? Between us? How can we affirm together these elementary values, these natural fertilities, how can we celebrate them and turn them into currency while becoming or remaining women?

According to Feuerbach, it's not possible to affirm a genus or a human kind without a god, and probably not without a trinity.[57] Women, traditionally mothers of God, lack their own God (or gods) with which, individually or as a community, to attain a specificity of their own (cf. 'Femmes divines'[58]).

III

To demand unpaid labour of a woman, for women to resist social remu-neration for work, also means a *repression, or an assent to the censor-ship, of our desire to trade amongst ourselves*. Little girls love playing at shopkeepers, much more than little boys do, and this quite sponta-neously, without being taught. Where do they acquire this taste that accompanies their rapid acquisition of language, their talkativeness? To what repression or censorship do these symbolic exchanges, more pre-cocious in girls than boys, get submitted? For the benefit of what form of male sociality? At the price of what sacrifice(s)? As long as women remain unaware of this repression and its denial, of their failure to rec-ognize it, then they perpetuate it. And it appears quite normal not to pay or to underpay a woman, to ask of her traditionally unpaid labour. Especially if she is working for the liberation of women? I'm using this expression in its broadest possible sense. To give an account of what one knows, what one has learnt, to a female audience is a contribution, for example, to women's liberation. Unless this learning doesn't help them to situate themselves socially and culturally as women, unless it discourages their search for their own identity, makes them feel that there is no hope for a future any different from the past, other than, at best, becoming men.

It appears to be impossible, at least in any profound and lasting way, to modify social relations, language, art in general, without modifying the economic system of exchange. They go hand in hand. Sometimes the one predominates, sometimes the other, but changes in both are indispensable for any social mutation. We can neither decide nor hope to liberate ourselves from a given order without changing the forms of that order. The one demands the other. A change in economic style wouldn't necessarily entail any real change in *relations between women*. On the other hand, a reordering of social relationships between women necessitates the setting up of an economic system of their own. And, in the first place, respect for a system of exchange.

In the absence of an exchange system, the law amongst women is consumption without rites. The totemic meal, of course, allows the mur-der of the victim to be exorcized. Without some rite, this consumption becomes dangerous and gives rise to various forms of pathology. Thus that which is blindly sacrificed becomes persecuting and engenders persecution between male and female consumers. Freud describes for us the murder of the father, the institution of the primal horde through the devouring of the primogenitor, and the risk of conflict between 'brothers' before and after this ritual crime. Isn't this a more serious risk without a rite? And without modification of the kind of society?

Perhaps it is not indispensable for every society to found itself upon a sacrifice. But if this is to be avoided, it is important to assure the functioning of society in some other manner. We need to modify our relationship with the spatial-temporal order, to become faithful once more to micro- and macrocosmic rhythms. Which supposes that we reduce – without a new sacrifice – the concentrations of time and space which are built on a sacrifice: of men, of animals, in a less obvious way of the vegetable, of the vegetative, of its qualities, of our elementary food and space, etc.

IV

Certainly our societies presuppose that *the mother should nurture the child without payment*, before and after the birth, and that she should continue to nurture both man and society – *a totem before any designated, identified or represented totem*. To become aware of this is essential if a woman, women, are to find a way of situating themselves without remaining in the position of obscure nurturers. This traditional role paralyses male society too, and allows us to go on destroying life's natural reserves. This society upholds the illusion that food should come to us free of charge and that, in any case, it will never run out. Nor will the supply of women ever run out, especially mothers. A certain number of fictional writings describe a world where the sexes are separated. But none, to my knowledge, imagines a world without mothers. Of course there are fictions and experiments of the 'test-tube baby' sort. But this is still entertaining the notion of the maternal function. An artificial womb isn't yet an artificial nurturer, at least not a post-natal one. Up to what age would one need to take care of these artificial children in order to dispense with mothers? How much would they cost? What changes would result from manufacturing babies in laboratories in this way – what economic, affective and cultural changes?

Estimating the cost of a child shocks almost anyone's imagination. You don't have to be an expert on the mind or the human psyche to worry about it.

Freud, who didn't, as far as I know, consider such a thing possible, maintains that *money is linked to the anal*,[59] and elsewhere he says that *children think that they are born through the anus*. He doesn't make the connexion between the child and the currency of exchange. At least I don't remember having read this anywhere in his work. But one might raise the question of the *transposition* – unavoidable in our social

regime – *of little girls playing at shopkeepers into mothers with a some-*
what possessive attitude towards their children, especially if they don't
have any paid work, if they don't have any money of their own and mis-
understand their relationship with the anal, which they apprehend only
in its aspect as rape – experienced and feared on account of the drives
and fantasies of men. The anal is something which women can only
experience in a passive way. It's as if they'd been anally castrated. Their
so-called desire for the penis – or phallus – could perhaps be seen as
submission to an economic, imaginary and symbolic order where the
anal prevails, and where, as far as the economy of anal drives and their
possible sublimation is concerned, women are amputated. Given their
social and cultural role, the *only* goods that women could *exchange(?)*
would be their children, and what they say or do *apropos of their chil-*
dren. They would exchange them – without any explicitly organized
market – in order to achieve their *own* status as traders, qua objects of
value and maternal subjects(?) or maternal function. In maternity they
have social value and ... are phallic, writes Freud, and others after him.
But then this phallic must belong to the anal, in different forms (especially oral).

The character of a society organized around such exchanges is still
largely anal, whether it is manufactured goods, currency, children, or, to
some extent, women that are exchanged. These different products can
be substituted for each other. Some are guaranteed by the 'fixed' standard of procreation, others are far more subject to inflation and devalu-
ation. The fuss caused by the problems of contraception, abortion and
the production of more or less artificial children can be understood in
terms of the fact that *procreation has been the value underlying our soci-*
eties for thousands of years. The question isn't expressed in these terms
– the 'work' is unpaid, the job is enveloped in an intangible aura of
sacredness, in masks commensurate with the repressions and ignorance
which it presupposes and continues to demand.

Women who continue to demand unpaid childbirth and unpaid child-
rearing from other women are a party – whether or not voluntarily – to
a system of values which is predominantly anal and sacrificial, where
the value of the child and of mothers is that of a relatively stable commodity beneath the fluctuations of currencies and economic regimes.

V

Deprived of rites and social institutions, women are left to polemicize
and settle their accounts privately. This is their habitual way of going

about things, between women and children, and especially between mothers and daughters. In this, their world could be compared to certain primitive societies, with no official sacrifice, no acknowledged sacrificial rite, no jurisprudence of their own. Vengeance is practised, outside of laws or rights, in the form of aggressions that may or may not be preconcerted. Thus a sort of international vendetta is set up, present more or less everywhere, which disorientates the female populace, the groups and micro-societies which are in the process of being formed. Real murders take place as a part of it, but also (insofar as they can be distinguished) cultural murders, murders of minds, emotions and intelligence, which women perpetuate amongst themselves.

Some intellectuals lack judicial status too. The way they behave derives from insufficient regulation of these sorts of social relations.

If there are social injustices in the marxist sense in the fact of the different status of jobs, there are injustices too in spheres which have been less thoroughly analysed: intellectual work is underpaid despite the fact that our societies live off the exploitation of intellectuals by industry, for example. Quite apart from the fact that most of the time it is intellectuals who have directly or indirectly invented our social and political modes of organization. The payment doesn't go to the place where the work is done, but to the place where the work is exploited. Intellectuals are seen as the king's fool whereas, in actual fact, they are the origin of the king. Unwaged at the site of its production, subject to a sacrificial misunderstanding (recognition often comes only with old age or after death), intellectual work entails a social disfunctioning. What's more, as victims, intellectuals turn into instigators of sacrifices. All this is possible because of a non-adjustment of values, particularly of thought and of the female as social resources. *For if intellectuals are underpaid, women remain unpaid.* Another fundamental disorder of society: the existence of its functional infrastructure isn't acknowledged because it comes free. There is no constitution, development or renewal of the social body without women's work: their cathartic function as loved mistress or wife, their function as reproducing mother, their functions as carer and housewife assuring life and survival. What allows the sacrificial rite or rhythm to exist is already based in the first place on this non-recognition, or on this oversight.

I bring the two together: women and (female) intellectuals. The two are linked to an interpretation and an evolution of the way in which the social organization is thought and conceived. The latter is often only interpreted, imagined and programmed partially and after the event. It is rarely *thought out in advance*, as a whole. Less and less? The fashion is for the past and forgetting what is still to be discovered of the future in the past. Myths, tales and sacred tests are analysed, occasionally with nostalgia, rarely with a view to modifying society as it is at present. They are consumed or reconsumed, as it were. The obscurities of our imaginary or symbolic horizon are analysed more or less adequately, but rarely with a view to setting up a new ethic The sacred, the religious, the popular are being invaded by technology which doesn't, however, open up a new world commensurate with what it consumes (in both senses) [*consomme ou consume*]. Although it promotes itself in various ways, and can sometimes inform/give form [*informe parfois*], it cannot create. Thinkers and women aren't rewarded for what they bring to the functioning of society: the most fully elaborated work of the mind and of nature, the two going together.

But any thought which fails to recognize its natural sources and resources isn't genuine thought. Or it's thought that endangers life. To speak or to try to think the sublime is legitimate if the sublime respects what has allowed it to be thought: nature, the micro- and macrocosm. All the rest is a technocratic machine which separates our heads from our bodies, from our feet, splitting us into semi ghosts, on the one hand, and bodies like machines or servants on the other [*des corps machines-serviteurs*]. Women who let themselves be consumed without pay belong to the same disorder.

In a society like ours, money not paid where it is due deregulates the mechanism, the organism. Certain cogs and certain strata function in a *primitive* mode in a highly technocratic entity. Could these little enclaves of another sort or style change the whole society? That's the wager of some (women). This wager is far from being a simple utopia, as others claim, but it requires an extremely rigorous ethical position if it's to avoid constantly providing fuel for that against which or despite which these 'cells' are trying to work. This wager requires the protection of especially designed places and space, so as not to fall back into an atopia so long as the scaffolding of the social order endures and recuperates the products of 'primitives', 'mutants', 'rebels' and 'others' ... For society refuses to acknowledge differences, in order to save(?) the city, to maintain its order, to make it evolve according to cycles which always throw things out once their best part has been absorbed, or which turn slowly enough to allow the digestion of the other consumed without poisoning, death, rebirth and resurrection of the social body.

Must we kill then? That's not the goal. Uncovering murders doesn't necessarily mean killing, but suspending hidden crime, aggression and sacrifice. This would force a rebalancing of the group, of groups and of individuals. To tell the other that he is a criminal, often involuntary, doesn't mean imposing any sanction on him other than that of becoming conscious of himself and of permitting the other to become so as well. Of course this will modify the economy of consciousness [*conscience*]. Masters are no longer its masters, with the alibi of helping others insofar as they alone respect the status of an intangible good conscience [*conscience*]. The master, the masters, split themselves into at least two sexes. The sacrifice then becomes that of the omnipotence of either one or the other, a sacrifice which reopens the world, whereas immolation normally leads to the constitution of a world which is *closed* by *periodic exclusion*. This sacrifice – if indeed it is one, since it involves a discipline rather than a sacrifice – comes down to the renunciation of the narcissistic self-sufficiency of an individual person or of a social body.

Perhaps this means recognizing that we are still and continue to be *open* to the world and to the other simply because we are alive and sensitive, subject to time and to the rhythms of the universe, a universe with which we share certain properties – properties which are different depending upon whether we are men or women. We are not living, for all that, in primitive societies, nor in a culture at pains to take its rhythms from the moment, the hour, and the season, so as to respect natural products and to respect ourselves as one of these. If we were, then sacrifice might seem pointless? Winter isn't summer, night isn't day, not all the parts of the universe equal each other. These rhythms ought to be sufficient to permit us to constitute societies. Why hasn't man been satisfied with them? Where does he get this excess of violence that he then needs to get rid of? Has his growth been stunted or stopped?

16 MARY ANN DOANE

Woman's Stake: Filming the Female Body

> We know that, for want of a stake, representation is not worth anything
>
> Michèle Montrelay

To those who still ask, 'What do women want?' the cinema seems to provide no answer. For the cinema, in its alignment with the fantasies of the voyeur, has historically articulated its stories through a conflation of its central axis of seeing/being seen with the opposition male/female. So much so that in a classical instance such as *Humoresque*, when Joan Crawford almost violently attempts to appropriate the gaze for herself, she must be represented as myopic (the moments of her transformation from spectacle to spectator thus captured and constrained through their visualization as the act of putting on glasses) and eventually eliminated from the text, her death equated with that of a point of view. Cinematic images of woman have been so consistently oppressive and repressive that the very idea of a feminist filmmaking practice seems an impossibility. The simple gesture of directing a camera toward a woman has become equivalent to a terrorist act.

This state of affairs – the result of a history which inscribes woman as subordinate – is not simply to be overturned by a contemporary practice that is more aware, more self-conscious. The impasse confronting feminist film makers today is linked to the force of a certain theoretical discourse which denies the neutrality of the cinematic apparatus itself. A machine for the production of images and sounds, the cinema generates and guarantees pleasure by a corroboration of the spectator's identity. Because that identity is bound up with that of the voyeur and the fetishist, because it requires for its support the attributes of the 'noncastrated', the potential for illusory mastery of the signifier, it is not accessible to the female spectator, who, in buying her ticket, must deny her sex. There are no images either *for* her or *of* her. There is a sense in which Peter Gidal, in attempting to articulate the relationship between his own filmmaking practice and feminist concerns, draws the most logical conclusion from this tendency in theory:

> In terms of the feminist struggle specifically, I have had a vehement refusal over the last decade, with one or two minor aberrations, to allow images of women into my films at all, since I do not see how those images can be separated from the dominant meanings. The ultra-left aspect of this may be nihilistic as well, which may be a critique of my position because it does not see much hope for representations for women, but I do not see how, to take the main example I gave round about 1969 before any knowledge on my part of, say, semiotics, there is any possibility of using the image of a naked woman – at that time I did not have it clarified to the point of any image of a woman – other than in an absolutely sexist and politically repressive patriarchal way in this conjuncture.[60]

This is the extreme formulation of a project which can define itself only in terms of negativity. If the female body is not necessarily always excluded within this problematic, it must always be placed within quotation marks. For it is precisely the massive reading, writing, filming of the female body which constructs and maintains a hierarchy along the lines of a sexual difference assumed as natural. The ideological complicity of the concept of the natural dictates the impossibility of a nostalgic return to an unwritten body.

Thus, contemporary filmmaking addresses itself to the activity of uncoding, de-coding, deconstructing the given images. It is a project of defamiliarization whose aim is not necessarily that of seeing the female body differently, but of exposing the habitual meanings/values attached to femininity as cultural constructions. Sally Potter's *Thriller*, for instance, is a rereading of the woman's role in opera, specifically in Puccini's *La Bohème*, in terms of its ideological function. Mimi's death, depicted in the opera as tragedy, is rewritten as a murder, the film itself invoking the conventions of the suspense thriller. In Babette Mangolte's *The Camera: Je/La Caméra: Eye*, what is at stake are the relations of power sustained within the camera–subject nexus. The discomfort of the subjects posing for the camera, together with the authority of the off-screen voice giving instructions ('Smile,' 'Don't smile,' 'Look to the left,' etc.), challenge the photographic image's claim to naturalism and spontaneity. And, most interestingly, the subjects, whether male or female, inevitably appear to assume a mask of 'femininity' in order to become photographic (filmable) – as though femininity were synonymous with the *pose*.[61] This may explain the feminist film's frequent obsession with the pose as position – the importance accorded to dance positions in *Thriller*, or those assumed by the hysteric in Terrel Seltzer's *The Story of Anna O.* – which we may see as the arrangements of the body in the interests of aesthetics and science. In their rigidity (the recurrent use of the tableau in these films) or excessive repetition (the multiple, seemingly unending caresses of the woman's breasts in Mangolte's *What Maisie Knew*), positions and gestures are isolated, deprived of the syntagmatic rationalization which, in the more classical text, conduces to their naturalization. These strategies of demystification are attempts to strip the body of its readings. The inadequacy of this formulation of the problem is obvious, however, in that the gesture of stripping in relation to a female body is already the property of patriarchy. More importantly, perhaps, the question to be addressed in this: what is left after the stripping, the uncoding, the deconstruction? For an uncoded body is clearly an impossibility.

Attempts to answer this question by invoking the positivity or specificity of a definition have been severely criticized on the grounds that the particular definition claims a 'nature' proper to the woman and is hence complicit with those discourses which set woman outside the social order. Since the patriarchy has always already said everything (everything and nothing) about woman, efforts to give those phrases a different intonation, to mumble, to stutter, to slur them, to articulate them differently, must be doomed to failure. Laura Mulvey and Peter Wollen's *Riddles of the Sphinx*, for instance, has been repeatedly criticized for its invocation of the sphinx as the figure of a femininity repressed by the Oedipal mythos. Femininity is something which has been forgotten or repressed, left outside the gates of the city; hence, what is called for is a radical act of remembering. The radicality of that act, however, has been subject to debate. As Stephen Heath points out,

> The line in the figure of the sphinx-woman between the posing of a question and the idea that women are the question is very thin; female sexuality is dark and unexplorable, women, as Freud puts it, are that half of the audience which is the enigma, the great enigma. This is the problem and the difficulty – the area of debate and criticism – of Mulvey and Wollen's film *Riddles of the Sphinx* where the sphinx is produced as a point of resistance that seems nevertheless to repeat, in its very terms, the relations of women made within patriarchy, their representation in the conjunction of such elements as motherhood as mystery, the unconscious, a voice that speaks far off from the past through dream or forgotten language. The film is as though poised on the edge of a politics of the unconscious, of the imagination of a politics of the unconscious ('what would the politics of the unconscious be like?'), with a simultaneous falling short, that politics and imagination not yet there, coming back with old definitions, the given images.[62]

What is forgotten in the critical judgement, but retrieved in Heath's claim that 'the force remains in the risk' – the risk, that is, of recapitulating the terms of patriarchy – is the fact that the sphinx is also, and crucially, subject to a kind of filmic disintegration. In the section entitled 'Stones', the refilming of found footage of the Egyptian sphinx problematizes any notion of perceptual immediacy in refinding an 'innocent' image of femininity. In fact, as the camera appears to get closer to its object, the graininess of the film is marked, thus indicating the limit of the material basis of its representation.

Most of this essay will be a lengthy digression, a prolegomenon to a much needed investigation of the material specificity of film in relation to the female body and its syntax. Given the power of a certain form of feminist theory which has successfully blocked attempts to provide a conceptualization of this body, the digression is, nevertheless, crucial.

The resistance to filmic and theoretical descriptions of femininity is linked to the strength of the feminist critique of essentialism – of ideas concerning an essential femininity, or of the 'real' woman not yet disfigured by patriarchal social relations. The force of this critique lies in its exposure of the inevitable alliance between 'feminine essence' and the natural, the given, or precisely what is outside the range of political action and thus not amenable to change. This unchangeable 'order of things' in relation to sexual difference is an exact formulation of patriarchy's strongest rationalization of itself. And since the essence of femininity is most frequently attached to the natural body as an immediate indicator of sexual difference, it is this body which must be refused. The body is always a function of discourse.

Feminist theory which grounds itself in anti-essentialism frequently turns to psychoanalysis for its description of sexuality because psychoanalysis assumes a necessary gap between the body and the psyche, so that sexuality is not reducible to the physical. Sexuality is constructed within social and symbolic relations; it is most *un*natural and achieved only after an arduous struggle. One is not born with a sexual identity (hence the significance of the concept of bisexuality in psychoanalysis). The terms of this argument demand that charges of phallocentrism be met with statements that the phallus is not equal to the penis, castration is bloodless, and the father is, in any case dead and only symbolic.

Nevertheless, the gap between body and psyche is not absolute; an image or symbolization of the body (which is not necessarily the body of biological science) is fundamental to the construction of the psychoanalytical discourse. Brief references to two different aspects of psychoanalytic theory will suffice to illustrate my point. Jean Laplanche explains the emergence of sexuality by means of the concept of propping or *anaclisis*. The drive, which is always sexual, leans or props itself upon the nonsexual or presexual instinct of self-preservation. His major example is the relation of the oral drive to the instinct of hunger whose object is the milk obtained from the mother's breast. The object of the oral drive (prompted by the sucking which activates the lips as an erotogenic zone) is necessarily displaced in relation to the first object of the instinct. The fantasmatic breast (henceforth the object of the oral drive) is a metonymic derivation, a symbol, of the milk: 'The object to be rediscovered is not the lost object, but its substitute by displacement; the lost object is the object of self-preservation, of hunger, and the object one seeks to refind is an object displaced in relation to that first object.'[63] Sexuality can only take form in a dissociation of subjectivity from the bodily function, but the concept of a bodily function is necessary in the explanation as, precisely, a support. We will see later how Laplanche de-naturalizes this body (which is simply a distribution of erotogenic zones) while retaining it as a cipher. Still, the body is there, as a prop.

The second aspect of psychoanalysis which suggests the necessity of a certain conceptualization of the body is perhaps more pertinent, and certainly more notorious, in relation to a discussion of feminism: the place of the phallus in Lacanian theory. Lacan and feminist theorists who subscribe to his formulations persistently claim that the phallus is not the penis; the phallus is a signifier (the signifier of lack). It does not *belong* to the male. The phallus is only important insofar as it can be put in circulation as a signifier. Both sexes define themselves in relation to this 'third term'. What is ultimately stressed here is the absolute necessity of positing only one libido (which Freud labels masculine) in relation to only one term, the phallus. Initially, both sexes, in desiring to conform to the desire of the other (the mother), define themselves in relation to the phallus in the mode of 'being'. Sexual difference, then, is inaugurated at the moment of the Oedipal complex when the girl continues to 'be' the phallus while the boy situates himself in the mode of 'having'. Positing two terms, in relation to two fully defined sexualities, as Jones and Horney do, binds the concept of sexuality more immediately, more directly, to the body as it expresses itself at birth. For Jones and Horney, there is an essential femininity which is linked to an expression of the vagina. And for Horney at least, there is a sense in which the little girl experiences an empirical, not a psychic, inferiority.[64]

But does the phallus really have nothing to do with the penis, no commerce with it at all? The ease of the description by means of which the boy situates himself in the mode of 'having' one would seem to indicate that this is not the case. And Lacan's justification for the privilege accorded to the phallus as signifier appears to guarantee its derivation from a certain representation of the bodily organ:

> The phallus is the privileged signifier of that mark in which the role of the logos is joined with the advent of desire. It can be said that this signifier is chosen because it is the most tangible element in the real of sexual copulation, and also the most symbolic in the literal (typographical) sense of the term, since it is equivalent there to the (logical) copula. It might also be said that, by virtue of its turgidity, it is the image of the vital flow as it is transmitted in generation.[65]

There is a sense in which all attempts to deny the relation between the phallus and the penis are feints, veils, illusions. The phallus, as signifier, may no longer *be* the penis, but any effort to conceptualize its function is inseparable from an imaging of the body. The difficulty in conceptualizing the relation between the phallus and the penis is evident in Parveen Adams's explanation of the different psychic trajectories of the girl and the boy.

Sexuality can only be considered at the level of the symbolic process. This lack is undifferentiated for both sexes and has nothing to do with the absence of a penis, a physical lack.

Nonetheless, the anatomical difference between the sexes does permit a differentiation within the symbolic process. . . . The phallus represents lack both for boys and girls. But the boy in having a penis has that which lends itself to the phallic symbol. The girl does not have a penis. What she lacks is not a penis as such, but the means to represent lack.[66]

The sexual differentiation is permitted but not demanded by the body and it is the exact force or import of this 'permitting' which requires an explanation. For it is clear that what is being suggested is that the boy's body provides an access to the processes of representation while the girl's body does not. From this perspective, a certain slippage can then take place by means of which the female body becomes an absolute tabula rasa of sorts: anything and everything can be written on it. Or more accurately, perhaps, the male body comes fully equipped with a binary opposition – penis/no penis, presence/absence, phonemic opposition – while the female body is constituted as 'noise',[67] an undifferentiated presence which always threatens to disrupt representation.

This analysis of the bodily image in psychoanalysis becomes crucial for feminism with the recognition that sexuality is inextricable from discourse, from language. The conjunction of semiotics and psychoanalysis (as exemplified in the work of Lacan and others) has been successful in demonstrating the necessity of a break in an initial plenitude as a fundamental condition for signification. The concept of lack is not arbitrary. The fact that the little girl in the above description has no means to represent lack results in her different relation to language and representation. The work of Michèle Montrelay is most explicit in this issue: '. . . for want of a stake, representation is not worth anything'.[68] The initial relation to the mother, the determinant of the desire of both sexes, is too full, too immediate, too present. This undifferentiated plenitude must be fissured through the introduction of lack before representation can be assured, since representation entails the absence of the desired object. 'Hence the repression that ensures that one does not think, nor see, nor take the desired object, even and above all if it is within reach: this object must remain lost.'[69] The tragedy of Oedipus lies in his refinding of the object. And as Montrelay points out, it is the sphinx as the figure of femininity which heralds this 'ruin of representation'.

In order for representation to be possible, then, a stake is essential. Something must be threatened if the paternal prohibition against incest is to take effect, forcing the gap between desire and its object. This theory results in a rather surprising interpretation of the woman's psychic oppression: her different relation to language stems from the fact that she has nothing to lose, nothing at stake. Prohibition, the law of limitation, cannot touch the little girl. For the little boy, on the other hand, there is most definitely something to lose. 'He experiments, not only with chance but also with the law and with his sexual organ: his body itself takes on the value of stake.'[70]

Furthermore, in repeating, doubling the maternal body with her own, the woman recovers the first stake of representation and thus undermines the possibility of losing the object of desire since she has, instead, become it.

> From now on, anxiety, tied to the presence of this body, can only be insistent, continuous. This body, so close, which she has to occupy, is an object in excess which must be 'lost', that is to say, repressed, in order to be symbolized. Hence the symptoms which so often simulate this loss: 'there is no longer anything, only the hole, emptiness ...' Such is the *leitmotif* of all feminine cure, which it would be a mistake to see as the expression of an alleged 'castration'. On the contrary, it is a defense produced in order to parry the avatars, the deficiencies, of symbolic castration.[71]

There are other types of defense as well, based on the woman's imaginary simulation of lack. Montrelay points to the anorexic, for instance, who diminishes her own body, dissolving the flesh and reducing the body to a cipher.[72] Or the woman can operate a performance of femininity, a masquerade, by means of an accumulation of accessories – jewelry, hats, feathers, etc. – all designed to mask the absence of a lack.[73] These defenses, however, are based on the woman's imaginary simulation of lack and exclude the possibility of an encounter with the symbolic. She can only mime representation.

Montrelay's work is problematic in several respects. In situating the woman's relation to her own body as narcissistic, erotic, and maternal, Montrelay insists that it is the 'real of her own body' which 'imposes itself', prior to any act of construction.[74] Furthermore, she does, eventually, outline a scenario within which the woman has access to symbolic lack, but it is defined in terms of a heterosexual act of intercourse in which the penis, even though it is described as 'scarcely anything', produces the 'purest and most elementary form of signifying articulation'.[75] Nevertheless, Montrelay's work points to the crucial dilemma confronting an anti-essentialist feminist theory which utilizes psychoanalysis. That is, while psychoanalysis does theorize the relative autonomy of psychic processes, the gap between body and psyche, it also requires the body as a prop, a support for its description of sexuality as a discursive function. Too often anti-essentialism is characterized by a paranoia in relation to all discussions of the female body (since ideas about a 'natural' female body or the female body and 'nature' are the linchpins of patriarchal ideology). This results in a position which simply repeats that of classical Freudian psychoanalysis in its focus upon the little boy's psychic development at the expense of that of the little girl. What is repressed here is the fact that psychoanalysis can conceptualize the sexuality of both the boy and the girl *only* by positing gender-specific bodies.

Even more crucially, as Montrelay's work demonstrates, the use of the concepts of the phallus and castration within a semiotically oriented psychoanalysis logically implies that the woman must have a different relation to language from that of the man. And from a semiotic perspective, her relation to language must be deficient since her body does not 'permit' access to what, for the semiotician, is the motor-force of language – the representation of lack. Hence, the greatest masquerade of all is that of the woman speaking (or writing, or filming), appropriating discourse. To take up a discourse for the woman (if not, indeed, by her), that is, the discourse of feminism itself, would thus seem to entail an absolute contradiction. How can she speak?

Yet, we know that women speak, even though it may not be clear exactly how this takes place. And unless we want to accept a formulation by means of which woman can only mimic man's relation to language, that is, assume a position defined by the penis-phallus as the supreme arbiter of lack, we must try to reconsider the relation between the female body and language, never forgetting that it is a relation between two terms and not two essences. Does woman have a stake in representation or, more appropriately, can we assign one to her? Anatomy is destiny only if the concept of destiny is recognized for what it really is: a concept proper to fiction.

The necessity of assigning to woman a specific stake informs the work of theorists such as Luce Irigaray and Julia Kristeva, and both have been criticized from an anti-essentialist perspective. Beverley Brown and Parveen Adams, for example, distinguish between two orders of argument about the female body which are attributed, respectively, to Irigaray and Kristeva:

> We can demand then: what is this place, this body, from which women speak so mutely?
>
> Two orders of reply to this question can be distinguished. In the first there is an attempt to find a real and natural body which is pre-social in a literal sense. The second, more sophisticated reply, says that the issue at stake is not the actual location of a real body, but that the positing of such a body seems to be a condition of the discursive in general.[76]

Although the second order of argument is described as 'more sophisticated', Brown and Adams ultimately find that both are deficient. I want briefly to address this criticism although it really requires an extended discussion impossible within the limits of this essay. The criticisms of Irigaray are based primarily on her essay, 'That Sex Which Is Not One',[77] in which she attempts to conceptualize the female body in relation to language/discourse, but independently of the penis/lack dichotomy. Irigaray valorizes certain features of the female body – the two lips (of the labia) which caress each other and define woman's auto-eroticism as a relation to duality, the multiplicity of sexualized zones spread across the body. Furthermore, Irigaray uses this representation of the body to specify a feminine language which is plural, polyvalent, and irreducible to a masculine language based on restrictive notions of unity and identity. Brown and Adams claim that 'her argument turns upon the possibility of discovering that which is already there – it is a case of "making visible" the previously "invisible" of feminine sexuality'.[78] While there are undoubtedly problems with the rather direct relation Irigaray often posits between the body and language, her attempt to provide the woman with an autonomous symbolic representation is not to be easily dismissed. Irigaray herself criticizes the logic which gives privilege to the gaze, thereby questioning the gesture of 'making visible' a previously hidden female sexuality. Her work is a radical rewriting of psychoanalysis which, while foregrounding the process of mimesis by which language represents the body, simultaneously constructs a distinction between a mimesis which is 'productive' and one which is merely 'reproductive' or 'imitative' – a process of 'adequation' and of 'specularization'.[79] An immediate dismissal of her work in the interests of an overwary anti-essentialism involves a premature rejection of 'the force that remains in the risk'.

The criticism addressed to Kristeva, on the other hand, is directed toward her stress on pre-Oedipal sexuality, allying it with a femininity whose repression is the very condition of Western discourse.[80] For Kristeva, the woman's negative relation to the symbolic determines her bond with a polymorphous, prelogical discourse which corresponds to the autonomous and polymorphous sexuality of the pre-Oedipal moment. Brown and Adams formulate their criticism in these terms: 'Setting up this apolitical autonomy of polymorphous sexuality is, in effect, the positing of sexuality as an impossible origin, a state of nature, as simply the eternal presence of sexuality at all.'[81] However, pre-Oedipal sexuality is not synonymous with 'nature'; it already assumes an organized distribution of erotogenic zones over the body and forms of relations to objects which are variable (whether human or nonhuman). Both male and female pass through, live pre-Oedipality. Hence, pre-Oedipality can only be equated with femininity retrospectively, *après coup*, after the event of the Oedipal complex, of the threat of castration, and the subsequent negative entry into the symbolic attributed to the woman. Insofar as Kristeva's description of pre-Oedipality is dependent upon notions of the drive, it involves a displacement of sexuality in relation to the body. As Laplanche points out, the drive is a metonymic derivation from the instinct which is itself attached to an erotogenic zone, a zone of *exchange*.

> The drive properly speaking, in the only sense faithful to Freud's discovery, is sexuality. Now sexuality, in its entirety, in the human infant, lies in *a movement which deflects the instinct, metaphorizes its aim, displaces and internalizes its object, and concentrates its source on what is ultimately a minimal zone, the erotogenic zone.* . . . This zone of exchange is also a zone for care, namely the particular and attentive care provided by the mother. These zones, then, attract the first erotogenic maneuvers from the adult. An even more significant factor, if we introduce the subjectivity of the first 'partner': these zones *focalize parental fantasies* and above all *maternal fantasies*, so that we may say, in what is barely a metaphor, that they are the points through which is *introduced into the child that alien internal entity* which is, properly speaking, the *sexual excitation*.[82]

The force of this scenario lies in its de-naturalization of the sexualized body. The conceptualization of the erotogenic zone as a zone of exchange demonstrates that the investment of the body with sexuality is always already social. Since it is ultimately *maternal* fantasies which are at issue here, it is apparent that, without an anchoring in the social, psychoanalysis can simply reiterate, reperform in its theorization, the vicious circle of patriarchy.

The rather long digression which structures this essay is motivated by the extreme difficulty of moving beyond the impasse generated by the opposition between essentialism and anti-essentialism. In the context of feminist film theory, both positions are formulated through a repression of the crucial and complex relation between the body and psychic processes, that is, processes of signification. From the point of view of essentialist theory, the goal of a feminist film practice must be production of images which provide a pure reflection of the real woman, thus returning the real female body to the woman as her rightful property. And this body is accessible to a transparent cinematic discourse. The position is grounded in a mis-recognition of signification as outside of, uninformed by, the psychic. On the other hand, the logical extension of anti-essentialist theory, particularly as it is evidenced in Gidal's description of his filmmaking practice, results in the absolute exclusion of the female body, the refusal of any attempt to figure or represent that body. Both the proposal of a pure access to a natural female body and the rejection of attempts to conceptualize the female body based on their contamination by ideas of 'nature' are inhibiting and misleading. Both positions deny the necessity of posing a complex relation between the body and psychic/signifying processes, of using the body, in effect, as a 'prop'. For Kristeva is right – the positing of a body *is* a condition of discursive practices. It is crucial that feminism move beyond the opposition between essentialism and anti-essentialism. This move will entail the necessary risk taken by theories which attempt to define or construct a feminine specificity (not essence), theories which work to provide the woman with an autonomous symbolic representation.

What this means in terms of the theorization of a feminist filmmaking practice can only be sketched here. But it is clear from the preceding exploration of the theoretical elaboration of the female body that the stake does not simply concern an isolated image of the body. The attempt to 'lean' on the body in order to formulate the woman's different relation to speech, to language, clarifies the fact that what is at stake is, rather, the syntax which constitutes the female body as a term. The most interesting and productive recent films dealing with the feminist problematic are precisely those which elaborate a new syntax, thus 'speaking' the female body differently, even haltingly or inarticulately from the perspective of a classical syntax. For instance, the circular camera movements which carve out the space of the mise-en-scène in *Riddles of the Sphinx* are in a sense more critical to a discussion of the film than the status of the figure of the sphinx as feminine. The film effects a continual displacement of the gaze which 'catches' the woman's body only accidentally, momentarily, refusing to hold or fix her in the frame. The camera consistently transforms its own framing to elide the possibility of a fetishism of the female body. Chantal Akerman's *Jeanne Dielman, 23 Quai du Commerce – 1080 Bruxelles* constructs its syntax by linking together scenes which, in the classical text, would be concealed, in effect negated, by temporal ellipses. The specificity of the film lies in the painful duration of that time 'inbetween' events, that time which is exactly proper to the woman (in particular, the housewife) within a patriarchal society. The obsessive routine of Jeanne Dielman's daily life, as both housewife and prostitute, is radically broken only by an instance of orgasm (corresponding quite literally to the 'climax' of the narrative) which is immediately followed by her murder of the man. Hence, the narrative structure is a parodic 'mime' that distorts, undoes the structure of the classical narrative through an insistence upon its repressions.

The analysis of the elaboration of a special syntax for a different articulation of the female body can also elucidate the significance of the recourse, in at least two of these films, to the classical codification of suspense. Both *Jeanne Dielman* and Sally Potter's *Thriller* construct a suspense without expectation. *Jeanne Dielman*, although it momentarily 'cites' the mechanism of the narrative climax, articulates an absolute refusal of the phatic function of suspense, its engagement with and constraint of the spectator as consumer, devourer of discourse. *Thriller*, on the other hand, 'quotes' the strategies of the suspense film (as well as individual films of this genre – for example, *Psycho*) in order to undermine radically the way in which the woman is 'spoken' by another genre altogether, that of operatic tragedy. This engagement with the condification of suspense is an encounter with the genre which Roland Barthes defines as the most intense embodiment of the 'generalized distortion' which 'gives the language of narrative its special character':

> 'Suspense' is clearly only a privileged – or 'exacerbated' – form of distortion: on the one hand, by keeping a sequence open (through emphatic procedures of delay and renewal), it reinforces the contact with the reader (the listener), has a manifestly phatic function; while on the other, it offers the threat of an uncompleted sequence, of an open paradigm (if, as we believe, every sequence has two poles), that is to say of a logical disturbance, it being this disturbance which is consumed with anxiety and pleasure (all the more so because it is always made right in the end). 'Suspense', therefore, is a game with structure, designed to endanger and glorify it, constituting a veritable 'thrilling' of intelligibility: by representing order (and no longer series) in its fragility, 'suspense' accomplishes the very idea of language .... [83]

It is precisely this 'idea of language' which is threatened by both *Jeanne Dielman* and *Thriller* in their attempts to construct another syntax which would, perhaps, collapse the fragile order, revealing the ending too soon.

While I have barely approached the question of an exact formulation of the representation of the female body attached to the syntactical constructions of these films, it is apparent that this syntax is an area of intense concern of reworking, rearticulating the specular imaging of woman, for whom, in the context of a current filmmaking, the formulation of a stake is already in process.

Notes

1 Joan Riviere, 'Womanliness as a Masquerade', *International Journal of Psychoanalysis* X (1929); all page numbers are given in the text. See also the collection of Riviere's essays, Athol Hughes (ed.), *Joan Riviere: The Inner World and Joan Riviere* (London: Karnac Books, 1990).

2 See Joan Copjec, 'The Sartorial Superego', *October* 50 (1989); and Jane Gaines and Charlotte Herzog (eds), *Fabrications: Costume and the Female Body* (London: Routledge, 1990).

3 Stephen Heath, 'Joan Riviere and the Masquerade', in Victor Burgin, James Donald and Cora Kaplan (eds), *Formations of Fantasy* (London: Methuen, 1986), p. 56.

4 Judith Butler, *Gender Trouble: Feminism and the Subversion of Identity* (London: Routledge, 1990), p. 48.

5 Christine Holmlund, 'I love Luce: The Lesbian Mimesis and Masquerade in Irigaray, Freud, and Mainstream Film', *New Formations*. 9 (1990) See also Mary Ann Doane, 'Masquerade Reconsidered: Further Thoughts on the Female Spectator', *Femmes Fatales: Feminism, Film Theory, Psychoanalysis* (London: Routledge, 1991): Riviere's masquerading patient 'obsessively turns around and reinscribes her sexuality, born as it is of power and its effects, within another field of power relations – that of race', a factor Riviere, and commentators on her essay, ignore (p. 38).

6 Laura Mulvey, 'Visual Pleasure and Narrative Cinema', *Screen* 16 (3) (Autumn 1975).

7 See Constance Penley, ' "A Certain Refusal of Difference" ', in *The Future of an Illusion: Film, Feminism, and Psychoanalysis* (London: Routledge, 1989); and Tania Modleski, *Loving with a Vengeance: Mass-Produced Fantasies for Women* (New York: Methuen, 1982).

8 Gaines and Herzog (eds), *Fabrications*, p. 24.

9 Mulvey, 'Afterthoughts on "Visual Pleasure and Narrative Cinema" inspired by *Duel in the Sun*', *Framework* 6 (15–17) (Summer 1981).

10 Paul Willemen, quoted in Kenneth A. MacKinnon, *Misogyny in the Movies: The De Palma Question* (London: Associated Universities Press, 1990), p. 54.

11 Penley, *The Future of an Illusion*, p. 49.

12 Doane, 'Film and the Masquerade: Theorizing the Female Spectator', *Femmes Fatales*, p. 20.

13 Christian Metz, *The Imaginary Signifier* (Bloomington: Indiana University Press, 1981). See also Slavoj Žižek, *Enjoy Your Symptom! Jacques Lacan in Hollywood and Out* (New York and London: Routledge, 1992).

14 Doane, 'Film and the Masquerade', p. 22.

15 Ibid., p. 31.

16 Ibid., p. 18.

17 Butler, *Gender Trouble*, p. 51.

18 Luce Irigaray, *Speculum of the Other Woman*, trans. Gillian C. Gill (Ithaca: Cornell University Press, 1985).

19 Elizabeth Wright (ed.), *Feminism and Psychoanalysis: A Critical Dictionary* (Oxford: Blackwell, 1992), p. 178; Jane Gallop, *Feminism and Psychoanalysis: The Daughter's Seduction* (London: Macmillan, 1982).

20 Julia Kristeva, 'Women's Time', trans. Alice Jardine and Harry Blake, *Signs* 7 (1) (1981).

21 Luce Irigaray, *This Sex Which Is Not One*, trans. Catherine Porter (Ithaca: Cornell University Press, 1985), p. 186.

22 Luce Irigaray, 'Women on the Market', ibid., p. 191.

23 See, for instance, Ann Rosalind Jones, 'Writing the Body: Toward an Understanding of *écriture feminine*', *Feminist Studies* 7(2) (1981), Monique Plaza, '"Phallomorphic" power and the psychology of "woman"', *Feminist Issues* 1 (1) (1980).

24 Irigaray, 'When Our Lips Speak Together', pp. 209, 211.

25 Ibid., p. 216.

26 Margaret Whitford, *Luce Irigaray: Philosophy in the Feminine* (London: Routledge, 1991), p. 60.

27 Ibid., p. 94.

28 Irigaray, *This Sex Which Is Not One*, p. 220.

29 Irigaray, *Speculum*, pp. 119–23, and *This Sex Which Is Not One*, pp. 102–3; see also Hélène Cixous, *The Newly Born Woman*, trans. Betsy Wing (Manchester: Manchester University Press, 1986), pp. 63–132.

30 Irigaray, *This Sex Which Is Not One*, p. 103.

31 See Gayle Rubin, 'The Traffic in Women: Notes on the "Political Economy" of Sex', in Rayne R. Reiter (ed.), *Toward an Anthropology of Women* (New York: Monthly Review Press, 1974).

32 Steven Connor, *Theory and Cultural Value* (Oxford: Blackwell, 1992), p. 170; see also his criticisms of Irigaray's use of 'value' and Marxist theory, pp. 172, 181, and those of Rita Felski, *Beyond Feminist Aesthetics* (London: Hutchinson Radius, 1989), who accuses Irigaray of aestheticizing politics.

33 Connor, *Theory and Cultural Value*, p. 171.

34 Ibid., p. 172; see Gallop on prostitution as a money-relation, *Feminism and Psychoanalysis*, p. 90.

35 Irigaray, *This Sex Which Is Not One*, p. 173; Connor, *Theory and Cultural Value*, p. 172; and Margaret Atwood's novel, *The Handmaid's Tale* (London: Virago, 1985), for an effective defamiliarization of the contemporary workings of the 'proper name'.

36 Irigaray, *This Sex Which Is Not One*, p. 171.

37 Wright (ed.), *Feminism and Psychoanalysis*, p. 218.

38 Irigaray, *This Sex Which Is Not One*, p. 197; Dianne Chisholm writes that Irigaray is 'perhaps the single most important contributor to the psychoanalytic theory of female homosexuality', Wright (ed.), *Feminism and Psychoanalysis*, p. 217.

39 Whitford, *Luce Irigaray*, p. 34.

40 Ibid.

41 Mary Ann Doane, 'Film and the Masquerade', p. 20.

42 Irigaray, *This Sex Which Is Not One*, p. 177.
43 Robert Stam, *Reflexivity in Film and Literature, from 'Don Quixote' to Jean-Luc Godard* (Ann Arbor: UMI Research Press Studies in Cinema, 1985), p. 72.
44 Teresa de Lauretis, *Technologies of Gender: Essays on Theory, Film and Fiction* (London: Macmillan, 1987), p. 13; see also Teresa de Lauretis and Stephen Heath (eds), *The Cinematic Apparatus* (London: Macmillan, 1980).
45 Ibid., p. 13.
46 Doane, 'Film and the Masquerade', p. 23.
47 See also Teresa de Lauretis, *Alice Doesn't: Feminism, Semiotics, Cinema* (Bloomington: Indiana University Press, 1984), for a discussion of gender and narrative form.
48 Doane, 'Film and the Masquerade', p. 24.
49 Jane Gallop, *Feminism and Psychoanalysis*, p. 27.
50 Mary Ann Doane, 'Masquerade Reconsidered: Further Thoughts on the Female Spectator', *Femmes Fatales*, p. 37. Masquerade, despite its potential for feminist theory, has two drawbacks, Doane argues: as a reaction against masculine definitions, it 'makes femininity dependent upon masculinity for its very definition', and, second, Riviere does not discuss it as playful or pleasant, but as 'socially inappropriate' behaviour, interestingly in view of her elision of whether or not masquerade is a sign of pathology or normality (p. 38).

Reading 15 (Irigaray)

51 Particularly in *La Violence et le sacré* (Paris: Grasset, 1972), and in *Des Choses cachées depuis la fondation du monde* (Paris: Grasset, 1983).
52 [This type of interrogative statement – in the indicative, with a question mark at the end – is so characteristic of Irigaray's style, that we decided to keep it in the translation wherever it appeared in the original.] [*Notes in square brackets by Irigaray's translators, Diana Knight and Margaret Whitford.*]
53 Luce Irigaray, *Amante marine. De Friedrich Nietzsche* (Paris: Editions Minuit, 1980).
54 [This is a reference to Irigaray's view that in the male imaginary which dominates our culture, difference (e.g. sexual difference), can only be perceived in quantitative terms, *more* or *less* with reference to a single term, whereas in the female imaginary, these purely additive differences would have no place. This makes it difficult for female difference to be recognized in our culture (see in particular 'Le sujet de la science est-il sexué?' in *Parler n'est jamais neutre*, Paris: Editions Minuit, 1985) and 'Ethique de la difference sexuelle' in the book of the same title, Paris: Editions Minuit, 1984).]
55 [Irigaray argues that we live in a fundamentally homosexual economy in which *men* exchange [...] goods, words, ideas *and women*. Women are neither traders in their own right, nor do they have any legitimate objects of

exchange they can exchange amongst themselves. This is why the *only* goods they can exchange are their children (see section IV). See 'Women on the Market' and 'Commodities among Themselves' in *This Sex Which Is Not One*.]

56 [See note 53 above and Irigaray's description of the *plural* nature of female identity/sexuality as compared to the monolithic phallic nature of men's in 'This Sex Which Is Not One' in the book of the same title]

57 Ludwig Feuerbach, *L'Essence du christianisme*, trans. into French by J.-P. Osier (Paris: Maspero, 1968).

58 Luce Irigaray, 'Femmes divines', *Critique* 454 (March 1985), pp. 292–308.

59 [Irigaray uses both 'l'anal' and 'analité' (anality); we have translated both by 'the anal' here. For a longer discussion of women's relation to an anal economy, see 'The Blind Spot of an Old Dream of Symmetry', in *Speculum of the Other Woman* (Ithaca: Cornell University Press, 1985.]

Reading 16 (Doane)

60 Peter Gidal, transcription of a discussion following 'Technology and Ideology in/through/and Avant-Garde Film: An Instance', in *The Cinematic Apparatus*, ed. Teresa de Lauretis and Stephen Heath (New York: St Martins Press, 1980), p. 169.

61 This calls for a more thorough dissection and analysis of the assumptions underlying the cliché that male models are 'effeminate'.

62 Stephen Heath, 'Difference,' *Screen*, vol. 19, no. 3 (Autumn 1978), 73.

63 Jean Laplanche, *Life and Death in Psychoanalysis*, trans. Jeffrey Mehlman (Baltimore: Johns Hopkins), 1976, p. 20.

64 See, for example, 'The Denial of the Vagina', in *Psychoanalysis and Female Sexuality*, ed. Hendrick M. Ruitenbeek (New Haven: College and University Press, 1966), pp. 73–87; and *Feminine Psychology*, ed. Harold Kelman (New York: W. W. Norton, 1967).

65 Jacques Lacan, *Écrits: A Selection*, trans. Alan Sheridan (New York: W. W. Norton, 1977), p. 287.

66 Parveen Adams, 'Representation and Sexuality', *m/f*, no. 1 (1978), pp. 66–67. Even if the phallus is defined as logically prior to the penis, in that it is the phallus which bestows significance on the penis, a *relation* between the two is nevertheless posited, and this is my point.

67 I am grateful to Philip Rosen for this 'representation' of the problem.

68 Michèle Montrelay, 'Inquiry into Femininity', *m/f*, 1 (1978), p. 89.

69 Ibid.

70 Ibid., p. 90.

71 Ibid., pp. 91–2.

72 Ibid., p. 92.

73 This description is derived from Lacan's conceptualization of masquerade in relation to femininity. See *Écrits: A Selection*, pp. 289–90. Lacan, in turn, borrows the notion of masquerade from Joan Riviere; see 'Womanliness as Masquerade', in *Psychoanalysis and Female Sexuality*, pp. 209–20.

74 Montrelay, p. 91.
75 Ibid., p. 98.
76 Beverley Brown and Parveen Adams, 'The Feminine Body and Feminist Politics', *m/f*, 3 (1979), p. 37.
77 Luce Irigaray, 'This Sex Which Is Not One', trans. R. Albury and P. Foss, in *Language, Sexuality, Subversion*, ed. Paul Foss and Meaghan Morris (Darlington: Feral Publications, 1978), pp. 161–72. This is a translation of the second essay in *Ce sexe qui n'en est pas un* (Paris: Minuit, 1977), pp. 23–32.
78 Brown and Adams, 'The Feminine Body and Feminist Politics', p. 38.
79 Irigaray, *Ce sexe qui n'en est pas un*, pp. 129–30.
80 The critique of Kristeva is based on *About Chinese Women*, trans. Anita Barrows (New York: Urizen Books, 1977).
81 Brown and Adams, 'The Feminine Body and Feminist Politics', p. 39.
82 Laplanche, *Life and Death*, pp. 23–34.
83 Roland Barthes, 'Introduction to the Structural Analysis of Narratives', in *Image-Music-Text*, trans. Stephen Heath (New York: Hill and Wang, 1977), p. 119.

Select Bibliography

General

Bowie, Malcolm, *Psychoanalysis and the Future of Theory* (Oxford: Blackwell, 1991)

Elliott, Anthony, *Psychoanalytic Theory* (Oxford: Blackwell, 1994)

Jung, C. G., *The Basic Writings of C. G. Jung*, ed. Violet S. de Laslo (London: Modern Library, 1959)

Laplanche, J. and J. B. Pontalis, *The Language of Psychoanalysis*, trans. Donald Nicholson-Smith, with an introduction by Daniel Lagache (London: Karnac Books, 1988)

Meltzer, Françoise (ed.), *The Trial(s) of Psychoanalysis* (Chicago: Chicago University Press, 1988)

Roudinesco, Elisabeth, *Jacques Lacan and Co.: A History of Psychoanalysis in France 1925–1985* (Chicago: Chicago University Press, 1990)

Literary Critical Works

Berman, Jeffrey, *The Talking Cure: Literary Representations of Psychoanalysis* (New York: New York University Press, 1985)

Bersani, Leo, *The Freudian Body: Psychoanalysis and Art* (New York: Columbia University Press, 1986)

Bloom, Harold, *The Anxiety of Influence: A Theory of Poetry* (New York: Oxford University Press, 1973)

Bouson, J. Brooks, *The Empathetic Reader: A Study of the Narcissistic Character of the Drama of the Self* (Amherst: University of Massachusetts Press, 1989)

Brooks, Peter, *Body Works: Objects of Desire in Modern Narrative* (Cambridge, Mass., and London: Harvard University Press, 1993)

Brooks, Peter, *Psychoanalysis and Storytelling* (Oxford: Blackwell, 1993)

Brooks, Peter, *Reading for the Plot: Design and Intention in Narrative* (Oxford: Oxford University Press, 1984)

Crews, Frederick, *Out of My System: Psychoanalysis, Ideology and Critical Method* (Oxford: Oxford University Press, 1975)

Easthope, Antony, *Poetry and Phantasy* (Cambridge: Cambridge University Press, 1989)

Ellmann, Maud, (ed.), *Psychoanalytic Literary Criticism* (London: Longman, 1994)

Felman, Shoshana (ed.), *Psychoanalysis and Literature: The Question of Reading: Otherwise* (Baltimore: Johns Hopkins University Press, 1982)

Felman, Shoshana, *Writing and Madness: Literature/Philosophy/ Psychoanalysis* (Ithaca: Cornell University Press, 1985)

Gunn, Daniel, *Psychoanalysis and Fiction: An Exploration of Literary and Psychoanalytic Borders* (Cambridge: Cambridge University Press, 1988)

Hartman, Geoffrey, *Psychoanalysis and the Question of the Text* (New York: Johns Hopkins University Press, 1978)

Hertz, Neil, *The End of the Line: Essays on Psychoanalysis and the Sublime* (New York: Columbia University Press, 1985)

Holland, Norman H., *Holland's Guide to Psychoanalytic Psychology and Literature-and-Psychology* (Oxford: Oxford University Press, 1990)

Kaplan, Morton, and Robert Kloss, *The Unspoken Motive: A Guide to Psychoanalytic Literary Criticism* (New York: Free Press, 1973)

Kiell, Norman (ed.), *Psychoanalysis, Psychology, and Literature: A Bibliography* (Metuchen: Scarecrow Press, 1982)

Kofman, Sarah, *Freud and Fiction* (Illinois: Northeastern University Press, and Cambridge: Polity Press, 1991)

Kurzweil, Edith, and William Phillips, (eds.) *Literature and Psychoanalysis*, (New York: Columbia University Press, 1983)

Lukacher, Ned, *Primal Scenes: Literature, Philosophy and Psychoanalysis* (Ithaca: Cornell University Press, 1986)

Meaney, Gerardine, *(U)nlike Subjects: Women, Theory, Fiction* (London: Routledge, 1993)

Mollinger, Robert N., *Psychoanalysis and Literature: An Introduction* (New York: Nelson, 1981)

Natoli, Joseph P., and Frederick L. Rusch (eds.), *Psychocriticism: An Annotated Bibliography* (Westport, Conn.: Greenwood, 1984)

Rimmon-Kenan, Shlomith (ed.), *Discourse in Psychoanalysis and Literature* (London: Methuen, 1987)

Skura, Meredith, *The Literary Use of the Psychoanalytic Process* (New Haven: Yale University Press, 1981)

Smith, Joseph H., and William Kerrigan (eds), *Taking Chances: Derrida, Psychoanalysis and Literature* (Baltimore: Johns Hopkins University Press, 1984)

Timpanaro, Sebastiano, *The Freudian Slip: Psychoanalysis and Textual Criticism* (London: New Left Books, 1976)

Wright, Elizabeth, *Psychoanalytic Criticism: Theory into Practice* (London: Methuen, 1984)

Young, Robert (ed.), *Untying the Text: A Post-Structuralist Reader* (London: Routledge & Kegan Paul, 1981)

Sigmund Freud and the Case Histories

Abraham, Nicolas, and Maria Torok, *The Wolf Man's Magic Word*, trans. Nicholas Rand (Minneapolis: University of Minnesota Press, 1986)

Bernheimer, Charles, and Claire Kahane, (eds), *In Dora's Case* (London: Virago, 1985)

Freud, Sigmund. *The Standard Edition of the Complete Psychological Works of Sigmund Freud*, ed. James Strachey (London: Hogarth Press, 1953–74), 24 vols.

Gardiner, Muriel, *The Wolf-Man and Sigmund Freud* (London: Karnac Books, 1989)

Volosinov, Valentin, *Freudianism: A Marxist Critique* (New York: Academic Books, 1976)

Weber, Samuel, *The Legend of Freud* (Minneapolis: University of Minnesota Press, 1982)

Jacques Lacan

Bowie, Malcolm, *Lacan* (London: Fontana, 1991)

Clark, Michael, *Jacques Lacan: An Annotated Bibliography* (New York: Garland, 1988)

Davis, Robert Con (ed.), *The Fictional Father: Lacanian Readings of the Text* (Amherst: University of Massachusetts Press, 1981)

Davis, Robert Con (ed.), *Lacan and Narration: The Psychoanalytic Difference in Narrative Theory* (Baltimore: Johns Hopkins University Press, 1983)

Gallop, Jane, *Reading Lacan* (Ithaca: Cornell University Press, 1985)

Grosz, Elizabeth, *Jacques Lacan: A Feminist Introduction* (London: Routledge, 1990)

Lacan, Jacques, *Ecrits: A Selection* (London: Tavistock, 1980)

Lacan, Jacques, *The Ego in Freud's Theory and in the Technique of Psychoanalysis 1954–1955* (Cambridge: Cambridge University Press, 1988), vol. 2 of *Seminars*

Lacan, Jacques, *The Four Fundamental Concepts of Psychoanalysis* (New York: W. W. Norton, 1978)

Lacan, Jacques, *Freud's Papers on Technique, 1953–1954* (Cambridge: Cambridge University Press, 1988), vol. 1 of *Seminars*

Lacan, Jacques, *Speech and Language in Psychoanalysis: The Language of the Self* (Baltimore: Johns Hopkins University Press, 1981)

Laplanche, J. and J. B. Pontalis, *The Language of Psychoanalysis*, trans. Donald Nicholson-Smith, with an introduction by Daniel Lagache (London: Karnac Books, 1988)

Lemaire, Anika, *Jacques Lacan* (London: Routledge & Kegan Paul, 1977)

Mellard, James M., *Using Lacan, Reading Fiction* (Urbana and Chicago: University of Illinois Press, 1992)

Mitchell, Juliet, and Jacqueline Rose (eds), *Feminine Sexuality: Jacques Lacan and the Ecole Freudienne* (London: Macmillan, 1982)

Muller, J. P., and W. J. Richardson (eds), *Lacan and Language: A Reader's Guide to Ecrits* (New York: International Press, 1982)

Nordquist, Joan (ed.), *Jacques Lacan: A Bibliography* (Santa Cruz Reference and Research Services, 1987)

Ragland-Sullivan, Ellie, *Jacques Lacan and the Philosophy of Psychoanalysis* (Urbana and Chicago: University of Illinois Press, 1986)

Sarup, Madan, *Jacques Lacan* (Hemel Hempstead: Harvester, 1992)

Feminism and Psychoanalysis

Brennan, Teresa (ed.), *Between Feminism and Psychoanalysis* (London: Routledge, 1989)

Butler, Judith, *Gender Trouble: Feminism and the Subversion of Identity* (London: Routledge, 1990)

Clément, Catherine, *The Weary Sons of Freud* (London: Verso, 1987)

Feldstein, Richard, and Judith Roof (eds), *Feminism and Psychoanalysis* (Ithaca: Cornell University Press, 1989)

Flax, Jane, *Thinking Fragments: Psychoanalysis, Feminism, and Postmodernism in the Contemporary West* (Berkeley: University of California Press, 1990)

Gallop, Jane, *Feminism and Psychoanalysis: The Daughter's Seduction* (London: Macmillan, 1982)

Garner, Shirley Nelson, C. Kahane and M. Sprengnether, (eds), *The (M)Other Tongue: Essays in Feminist Psychoanalyist Interpretation* (Ithaca: Cornell University Press, 1985)

Hirsch, Marianne, *The Mother/Daughter Plot: Narrative, Psychoanalysis, Feminism* (Bloomington: Indiana University Press, 1989)

Jardine, Alice, *Gynesis* (Ithaca: Cornell University Press, 1985)

Kofman, Sarah, *The Enigma of Woman: Woman in Freud's Writings* (Ithaca: Cornell University Press, 1985)

Mitchell, Juliet, *Psychoanalysis and Feminism* (Harmondsworth: Pelican, 1974)

Moi, Toril, *Sexual/Textual Politics* (London: Routledge, 1990)

Sayers, Janet, *Sexual Contradictions: Psychology, Psychoanalysis, and Feminism* (London: Tavistock, 1987)

Wright, Elizabeth (ed.), *Feminism and Psychoanalysis: A Critical Dictionary* (Oxford: Blackwell, 1992)

Wyatt, Jean, *Reconstructing Desire: The Role of the Unconscious in Women's Reading and Writing* (Chapel Hill: University of North Carolina Press, 1990)

French Feminist Theory

Franklin, Sarah, *Luce Irigaray and the Feminist Critique of Language* (University of Kent at Canterbury Women's Studies Occasional Papers No. 6, 1985)

Fraser, Nancy, and Sandra Lee Bartky (eds), *Revaluing French Feminism: Critical Essays on Difference, Agency, and Culture* (Bloomington: Indiana University Press, 1992)

Grosz, Elizabeth, *Sexual Subversions: Three French Feminists* (Sydney: Allen and Unwin, 1989)

Irigaray, Luce, *The Marine Lover of Friedrich Nietzsche* (New York: Columbia University Press, 1991)

Irigaray, Luce, *Speculum of the Other Woman* (Ithaca: trans. Gillian C. Gill Cornell University Press, 1985)

Irigaray, Luce, *This Sex Which Is Not One* (Ithaca: trans. Catherine Porter Cornell University Press, 1985)

Marks, Elaine, and Isabelle de Courtivron (eds), *New French Feminisms: An Anthology* (Brighton: Harvester, 1981)

Whitford, Margaret (ed.), *The Irigaray Reader* (Oxford: Blackwell, 1991)

Whitford, Margaret, *Luce Irigaray: Philosophy in the Feminine* (London: Routledge, 1991)

Film and Psychoanalysis

Creed, Barbara, *The Monstrous-Feminine: Film, Feminism, Psychoanalysis* (London: Routledge, 1993)

Doane, Mary Ann, *Femmes Fatales: Feminism, Film Theory, Psychoanalysis* (London: Routledge, 1991)

Holmlund, Christine, 'I Love Luce: The Lesbian Mimesis and Masquerade in Irigaray, Freud, and Mainstream Film', *New Formations* 9 (1990)

Lauretis, Teresa de, *Technologies of Gender: Essays on Theory, Film and Fiction* (London: Macmillan, 1987)

Metz, Christian, *The Imaginary Signifier* (Bloomington: Indiana University Press, 1981)

Mulvey, Laura, 'Visual Pleasure and Narrative Cinema', *Screen*, 16 (3) (Autumn 1975).

Mulvey, Laura, 'Afterthoughts on "Visual Pleasure and Narrative Cinema", inspired by *Duel in the Sun* (King Vidor, 1946)', *Framework*, 10 (1979)

Penley, Constance (ed.), *Feminism and Film Theory* (London: Routledge, 1988)

Rose, Jacqueline, *Sexuality in the Field of Vision* (London: Verso, 1986)

Silverman, Kaja, *The Acoustic Mirror: The Female Voice in Psychoanalysis and Cinema* (Bloomington: Indiana University Press, 1988)

Žižek, Slavoj, *Enjoy Your Symptom! Jacques Lacan in Hollywood and Out* (New York and London: Routledge, 1992)

Edgar Allan Poe

Derrida, Jacques, 'The purveyor of truth', *Yale French Studies*, 52 (1975)

Muller, J. P., and W. J. Richardson (eds.), *The Purloined Poe* (Baltimore: Johns Hopkins University Press, 1988)

Julia Kristeva

Fletcher, John, and Andrew Benjamin (eds), *Abjection, Melancholia and Love: The Work of Julia Kristeva* (London: Routledge, 1990)

Kristeva, Julia, *About Chinese Women*, trans. Anita Barrows (London: Boyars, 1977)

Kristeva, Julia, *Black Sun: Depression and Melancholia* (New York: trans. Léon S. Roudiez, Columbia University Press, 1989)

Kristeva, Julia, *Desire in Language: A Semiotic Approach to Literature and Art* (Oxford: Blackwell, 1980)

Kristeva, Julia, *In the Beginning Was Love: Psychoanalysis and Faith* (New York: Columbia University Press, 1987)

Kristeva, Julia, *Language: the Unknown* (New York: trans. A. M. Menke, Columbia University Press, 1989)

Kristeva, Julia, *Nations Without Nationalism* (New York: trans. Léon S. Roudiez, Columbia University Press, 1993)

Kristeva, Julia, *Powers of Horror: An Essay on Abjection* (New York: trans. Léon S. Roudiez, Columbia University Press, 1982)

Kristeva, Julia, *Proust and the Sense of Time* (New York: trans. S. Bann, Columbia University Press, 1993)

Kristeva, Julia, *Revolution in Poetic Language* (New York: trans. Léon S. Roudiez, Columbia University Press, 1984)

Kristeva, Julia, *Strangers to Ourselves* (New York: trans. Léon S. Roudiez, Columbia University Press, 1991)

Kristeva, Julia, *Tales of Love* (New York: Columbia University Press, 1987)

Lechte, John, *Julia Kristeva* (London: Routledge, 1990)

Minow-Pinkney, Makiko, *Virginia Woolf and the Problem of the Subject: Feminine Writing in the Major Novels* (Brighton: Harvester, 1987)

Moi, Toril (ed.), *The Kristeva Reader* (Oxford: Blackwell, 1986)

Oliver, Kelly, *Reading Kristeva: Unraveling the Double-bind* (Bloomington: Indiana University Press, 1993)

Masquerade

Copjec, Joan, 'The Sartorial Superego', *October*, 50, (1989)

Gaines, Jane, and Charlotte Herzog, (eds), *Fabrications: Costume and the Female Body* (London: Routledge, 1990)

Garber, Marjorie, *Vested Interests: Cross-Dressing and Cultural Anxiety* (Harmondsworth: Penguin, 1992)

Heath, Stephen, 'Joan Riviere and the Masquerade', in Victor Burgin, James Donald and Cora Kaplan (eds), *Formations of Fantasy* (London: Methuen, 1986)

Hughes, Athol (ed.), *Joan Riviere: The Inner World and Joan Riviere* (London: Karnac Books, 1990)

Riviere, Joan, 'Womanliness as a Masquerade', *International Journal of Psychoanalysis*, X (1929)

Henry James

James, Henry, *The Turn of the Screw*, ed. Robert Kimbrough (New York: W. W. Norton, 1966)

Wilson, Edmund, 'The Ambiguity of Henry James', in *The Triple Thinkers* (New York: Octagon Books, 1977, and Harmondsworth: Penguin, 1965)

Melanie Klein

Grosskurth, Phyllis, *Melanie Klein: Her World and Her Work* (London: Maresfield Books, 1986)

Heimann, P., S. Isaacs, M. Klein and J. Riviere (eds), *Developments in Psycho-Analysis* (London: Hogarth Press, 1952)

Hinshelwood, R. D., *A Dictionary of Kleinian Thought* (London: Free Association Books, 1989)

Klein, Melanie, *Envy and Gratitude and Other Works 1946–1963* (London: Virago, 1988)

Klein, Melanie, *Love, Guilt and Reparation and Other Works 1921–1945* (London: Virago, 1988)

Klein, Melanie, *Narrative of a Child Analysis* (London: Virago, 1989)

Klein, Melanie, *The Psycho-Analysis of Children* (London: Virago, 1989)

Mitchell, Juliet (ed.), *The Selected Melanie Klein* (Harmondsworth: Penguin, 1986)

Segal, Hanna, *Melanie Klein* (Harmondsworth: Penguin, 1981)

Women: A Cultural Review, 'Positioning Klein', 1/2 (1990)

Index